Daily Selections From The
New International Version

Light to Live By

D0017840

ZONDERVAN
PUBLISHING HOUSE

OF THE ZONDERVAN CORPORATION | GRAND RAPIDS, MICHIGAN 49506

Library of Congress Cataloging in Publication Data

Bible. English. New international. Selections. 1979.
   Light to live by.
      1. Devotional calendars. I. Lockyer, Herbert.
II. Title.
BS195.N37   1979   242'.2   79-17397
ISBN 0-310-28211-X: Paper
ISBN 0-310-28210-1: All-Occasion
ISBN 0-310-28240-3: Christmas
ISBN 0-310-28230-6: Graduation

Printed in the United States of America

With Love Christmas 1980

Cindy

Blessed is the man who listens to me, watching daily at my doors, waiting at my doorway.

—Proverbs 8:34

preface

These daily readings, selected and arranged by Dr. Herbert Lockyer, are from *The New International Version* of the Bible. This contemporary version is based upon accurate and faithful translation of the best manuscripts of the original languages as well as a sensitive feeling for the style of the English language. Therefore this collection of daily Bible readings by the renowned author of the *All* series will be highly pleasing to both the heart and the mind. The readings are assembled around themes for profitable meditation. Because of the limitation of space for each day, it is not possible to cite all references on a given word or subject. These meditations will be helpful for further study if the context of each given reference is examined.

The Publishers

In the beginning was the Word.

Jan/1

In the beginning was the Word, and the Word was with God, and the Word was God. He was with God in the beginning. —A faith and knowledge resting on the hope of eternal life, which God, who does not lie, promised before the beginning of time.—In the beginning God created the heavens and the earth.—"I am the Alpha and the Omega," says the Lord God, "who is, and who was, and who is to come, the Almighty." . . . "I am the Alpha and the Omega, the First and the Last, the Beginning and the End."—It is a land the Lord your God cares for; the eyes of the Lord your God are continually on it from the beginning of the year to its end. "The Lord possessed me at the beginning of his work, before his deeds of old; I was appointed from eternity, from the beginning, before the world began. . . . Before the hills, I was given birth. . . . I was there when he set the heavens in place."—"In the beginning, O Lord, you laid the foundations of the earth. . . . Your years will never end." . . . Jesus Christ is the same yesterday and today and forever.

John 1:1,2; Titus 1:2; Gen. 1:1; Rev. 1:8; 22:13; Deut. 11:12; Prov. 8:22-27; Heb. 1:10-12; 13:8.

jan/2

Your strength will equal your days.—"It is not by strength that one prevails."—Jonathan went to David . . . and helped him find strength in God.—In your hands are strength and power to exalt and give strength to all.—"My grace is sufficient for you, for my power is made perfect in weakness." . . . For when I am weak, then I am strong.—I pray that out of his glorious riches he may strengthen you with power through his Spirit in your inner being.—Being strengthened with all power according to his glorious might so that you may have great endurance and patience.—But the Lord stood at my side and gave me strength, so that through me the message might be fully proclaimed and all the Gentiles might hear it.—God is our refuge and strength, an ever present help in trouble.—When we were still powerless, Christ died for the ungodly.—"Worthy is the Lamb, who was slain, to receive . . . strength."—Those who hope in the Lord will renew their strength.—If you falter in times of trouble, how small is your strength!—Awake, awake, O Zion, clothe yourself with strength.

Deut. 33:25; 1 Sam. 2:9; 23:16; 1 Chron. 29:12; 2 Cor. 12:9-10; Eph. 3:16; Col. 1:11; 2 Tim. 4:17; Ps. 46:1; Rom. 5:6; Rev. 5:12; Isa. 40:31; Prov. 24:10; Isa. 52:1.

jan /3

O Lord, our Lord, how majestic is your name in all the earth!—He will be called Wonderful Counselor, Mighty God, Everlasting Father, Prince of Peace. . . . "Give thanks to the Lord, call on his name; . . . proclaim that his name is exalted." . . . I am the Lord; that is my name!" . . . Our Redeemer—the Lord Almighty is his name.—"The virgin will be with child and give birth to a son, and they will call him Immanuel"—which means, "God with us."—Repentance and forgiveness of sins will be preached in his name to all nations.—"You are to give him the name Jesus, because he will save his people from their sins."—God exalted him to the highest place and gave him the name that is above every name, that at the name of Jesus every knee should bow,—Yet to all who received him, to those who believed in his name, he gave the right to become children of God.—You may ask me for anything in my name, and I will do it.—By believing you may have life in his name.—On his robe and on his thigh he has this name written: KING OF KINGS AND LORD OF LORDS. —Remain true to my name—His name will be on their foreheads.

Ps. 8:1; Isa. 9:6; 12:4; 42:8; 47:4; Matt. 1:23; Luke 24:47; Matt. 1:21; Phil. 2:9, 10; John 1:12; 14:14; 20:31; Rev. 19:16; 2:13; 22:4.

Jan / 4

Comfort, comfort my people, says your God. . . . The Lord will surely comfort Zion. . . . "I, even I, am he that comforts you."—The Father of compassion and the God of all comfort, who comforts us in all our troubles, so that we can comfort those in any trouble with the comfort we ourselves have received from God. . . . But God, who comforts the downcast, comforted us by the coming of Titus, and not only by his coming but also by the comfort you had given him.—Any comfort from his love.—These are the only Jews among my fellow workers for the kingdom of God, and they have proved a comfort to me.—Your rod and your staff, they comfort me.—[Simeon] was waiting for the consolation of Israel, and the Holy Spirit was upon him.—For just as the sufferings of Christ flow over into our lives, so also through Christ our comfort overflows. If we are distressed, it is for your comfort and salvation; if we are comforted, it is for your comfort, which produces in you patient endurance of the same sufferings we suffer. And our hope for you is firm, because we know that just as you share in our sufferings, so also you share in our comfort.

Isa. 40:1; 51:3, 12; 2 Cor. 1:3-4; 7:6; Phil. 2:1; Col. 4:11; Ps. 23:4; Luke 2:5; 2 Cor. 1:5-7

jan /5

Man goes out to his work, to his labor until evening.—"The work of my hands . . . My own hands stretched out the heavens."—Jesus said to them, "My Father is always at his work to this very day, and I, too, am working." . . . "My food," said Jesus, "is to do the will of him who sent me and to finish his work." . . . "As long as it is day, we must do the work of him who sent me. Night is coming when no one can work." . . . "What must we do to do the works God requires?" Jesus answered, "The work of God is this: to believe in the one he has sent." . . . "I have brought you glory on earth by completing the work you gave me to do."—Your work produced by faith, your labor prompted by love.—Do your best to present yourself to God as one approved, a workman who does not need to be ashamed.—God is not unjust; he will not forget your work and the love you have shown him as you have helped his people and continue to help them.—His work will be shown for what it is, because the Day will bring it to light. . . . The fire will test the quality of each man's work. . . . Always give yourselves fully to the work of the Lord, because you know that your labor in the Lord is not in vain.

Ps. 104:23; Isa. 45:11-12; John 5:17; 4:34; 9:4; 6:28-29; 17:4; 1 Thess. 1:3; 2 Tim. 2:15; Heb. 6:10; 1 Cor. 3:13; 1 Cor. 15:58.

jan/6

But whatever was to my profit I now consider loss for the sake of Christ. What is more, I consider everything a loss compared to the surpassing greatness of knowing Christ Jesus my Lord, for whose sake I have lost all things. I consider them rubbish, that I may gain Christ and be found in Him.—"What good will it be for a man if he gains the whole world, yet forfeits his soul? Or what can a man give in exchange for his soul?"—Sorrowful, yet always rejoicing; poor, yet making many rich; having nothing, and yet possessing everything.—"The ground of a certain rich man produced a good crop. He thought to himself, 'What shall I do? I have no place to store my crops.' Then he said, 'This is what I'll do. I will tear down my barns and build bigger ones, and there will I store all my grain and my goods. And I'll say to myself, "You have plenty of good things laid up for many years. Take life easy; eat, drink and be merry."' But God said to him, 'You fool! This very night your life will be demanded from you. Then who will get what you have prepared for yourself?' This is how it will be with anyone who stores up things for himself but is not rich toward God."

Phil. 3:7-9; Matt. 16:26; 2 Cor. 6:10; Luke 2:6-21.

Jan /7

Let my lover come into his garden and taste its choice fruits.—Tell the righteous it will be well with them, for they will enjoy the fruit of their deeds.—"Make a tree good and its fruit will be good, or make a tree bad and its fruit will be bad, for a tree is recognized by its fruit." . . . "Every tree that does not bear good fruit is cut down and thrown into the fire."—" 'For three years now I've been coming to look for fruit on this fig tree and haven't found any. Cut it down! Why should it use up the soil?' "—"No branch can bear fruit by itself; it must remain in the vine. Neither can you bear fruit unless you remain in me. . . . If a man remains in me and I in him, he will bear much fruit."—The fruit of the Spirit is love, joy, peace, patience, kindness, goodness, faithfulness, gentleness and self-control.—The fruit of the light consists in all goodness, righteousness and truth.—Bearing fruit in every good work, growing in the knowledge of God.—Filled with the fruit of righteousness that comes through Jesus Christ—to the glory and praise of God.—The wisdom that comes from heaven is first of all pure; then peace loving, considerate, submissive, full of mercy and good fruit, impartial and sincere.

Song of Songs 4:16; Isa. 3:10; Matt. 12:33; 7:19; Luke 13:7; John 15:4-5; Gal. 5:22-23; Eph. 5:9; Col. 1:10; Phil. 1:11; James 3:17.

Jan /8

Of the increase of his government and peace there will be no end. . . . The zeal of the Lord Almighty will accomplish this.—He put on the garments of vengeance and wrapped himself in zeal as in a cloak.—When they heard this, they praised God. Then they said to Paul: "You see, brother, how many thousands of Jews have believed, and all of them are zealous for the law."—"I was thoroughly trained in the law of our fathers and was just as zealous for God as any of you are today."—For I can testify about them that they are zealous for God, but their zeal is not based on knowledge.—His disciples remembered that it is written: "Zeal for your house will consume me."—Where are your zeal and your might? Your tenderness and compassion are withheld from us.—Those people are zealous to win you over, but for no good. What they want is to alienate you from us, so that you may be zealous for them. It is fine to be zealous, provided the purpose is good, and to be so always.—He was zealous for the honor of his God.

Isa. 9:7; 59:17; Acts 21:20; 22:3; Rom. 10:2; John 2:17; Isa. 63:15; Gal. 4:17-18; Num. 25:13.

jan/9

If you are willing and obedient, you will eat the best from the land.—Obedience that comes from faith. . . . You wholeheartedly obeyed the form of teaching to which you were entrusted. . . . "All day long I have held out my hands to a disobedient and obstinate people."—A large number of priests became obedient to the faith. . . . "We must obey God rather than men! . . . The Holy Spirit, whom God has given to those who obey him."—We take captive every thought to make it obedient to Christ.— Obedience, which leads to righteousness.—He humbled himself and became obedient to death.—Through the obedience of the one man the many will be made righteous.—Although he was a son, he learned obedience from what he suffered and, once made perfect, he became the source of eternal salvation for all who obey him.—Chosen according to the foreknowledge of God the Father, by the sanctifying work of the Spirit, for obedience to Jesus Christ and sprinkling by his blood. . . . You have purified yourselves by obeying the truth.—Confident of your obedience, I write to you, knowing that you will do even more than I ask.

Isa. 1:19; Rom. 1:5; 6:17; 10:21; Acts 6:7; 5:29, 32; 2 Cor. 10:5; Rom. 6:16; Phil. 2:8; Rom. 5:19; Heb. 5:8-9; 1 Peter 1:2, 22; Philem. 21.

Jan/10

[God] said, "This is the resting place, let the weary rest"; and, "This is the place of repose"—But they would not listen. . . . My people will live in undisturbed places of rest.—"Come to me, all you who are weary and burdened, and I will give you rest. . . . You will find rest for your souls."—"Where will my resting place be?" . . . In that day the Root of Jesse will stand as a banner for the people; the nations will rally to him, and his place of rest will be glorious.—To whom did God swear that they would never enter his rest if not to those who disobeyed? So we see that they were not able to enter, because of their unbelief. . . . Now we who have believed enter that rest, just as God has said. . . . It still remains that some will enter that rest, and those who formerly had the gospel preached to them did not go in, because of their disobedience.—Then I heard a voice from heaven say, "Write: Blessed are the dead who die in the Lord from now on." "Yes," says the Spirit, "they will rest from their labor, for their deeds will follow them." . . . "He will wipe every tear from their eyes. There will be no more death or mourning or crying or pain, for the old order of things has passed away."

Isa. 28:12; 32:18; Matt. 11:28, 29; Isa. 66:1; 11:10; Heb. 3:18-19; 4:3, 6; Rev. 14:13; 21:4.

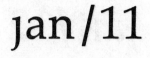

Jan/11

"Gather to me my consecrated ones, who made a covenant with me by sacrifice."—He will raise a banner for the nations and gather the exiles of Israel. . . . You, O Israelites, will be gathered up one by one. . . . He gathers the lambs in his arms and carries them close to his heart.—He will send his angels with a loud trumpet call, and they will gather his elect from the four winds, from one end of the heavens to the other.—He prophesied that Jesus would die for the Jewish nation, and not only for that nation but also for the scattered children of God, to bring them together and make them one.—"O Jerusalem, Jerusalem, . . . how often I have longed to gather your children together, as a hen gathers her chicks under her wings, but you were not willing!"—They gathered the kings together to the place that in Hebrew is called Armageddon. . . . I saw the beast and the kings of the earth and their armies gathered together to make war. . . .—"For where two or three come together in my name, there am I with them."—Concerning the coming of our Lord Jesus Christ and our being gathered to him, we ask you, brothers, not to become easily unsettled or alarmed by some prophecy, report or letter . . . saying that the day of the Lord has already come.

Ps. 50:5; Isa. 11:12; 27:12; 40:11; Matt. 24:31; John 11:51-52; Luke 13:34; Rev. 16:16; 19:19; Matt. 18:20; 2 Thess. 2:1-2.

Jan / 12

This is the message we have heard from him and declare to you: God is light; in him there is no darkness at all. If we claim to have fellowship with him yet walk in the darkness, we lie and do not live by the truth. But if we walk in the light, as he is in the light, we have fellowship with one another, and the blood of Jesus, his Son, purifies us from every sin.—They devoted themselves to the apostles' teaching and to the fellowship. . . . All the believers were together and had everything in common.—God, who has called you into fellowship with his Son Jesus Christ our Lord, is faithful.—Do not be yoked together with unbelievers. For what do righteousness and wickedness have in common? Or what fellowship can light have with darkness?—I want to know Christ . . . and the fellowship of sharing in his sufferings. . . . If you have any encouragement from being united with Christ, if any comfort from his love, if any fellowship with the Spirit . . . having the same love, being one in spirit and purpose.—You are all sons of God through faith in Christ Jesus. . . . You are all one in Christ.—Both the one who makes men holy and those who are made holy are of the same family. So Jesus is not ashamed to call them brothers.

1 John 1:5-7; Acts 2:42, 44; 1 Cor. 1:9; 2 Cor. 6:14; Phil. 3:10; 2:1-2; Gal. 3:26, 28; Heb. 2:11.

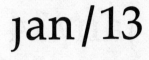

jan/13

He leads me beside quiet waters. . . . He guides me in paths of righteousness. . . . He guided them safely, so they were unafraid.—I will lead the blind by ways they have not known, along unfamiliar paths I will guide them. . . . Who led them through the depths. . . . He who has compassion on them will guide them and lead them beside springs of water.—Small is the gate and narrow the road that leads to life, and only a few find it.—He calls his own sheep by name and leads them out. . . . When he, the Spirit of truth, comes, he will guide you into all truth.—God's kindness leads you toward repentance. . . . Those who are led by the Spirit of God are sons of God.—If you are led by the Spirit, you are not under law.—You led your people like a flock.—"I am the Lord your God, who directs you in the way you should go." . . . I have made him a witness to the peoples, a leader and commander of the peoples.—"'Lead us not into temptation, but deliver us from the evil one.'"—"For the Lamb at the center of the throne will be their shepherd; he will lead them to springs of living water. And God will wipe away every tear from their eyes."

Pss. 23:2-3; 78:53; Isa. 42:16; 63:13; 49:10; Matt. 7:14; John 10:3; 16:13; Rom. 2:4; 8:14; Gal. 5:18; Ps. 77:20; Isa. 48:17; 55:4; Matt. 6:13; Rev. 7:17.

jan/14

"Watchman, what is left of the night?
Watchman, what is left of the night?" The
watchman replies, "Morning is coming, but also
the night." . . . Israel's watchmen are blind, they
all lack knowledge.—"Therefore keep watch,
because you do not know on what day your Lord
will come." . . . "My soul is overwhelmed with
sorrow to the point of death. Stay here and keep
watch with me." . . . "Watch and pray so that you
will not fall into temptation."—"What I say to
you, I say to everyone, 'Watch!'"—Be on your
guard; stand firm in the faith.—So then, let us not
be like others, who are asleep, but let us be alert
and self-controlled.—They keep watch over you as
men who must give an account.—"Wake up!
Strengthen what remains and is about to die." . . .
"Behold, I come like a thief! Blessed is he who
stays awake and keeps his clothes with him, so
that he may not go naked and be shamefully
exposed."—"Therefore keep watch, because you
do not know the day or the hour."—Understand
the present time. The hour has come for you to
wake up from your slumber, because our salvation
is nearer now than when we first believed. The
night is nearly over; the day is almost here.

---

*Isa. 21:11-12; 56:10; Matt. 24:42; 26:38, 41; Mark
13:37; 1 Cor. 16:13; 1 Thess. 5:6; Heb. 13:17; Rev.
3:2; 16:15; Matt. 25:13; Rom. 13:11-12.*

Jan/15

I will . . . love them freely.—Freely you have received, freely give.—All have sinned and fall short of the glory of God, and are justified freely by his grace through the redemption that came by Christ Jesus. . . . How much more did God's grace and the gift that came by the grace of the one man, Jesus Christ, overflow to the many! . . . He who did not spare his own Son, but gave him up for us all—how will he not also, along with him, graciously give us all things?—We have not received the spirit of the world but the Spirit who is from God, that we may understand what God has freely given us.—Was it a sin for me to lower myself in order to elevate you by preaching the gospel of God to you free of charge? I robbed other churches by receiving support from them so as to serve you.—"To him who is thirsty I will give to drink without cost from the spring of the water of life." . . . The Spirit and the bride say, "Come!" And let him who hears say, "Come!" Whoever is thirsty, let him come; and whoever wishes, let him take the free gift of the water of life.— Remember this: Whoever sows sparingly will also reap sparingly, and whoever sows generously will also reap generously.

Hos. 14:4; Matt. 10:8; Rom. 3:23-24; 5:15; 8:32; 1 Cor. 2:12; 2 Cor. 11:7-8; Rev. 21:6; 22:17; 2 Cor. 9:6.

Jan/16

He will bear their iniquities. . . . He bore the sin of many. . . . The Lord has laid on him the iniquity of us all—"Look, the Lamb of God, who takes away the sin of the world!"—God made him who had no sin to be sin for us, so that in him we might become the righteousness of God.—"I, even I, am he who blots out your transgressions, for my own sake. . . . I have swept away your offenses like a cloud, your sins like the morning mist."—Christ died for our sins according to the Scriptures.—For all have sinned and fall short of the glory of God. . . . "Blessed are they whose transgressions are forgiven, whose sins are covered. . . . Blessed is the man whose sin the Lord will never count against him." . . . Where sin increased, grace increased all the more. . . . For sin shall not be your master, because you are not under law, but under grace.—But now he has appeared once for all at the end of the ages to do away with sin by the sacrifice of himself. . . . When this priest had offered for all time one sacrifice for sins, he sat down at the right hand of God.—If we claim to be without sin, we deceive ourselves and the truth is not in us. . . . The blood of Jesus, His Son, purifies us from every sin.

Isa. 53:11-12, 6; John 1:29; 2 Cor. 5:21; Isa. 43:25; 44:22; 1 Cor. 15:3; Rom. 3:23; 4:7-8; 5:20; 6:14; Heb. 9:26; 10:12; 1 John 1:8, 7.

Jan/17

You will fill me . . . with eternal pleasures at your right hand. . . . The saving power of his right hand.—"I will uphold you with my righteous right hand. . . . I am the Lord, your God, who takes hold of your right hand." . . . "My right hand spread out the heavens."—"I am," said Jesus. "And you will see the Son of Man sitting at the right hand of the Mighty One and coming on the clouds of heaven."—"'I saw the Lord always before me. Because he is at my right hand, I will not be shaken.'"—God exalted him to his own right hand. . . . Stephen . . . saw . . . Jesus standing at the right hand of God. "Look," he said, "I see heaven open and the Son of Man standing at the right hand of God."—Christ Jesus . . . is at the right hand of God and is also interceding for us.—[God] raised him from the dead and seated him at his right hand in the heavenly realms.—The right hand of fellowship.—In his right hand he held seven stars. . . . Then I saw in the right hand of him who sat on the throne a scroll with writing on both sides and sealed with seven seals. . . . He came and took the scroll from the right hand of him who sat on the throne.

Pss. 16:11; 20:6; Isa. 41:10, 13; 48:13; Mark 14:62; Acts 2:25; 5:31; 7:55-56; Rom. 8:34; Eph. 1:20; Gal. 2:9; Rev. 1:16; 5:1, 7.

Jan/18

On his head are many crowns. . . . On his robe and on his thigh he has this name written: KING OF KINGS AND LORD OF LORDS.—God, the blessed and only Ruler, the King of kings, and Lord of lords. . . . To him be honor and might forever.—"My kingdom is not of this world. . . . My kingdom is from another place. . . . I am a king. In fact, for this reason I was born."—When this priest had offered for all time one sacrifice for sins, he sat down at the right hand of God. Since that time he waits for his enemies to be made his footstool.—He must reign until he has put all enemies under his feet. The last enemy to be destroyed is death.—"'Your kingdom come . . . Yours is the kingdom and the power and the glory forever.'"—Do not be afraid, little flock, for your Father has been pleased to give you the kingdom.—But thanks be to God! He gives us the victory through our Lord Jesus Christ.—He raised him from the dead and seated him at his right hand in the heavenly realms, far above all rule and authority, power and dominion, and every title that can be given, not only in the present age but also in the one to come.—"Your king is coming."

Rev. 19:12, 16; Tim. 6:15-16; John 18:36-37; Heb. 10:12-13; 1 Cor. 15:25-26; Matt. 6:10, 13; Luke 12:32; 1 Cor. 15:57; Eph. 1:20-21; John 12:15.

Jan / 19

Have you . . . walked in the recesses of the deep?—Was it not you who dried up the sea, the waters of the great deep, who made a road in the depths of the sea so that the redeemed might cross over? . . . Woe to those who go to great depths to hide their plans from the Lord.—Some [seed] fell on rocky places, where it did not have much soil. It sprang up quickly, because the soil was shallow.—I will show you what he is like who comes to me and hears my words and puts them into practice. He is like a man building a house, who dug deep down and laid the foundation on rock . . . "Put out into deep water, and let down the nets for a catch."—Neither height nor depth, nor anything else in all creation, will be able to separate us from the love of God that is in Christ Jesus our Lord.—I pray that . . . Christ may dwell in your hearts through faith. And I pray that you, being rooted and established in love, may have power, together with all the saints, to grasp how wide and long and high and deep is the love of Christ.—"No eye has seen, no ear has heard, no mind has conceived what God has prepared for those who love him"—but God has revealed it to us by his Spirit. The Spirit searches all things, even the deep things of God.

Job 38:16; Isa. 51:10; 29:15; Matt. 13:5; Luke 6:47-48; 5:4; Rom. 8:39; Eph. 3:16-18; 1 Cor. 2:9-10.

Jan/20

Therefore, just as sin entered the world through one man, and death through sin, and in this way death came to all men, because all sinned. . . . The wages of sin is death.—On this mountain he will destroy the shroud that enfolds all peoples, the sheet that covers all nations; he will swallow up death forever.—He poured out his life unto death.—"My soul is overwhelmed with sorrow to the point of death."—Christ died for our sins according to the Scriptures.—Christ died for the ungodly.—[God] has reconciled you by Christ's physical body through death to present you holy in his sight.—We know that since Christ was raised from the dead, he cannot die again; death no longer has mastery over him.—I am the Living One; I was dead, and behold I am alive for ever and ever! And I hold the keys of death and Hades.—"Death has been swallowed up in victory."—Christ Jesus, who has destroyed death and has brought life and immortality to light through the gospel.—By the grace of God he might taste death for everyone. . . . By his death he might destroy him who holds the power of death—that is, the devil—and free those who all their lives were held in slavery by their fear of death.—There will be no more death.

Rom. 5:12; 6:23; Isa. 25:7-8; 53:12; Matt. 26:38; 1 Cor. 15:3; Rom. 5:6; Col. 1:22; Rom. 6:9; Rev. 1:18; 1 Cor. 15:54; 2 Tim. 1:10; Heb. 2:9, 14-15; Rev. 21:4.

Jan/21

Lord, who may dwell in your sanctuary? . . .
[He] who keeps his oath even when it hurts. . . .
[God] will hear them and afflict them—men who
never change their ways and have no fear of
God.—He changes times and seasons.—"No
decree or edict that the king issues can be
changed."—The heavens are the work of your
hands. . . . Like clothing you will change them
and they will be discarded.—The Lord Jesus
Christ, who, by the power that enables him to
bring everything under his control, will transform
our lowly bodies so that they will be like his
glorious body.—Fools [that] exchanged the glory
of the immortal God for images made to look like
mortal man. . . . They exchanged the truth of God
for a lie.—Listen, I tell you a mystery: We will not
all sleep, but we will all be changed—in a
flash.—We, who with unveiled faces all reflect the
Lord's glory, are being transformed into his
likeness with ever-increasing glory, which comes
from the Lord, who is the Spirit.—But you remain
the same, and your years will never end.—Jesus
Christ is the same yesterday and today and
forever.—Lord, you have been our dwelling place
throughout all generations. . . . from everlasting
to everlasting you are God.

*Pss. 15:1, 4; 55:19; Dan. 2:21; 6:15; Ps. 102:25-26;
Phil. 3:21; Rom. 1:22, 25; 1 Cor. 15:51-52; 2 Cor.
3:18; Ps. 102:27; Heb. 13:8; Ps. 90:1-2.*

Jan/22

"The wisdom of the wise will perish, the intelligence of the intelligent will vanish." . . . He will be . . . a rich store of salvation and wisdom and knowledge.—Jesus grew in wisdom and stature, and in favor with God and men.—The foolishness of God is wiser than man's wisdom. . . . Christ the power of God and the wisdom of God. . . . Christ Jesus, who has become for us wisdom from God.—Not according to worldly wisdom but according to God's grace.—We are fools for Christ, but you are so wise in Christ!—If any of you lacks wisdom, he should ask God, who gives generously to all.—"If you believe, you will receive whatever you ask for in prayer."—Who is wise and understanding among you? Let him show it by his good life, by deeds done in the humility that comes from wisdom. . . . The wisdom that comes from heaven is first of all pure; then peace loving, considerate, submissive, full of mercy and good fruit, impartial and sincere.—We speak of God's secret wisdom, a wisdom that has been hidden and that God destined for our glory before time began.—"Worthy is the Lamb, who was slain, to receive power and wealth and wisdom and strength and honor and glory and praise!"

Isa. 29:14; 33:6; Luke 2:52; 1 Cor. 1:25, 24, 30; 2 Cor. 1:12; 1 Cor. 4:10; James 1:5; Matt. 21:22; James 3:13, 17; 1 Cor. 2:7; Rev. 5:12.

Jan/23

He gave [Moses] the two tablets of the Testimony, the tablets of stone inscribed by the finger of God.—On them were all the commandments the Lord proclaimed to you.—Bind them on your fingers; write them on the tablet of your heart.—Suddenly the fingers of a human hand appeared and wrote on the plaster of the wall. . . . The king watched the hand as it wrote. . . . He was so frightened that his knees knocked together. . . . "[God] sent the hand that wrote. . . ."—The magicians said to Pharaoh, "This is the finger of God."—When I consider your heavens, the work of your fingers. . . . —They bow down to the work of their hands, to what their fingers have made. . . . The incense altars their fingers have made.—[The Pharisees] tie up heavy loads and put them on men's shoulders, but they themselves are not willing to lift a finger to move them.—But if I drive out demons by the finger of God, then the kingdom of God has come to you.—"Unless I see the nail marks in his hands and put my finger where the nails were, and put my hand into his side, I will not believe it." . . . [Jesus] said to Thomas, "Put your finger here; see my hands. . . . Stop doubting and believe."

Exod. 31:18; Deut. 9:10; Prov. 7:3; Dan. 5:5-6, 24; Exod. 8:19; Ps. 8:3; Isa. 2:8; 17:8; Matt. 23:4; Luke 11:20; John 20:25, 27.

Jan /24

Against all hope, Abraham in hope believed and so became the father of many nations. . . . We rejoice in the hope of the glory of God. . . . May the God of hope fill you with all joy and peace as you trust in him, so that you may overflow with hope by the power of the Holy Spirit.—A faith and knowledge resting on the hope of eternal life. . . . We wait for the blessed hope—the glorious appearing of our great God and Savior, Jesus Christ.—If only for this life we have hope in Christ, we are to be pitied more than all men.—We know that when he appears, we shall be like him, for we shall see him as he is. Everyone who has this hope in him purifies himself, just as he is pure.—The faith and love that spring from the hope that is stored up for you in heaven. . . . Christ in you, the hope of glory.—By faith we eagerly await through the Spirit the righteousness for which we hope.—He has given us new birth into a living hope through the resurrection of Jesus Christ from the dead. . . . Set your hope fully on the grace to be given you when Jesus Christ is revealed.—We have this hope as an anchor for the soul, firm and secure. . . . Now faith is being sure of what we hope for and certain of what we do not see.

Rom. 4:18; 5:2; 15:13; Titus 1:2; 2:13; 1 Cor. 15:19; 1 John 3:2-3; Col. 1:5, 27; Gal. 5:5; 1 Peter 1:3, 13; Heb. 6:19; 11:1.

jan/25

"The god who answers by fire—he is God."—The Lord your God is a consuming fire.—The angel of the Lord appeared to [Moses] in flames of fire.—He will baptize you with the Holy Spirit and with fire.—They saw what seemed to be tongues of fire that separated and came to rest on each of them.—"Is not my word like fire?" declares the Lord.—The Light of Israel will become a fire, their Holy One a flame. . . . See, the Lord is coming with fire, . . . his rebuke with flame of fire. . . . When you walk through the fire, you will not be burned.—His work will be . . . revealed with fire, and the fire will test the quality of each man's work.—The Lord Jesus is revealed from heaven in blazing fire with his powerful angels.—Consider what a great forest is set on fire by a small spark. The tongue also is a fire. . . . It . . . sets the whole course of his life on fire, and is itself set on fire by hell.—All kinds of trials . . . have come so that your faith—of greater worth than gold, which perishes even though refined by fire—may be proved genuine and may result in praise.—I saw what looked like a sea of glass mixed with fire and, standing beside the sea, those who had been victorious over the beast.

1 Kings 18:24; Deut. 4:24; Exod. 3:2; Matt. 3:11; Acts 2:3; Jer. 23:29; Isa. 10:17; 66:15; 43:2; 1 Cor. 3:13; 2 Thess. 1:7; James 3:5-6; 1 Peter 1:6-7; Rev. 15:2.

jan/26

I may rejoice in your salvation. . . . Sing to God, sing praise to his name, . . . and rejoice before him.—Once more the humble will rejoice in the Lord; the needy will rejoice in the Holy One of Israel. . . . The wilderness will rejoice and blossom. . . . It will rejoice greatly and shout for joy. . . . As a bridegroom rejoices over his bride, so will your God rejoice over you.—He will be a joy and delight to you, and many will rejoice because of his birth. . . . My spirit rejoices in God my Savior. . . . Rejoice in that day and leap for joy, because great is your reward in heaven.—Rejoicing because they had been counted worthy of suffering disgrace for the Name.—We rejoice in the hope of the glory of God.—Love does not delight in evil but rejoices with the truth.—Sorrowful, yet always rejoicing.—Rejoice in the Lord always. I will say it again: Rejoice!—I rejoice in what was suffered for you, and I fill up in my flesh what is still lacking in regard to Christ's afflictions.—Be joyful always; pray continually.—But rejoice that you participate in the sufferings of Christ, so that you may be overjoyed when his glory is revealed.—Finally, my brothers, rejoice in the Lord!

Pss. 9:14; 68:4; Isa. 29:19; 35:1-2; 62:6; Luke 1:14, 47; 6:23; Acts 5:41; Rom. 5:2; 1 Cor. 13:6; 2 Cor. 6:10; Phil. 4:4; Col. 1:24; 1 Thess. 5:16-17; 1 Peter 4:13; Phil. 3:1.

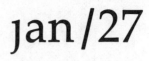

Jan/27

With fire and with his sword the Lord will execute judgment upon all men.—May the praise of God be in their mouths and a double-edged sword in their hands.—The sword of the Spirit, which is the word of God.—The word of God is living and active. Sharper than any double-edged sword, it penetrates even to dividing soul and spirit, joints and marrow; it judges the thoughts and attitudes of the heart.—Gird your sword upon your side, . . . clothe yourself with splendor and majesty.—He made my mouth like a sharpened sword, in the shadow of his hand he hid me. . . . Let the earth hear. . . . The Lord is angry with all nations; his wrath is upon all their armies. . . . My sword has drunk its fill in the heavens. . . . The sword of the Lord is bathed in blood.—Out of his mouth came a sharp double-edged sword. His face was like the sun shining in all its brilliance.—Out of his mouth comes a sharp sword with which to strike down the nations. "He will rule them with an iron scepter."—"Do not suppose that I have come to bring peace to the earth. I did not come to bring peace, but a sword."—"Awake, O sword, against my shepherd!"—They will beat their swords into plowshares and their spears into pruning hooks.

Isa. 66:16; Ps. 149:6; Eph. 6:17; Heb. 4:12; Ps. 45:3; Isa. 49:2; 34:1-2, 5-6; Rev. 1:16; 19:15; Matt. 10:34; Zech. 13:7; Isa. 2:4.

Jan/28

O God our Savior, the hope of all the ends of the earth. . . . It is better to take refuge in the Lord than to trust in princes.—Therefore we are always confident and know that as long as we are at home in the body we are away from the Lord. . . . We are confident, I say, and would prefer to be away from the body and at home with the Lord. . . . I am glad I can have complete confidence in you.—In him and through faith in him we may approach God with freedom and confidence. —Being confident of this, that he who began a good work in you will carry it on to completion until the day of Jesus Christ. . . . Put no confidence in the flesh.—Confident of your obedience, I write to you, knowing that you will do even more than I ask.—We have come to share in Christ if we hold firmly till the end the confidence we had at first. . . . Do not throw away your confidence; it will be richly rewarded.—And now, dear children, continue in him, so that when he appears we may be confident and unashamed before him at his coming. . . . Dear friends, if our hearts do not condemn us, we have confidence before God. . . . This is the assurance we have in approaching God: that if we ask anything according to his will, he hears us.

Pss. 65:5; 118:9; 2 Cor. 5:6, 8; 7:16; Eph. 3:12; Phil. 1:6; 3:4; Philem. 21; Heb. 3:14; 10:35; 1 John 2:28; 3:21; 5:14.

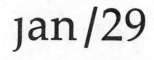

Jan/29

The Lord your God has enlarged your territory as he promised you. . . . He has declared that he will set you in praise, fame and honor high above all the nations he has made and that you will be a people holy to the Lord your God, as he promised.—"'The days are coming,' declares the Lord, 'when I will fulfill the gracious promise I made to the house of Israel and to the house of Judah.'"—Yet he did not waver through unbelief regarding the promise of God.—No matter how many promises God has made, they are "Yes" in Christ. . . . Since we have these promises, dear friends, let us purify ourselves from everything that contaminates body and spirit.—A faith and knowledge resting on the hope of eternal life, which God, who does not lie, promised before the beginning of time.—Imitate those who through faith and patience inherit what has been promised. . . . He who promised is faithful. . . . [Abraham] considered him faithful who had made the promise. . . . He has promised—He has given us his very great and precious promises, so that through them you may participate in the divine nature and escape the corruption in the world caused by evil desires.—This is what he has promised us—even eternal life.

Deut. 12:20; 26:19; Jer. 33:14; Rom. 4:20; 2 Cor. 1:20; 7:1; Titus 1:2; Heb. 6:12; 10:23; 11:11; 12:26; 2 Peter 1:4; 1 John 2:25.

Jan /30

You will keep in perfect peace, him whose mind
is steadfast.—When his heart became arrogant
and hardened with pride. . . . He was . . . given
the mind of an animal.—"'Love the Lord your
God . . . with all your mind.'"—Dressed and in
his right mind.—[God] gave them over to a
depraved mind. . . . The mind controlled by the
Spirit is life and peace. . . . Be transformed by the
renewing of your mind.—Be perfectly united in
mind and thought. . . . "Who has known the
mind of the Lord that he may instruct him?"—The
god of this age has blinded the minds of
unbelievers. . . . Be of one mind, live in
peace.—To be made new in the attitude of your
minds.—Like-minded, . . . being one in spirit
and purpose. . . . The peace of God, which
transcends all understanding, will guard your
hearts and your minds in Christ Jesus.—
Therefore, prepare your minds for action;
be self-controlled.—He is a double-minded man,
unstable in all he does. . . . Wash your hands, you
sinners, and purify your hearts, you
double-minded.—I have written both of [my
letters] as reminders to stimulate you to
wholesome thinking.

---

*Isa. 26:3; Dan. 5:20-21; Matt. 22:37; Mark 5:15;
Rom. 1:28; 8:6; 12:2; 1 Cor 1:10; 2:16; 2 Cor. 4:4;
13:11; Eph. 4:23; Phil. 2:2; 4:7; 1 Peter 1:13; James
1:8; 4:8; 2 Peter 3:1.*

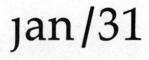

Jan/31

Your father's instruction . . . your mother's teaching. They will be a garland to grace your head and a chain to adorn your neck.—The glory of the one and only Son . . . full of grace and truth.—Justified freely by his grace through the redemption that came by Christ Jesus. . . . Receive God's abundant provision of grace. . . . Shall we sin because we are not under law but under grace? By no means!—The riches of God's grace that he lavished on us. . . . By grace you have been saved.—You know the grace of our Lord Jesus Christ, that though he was rich, yet for your sakes he became poor, so that you through his poverty might become rich. . . . God is able to make all grace abound to you.—The grace of God that brings salvation has appeared to all men.—Let us then approach the throne of grace with confidence.—"God opposes the proud but gives grace to the humble."—The God of all grace, who called you to his eternal glory in Christ.—But grow in the grace and knowledge of our Lord and Savior Jesus Christ.—Continue in the grace of God.—Each one should use whatever gift he has received to serve others, faithfully administering God's grace in its various forms.

Prov. 1:8-9; John 1:14; Rom. 3:24; 5:17; 6:15; Eph. 1:7-8; 2:5, 8; 2 Cor. 8:9; 9:8; Titus 2:11; Heb. 4:16; James 4:6; 1 Peter 5:10; 2 Peter 3:18, Acts 13:43; 1 Peter 4:10.

Bob Taylor

He will quiet you with his love.

feb /1

The Lord did not set his affection on you and choose you because you were more numerous than other people. . . . But . . . because [he] loved you.—"I will heal their waywardness and love them freely."—In his love and mercy he redeemed them.—He will quiet you with his love.—"For God so loved the world that he gave his one and only Son."—I pray that you, being rooted and established in love, may have power . . . to grasp how wide and long and high and deep is the love of Christ, and to know this love that surpasses knowledge.—Keep on loving each other as brothers.—If anyone loves the world, the love of the Father is not in him. . . . How great is the love the Father has lavished on us, that we should be called children of God! . . . This is love: not that we loved God, but that he loved us and sent his Son as an atoning sacrifice for our sins. . . . So we know and rely on the love God has for us. God is love. Whoever lives in love lives in God, and God in him. . . . There is no fear in love. But perfect love drives out fear. . . . We love because he first loved us. . . . Love comes from God. Everyone who loves has been born of God and knows God.

Deut. 7:7-8; Hos. 14:4; Isa. 63:9; Zeph. 3:17; John 3:16; Eph. 3:17-19; Heb. 13:1; 1 John 2:15; 3:1; 4:10, 16, 18-19, 7.

feb /2

"**H**onor your father and your mother, as the Lord your God has commanded you, so that you may live long and that it may go well with you in the land the Lord your God is giving you." . . . Be careful to obey all these regulations I am giving you, so that it may always go well with you and your children after you.—When the righteous prosper, the city rejoices.—Although a wicked man commits a hundred crimes and still lives a long time, I know that it will go better with God-fearing men, who are reverent before God. . . . It will not go well with [the wicked].—Tell the righteous it will be well with them, for they will enjoy the fruit of their deeds.—"He defended the cause of the poor and needy, and so all went well. Is that not what it means to know me?" declares the Lord.—" 'Well done, good and faithful servant! You have been faithful with a few things; I will put you in charge of many things. Come and share your master's happiness!' "—People were overwhelmed with amazement. "He has done everything well," they said.—"Be faithful, even to the point of death, and I will give you the crown of life."

Deut. 5:16; 12:28; Prov. 11:10; Eccl. 8:12-13; Isa. 3:10; Jer. 22:16; Matt. 25:21, 23; Mark 7:37; Rev. 2:10.

feb /3

The eternal God is your refuge, and underneath are the everlasting arms.—He who lives forever, whose name is holy. . . . I will make you the everlasting pride and the joy of all generations.—"Everyone who believes in him may have eternal life."—God's invisible qualities—his eternal power and divine nature. —For our light and momentary troubles are achieving for us an eternal glory that far outweighs them all.—His eternal purpose which he accomplished in Christ Jesus our Lord.—Now to the King eternal . . . the only God, be honor and glory for ever and ever.—He became the source of eternal salvation for all who obey him. . . . He entered the Most Holy Place once for all by his own blood, having obtained eternal redemption. . . . Who through the eternal Spirit offered himself unblemished to God. . . . Those who are called may receive the promised eternal inheritance.—The God of all grace, who called you to his eternal glory in Christ.—This is the testimony: God has given us eternal life, and this life is in his Son. . . . I write these things to you who believe in the name of the Son of God so that you may know that you have eternal life. . . . He is the true God and eternal life.

Deut. 33:27; Isa. 57:15; 60:15; John 3:15; Rom. 1:20; 2 Cor. 4:17; Eph. 3:11; 1 Tim. 1:17; Heb. 5:9; 9:12, 14-15; 1 Peter 5:10; 1 John 5:11, 13, 20.

feb /4

"Assemble the people before me to hear my
words so that they may learn to revere me as long
as they live in the land." . . . Hear, O Israel, the
decrees and laws I declare in your hearing today.
Learn them and be sure to follow them.—Instruct
a wise man and he will be wiser still; teach a
righteous man and he will add to his learning. . . .
Pleasant words . . . and . . . lips promote
instruction.—Stop doing wrong, learn to do
right! . . . The Sovereign Lord has given me an
instructed tongue.—Take my yoke upon you and
learn from me.—"It is written in the Prophets:
'They will all be taught by God.'"—Learn from us
the meaning of the saying, "Do not go beyond
what is written."—Children . . . should learn first
of all to put their religion into practice.—Always
learning but never able to acknowledge the
truth. . . . But as for you, continue in what you
have learned and have become convinced of.—I
have learned to be content whatever the
circumstances.—Although he was a son, he
learned obedience from what he suffered and,
once made perfect, he became the source of eternal
salvation.—They sang a new song. . . . No one
could learn the song except the 144,000 who had
been redeemed from the earth.

---

*Deut. 4:10; 5:1; Prov. 1:5; 9:9; 16:21, 23; Isa. 1:16-
17; 50:4; Matt. 11:29; John 6:45; 1 Cor. 4:6; 1 Tim.
5:4; 2 Tim. 3:7, 14; Phil. 4:11; Heb. 5:8-9; Rev. 14:3.*

feb /5

All glorious . . . within.—"You clean the outside of the cup and dish, but inside they are full of greed and self-indulgence. Blind Pharisee! First clean the inside of the cup and dish, and then the outside will be clean."—"What comes out of a man is what makes him 'unclean.' For from within, out of men's hearts, come evil thoughts, sexual immorality, theft, murder, . . . arrogance and folly. All these evils come from inside and make a man 'unclean.'"—"The kingdom of God does not come visibly. . . . because the kingdom of God is within you."—"Whoever drinks the water I give him will never thirst. Indeed, the water I give him will become in him a spring of water welling up to eternal life." . . . "The words I say to you are not just my own. Rather, it is the Father, living in me, who is doing his work."—You, however, are controlled not by the sinful nature but by the Spirit, if the Spirit of God lives in you. . . . The Spirit of him who raised Jesus from the dead is living in you.—I pray that out of his glorious riches he may strengthen you with power through his Spirit in your inner being.—You, dear children, are from God and have overcome them, because the one who is in you is greater than the one who is in the world.

Ps. 45:13; Matt. 23:25-26; Mark 7:20-23; Luke 17:20-21; John 4:14; 14:10; Rom. 8:9, 11; Eph. 3:16; 1 John 4:4.

feb/6

"But as for you, be strong and do not give up,
for your work will be rewarded."—"O great and
powerful God, whose name is the Lord Almighty,
great are your purposes and mighty are your
deeds."—"'Be strong,' . . . declares the Lord,
'and work.'"—Jesus said to them, "My Father is
always at his work to this very day, and I, too, am
working." . . . Then they asked him, "What must
we do to do the works God requires?" Jesus
answered, "The work of God is this: to believe in
the one he has sent." . . . "As long as it is day, we
must do the work of him who sent me. Night is
coming, when no one can work."—Am I not an
apostle? Have I not seen Jesus our Lord? Are you
not the result of my work in the Lord? . . .
Whatever you do, do it all for the glory of God.—
For we are God's workmanship, created in Christ
Jesus to do good works, which God prepared in
advance for us to do.—God is not unjust; he will
not forget your work and the love you have shown
him as you have helped his people and continue to
help them.—"Wake up! Strengthen what remains
and is about to die, for I have not found your
deeds complete in the sight of my God." . . .
"Yes," says the Spirit, "they will rest from their
labor, for their deeds will follow them."

---

*2 Chron. 15:7; Jer. 32:18-19; Hag. 2:4; John 5:17;
6:28-29; 9:4; 1 Cor. 9:1; 10:31; Eph. 2:10; Heb. 6:10;
Rev. 3:2; 14:13.*

feb/7

"You are my witnesses. Is there any God besides me?"—"They will be mine," says the Lord Almighty, "in the day when I make up my treasured possession."—"You are the salt of the earth. . . . You are the light of the world." . . . "Whoever does the will of my Father in heaven is my brother and sister and mother." . . . "I am sending you out like sheep among wolves. Therefore be as shrewd as snakes and as innocent as doves." . . . You are worth more than many sparrows."—"I am the vine; you are the branches." . . . "You are my friends. . . . I no longer call you servants."—We are God's fellow workers; you are God's field, God's building.—You yourselves are our letter, written on our hearts, known and read by everybody.—Children of God without fault in a crooked and depraved generation, in which you shine like stars in the universe as you hold out the word of life.—We sent Timothy, who is our brother and God's fellow worker.—You also, like living stones, are being built into a spiritual house to be a holy priesthood, offering spiritual sacrifices acceptable to God through Jesus Christ. . . . You are a chosen people, a royal priesthood, a holy nation, a people belonging to God.

Isa. 44:8; Mal. 3:17; Matt. 5:13-14; 12:50; 10:16, 31; John 15:5, 14-15; 1 Cor. 3:9; 2 Cor. 3:2; Phil. 2:15-16; 1 Thess. 3:2; 1 Peter 2:5, 9.

feb /8

Truly you are a God who hides himself, O God and Savior of Israel.—"Shall I hide from Abraham what I am about to do?"—O my God, I cry out by day, but you do not answer. . . . My soul is in anguish. How long, O Lord, how long?—The Almighty is beyond our reach.—"You do not realize now what I am doing, but later you will understand." . . . "Where I am going, you cannot follow now, but you will follow later." . . . At first his disciples did not understand all this. Only after Jesus was glorified did they realize that these things had been written about him and that they had done these things to him.—"How long, Sovereign Lord, holy and true, until you judge the inhabitants of the earth?"—[Trials] have come so that your faith—of greater worth than gold, which perishes even though refined by fire—may be proved genuine and may result in praise, glory and honor when Jesus Christ is revealed.—For we know in part, . . . but when perfection comes, the imperfect disappears. Now I know in part; then I shall know fully, even as I am fully known.

Isa. 45:15; Gen. 18:17; Pss. 22:2; 6:3; Job 37:23; John 13:7, 36; 12:16; Rev. 6:10; 1 Peter 1:7; 1 Cor. 13:9-10, 12.

feb/9

"Am I only a God nearby, . . . and not a God far away? Can anyone hide in secret places so that I cannot see him?"—For darkness is as light to you.—Consider what God has done: Who can straighten what he has made crooked? When times are good, be happy; but when times are bad, consider: God has made the one as well as the other.—"Blessed are the poor in spirit, for theirs is the kingdom of heaven. . . . Blessed are the meek, for they will inherit the earth."—"But many who are first will be last, and the last first."—"I was found by those who did not seek me; I revealed myself to those who did not ask for me." . . . Consider therefore the kindness and sternness of God: sternness to those who fell, but kindness to you, provided that you continue in his kindness.—Known, yet regarded as unknown; dying, and yet we live on; . . . sorrowful, yet always rejoicing; poor, yet making many rich; having nothing, and yet possessing everything. . . . When I am weak, then am I strong.—"I know your afflictions and your poverty—yet you are rich! . . . You say, 'I am rich; I have acquired wealth and do not need a thing.' But you do not realize that you are wretched, pitiful, poor, blind and naked."

Jer. 23:23-24; Ps. 139:12; Eccl. 7:13-14; Matt. 5:3, 5; Mark 10:31; Rom. 10:20; 11:22; 2 Cor. 6:9-10; 12:10; Rev. 2:9; 3:17.

feb/10

The Lord gives wisdom, and from his mouth come knowledge and understanding.—Wisdom is a shelter as money is a shelter, but the advantage of knowledge is this: that wisdom preserves the life of its possessor.—God gave Solomon wisdom and very great insight.—To turn the hearts of the fathers to their children and the disobedient to the wisdom of the righteous.—It is because of him that you are in Christ Jesus, who has become for us wisdom from God—that is, our righteousness, holiness and redemption. . . . We speak of God's secret wisdom, a wisdom that has been hidden and that God destined for our glory before time began.—The holy Scriptures, which are able to make you wise for salvation through faith in Christ Jesus.—Has not God made foolish the wisdom of the world? For since in the wisdom of God the world through its wisdom did not know him. . . . Greeks look for wisdom. . . . But to those whom God has called, both Jews and Greeks, Christ the power of God and the wisdom of God. For the foolishness of God is wiser than man's wisdom.—If any of you lacks wisdom, he should ask God, who gives generously to all without finding fault, and it will be given to him.

Prov. 2:6; Eccl. 7:12; 1 Kings 4:29; Luke 1:17; 1 Cor. 1:30; 2:7; 2 Tim. 3:15; 1 Cor. 1:20-22, 24-25; James 1:5.

feb/11

Because you did not serve the Lord your God
joyfully and gladly in the time of prosperity,
therefore in hunger and thirst, in nakedness and
dire poverty, you will serve the enemies the Lord
sends against you.—"Drink deeply and delight in
her overflowing abundance." . . . Turn to the
Lord, . . . for he will freely pardon.—"'I will heal
my people and will let them enjoy abundant peace
and security.'"—The Lord, . . . God, . . .
abounding in love and faithfulness.—You
have . . . set my feet in a spacious place. . . . The
righteous will flourish; prosperity will abound till
the moon is no more.—"Bless those who curse
you, pray for those who mistreat you."—God's
abundant provision of grace and of the gift of
righteousness.—Now to him who is able to do
immeasurably more than all we ask or imagine,
according to his power that is at work within
us.—The grace of our Lord was poured out on me
abundantly, along with the faith and love that are
in Christ Jesus.—"Bring the whole tithe into the
storehouse, that there may be food in my house.
Test me in this," says the Lord Almighty, "and see
if I will not throw open the floodgates of heaven
and pour out so much blessing that you will not
have room enough for it."

---

*Deut. 28:47-48; Isa. 66:11; 55:7; Jer. 33:6; Exod.
34:6; Pss. 31:8; 72:7; Luke 6:28; Rom. 5:17; Eph.
3:20; 1 Tim. 1:14; Mal. 3:10.*

feb/12

[**Rebekah**] went to inquire of the Lord.—But I pray to you, O Lord.—Then Jesus told his disciples a parable to show them that they should always pray and not give up. . . . One day Jesus was praying in a certain place. When he finished, one of his disciples said to him, "Lord teach us to pray."—"When you pray, go into your room, close the door and pray to your Father, who is unseen. Then your Father, who sees what is done in secret, will reward you." . . . "If you believe, you will receive whatever you ask for in prayer."—Be . . . faithful in prayer.—Pray in the Spirit on all occasions with all kinds of prayers and requests. With this in mind, be alert and always keep on praying for all the saints.—In everything, by prayer and petition, with thanksgiving, present your requests to God.—I want men everywhere to lift up holy hands in prayer.—Peter was kept in prison, but the church was earnestly praying to God for him. . . . The Lord sent his angel and rescued me. . . . [Peter] went to the house of Mary . . . where many people had gathered and were praying.—The prayer of a righteous man is powerful and effective.—Golden bowls full of incense, which are the prayers of the saints.

Gen. 25:22; Ps. 69:13; Luke 18:1; 11:1; Matt. 6:6-8; 21:22; Rom. 12:12; Eph. 6:18; Phil. 4:6; 1 Tim. 2:8; Acts 12:5, 11-12; James 5:16; Rev. 5:8.

feb/13

What other nation is so great as to have their gods near them the way the *Lord* our God is near us whenever we pray to him? . . . You will be blessed in the city and blessed in the country. . . . You will be blessed when you come in and blessed when you go out.—"But who am I, and who are my people, that we should be able to give as generously as this? Everything comes from you, and we have given you only what comes from your hand."—"Lord, you know all things."—We know that in all things God works for the good of those who love him, who have been called according to his purpose. . . . For from him and through him and to him are all things.—All this is from God, who reconciled us to himself through Christ and gave us the ministry of reconciliation.—To bring all things in heaven and on earth together under one head, even Christ.—I can do everything through him who gives me strength.—Hope in God, who richly provides us with everything for our enjoyment.—Above all, love each other deeply, because love covers over a multitude of sins. . . . In all things God may be praised through Jesus Christ.—"You are worthy, our Lord and God, to receive glory and honor and power, for you created all things."

Deut. 4:7; 28:3, 6; 1 Chron. 29:14; John 21:17; Rom. 8:28; 11:36; 2 Cor. 5:18; Eph. 1:10; Phil. 4:13; 1 Tim. 6:17; 1 Peter 4:8, 11; Rev. 4:11.

feb/14

These forty years the Lord your God has been
with you, and you have not lacked anything. . . .
In any of the towns of the land that the Lord your
God is giving you, do not be hardhearted or
tightfisted toward your poor brother.—"Since the
people began to bring their contributions to the
temple of the Lord, we have had enough to eat and
plenty to spare, because the Lord has blessed his
people, and this great amount is left over."—Then
Jesus asked them, "When I sent you without
purse, bag or sandals, did you lack anything?"
"Nothing," they answered.—They all ate and
were satisfied, and the disciples picked up twelve
basketfuls of broken pieces that were left
over.—Such confidence as this is ours through
Christ before God. . . . God is able to make all
grace abound to you, so that in all things at all
times, having all that you need, you will abound
in every good work. . . . "My grace is sufficient for
you."—[Boaz] offered [Ruth] some roasted grain.
She ate all she wanted and had some left
over.—Now to him who is able to do
immeasurably more than all we ask or imagine,
according to his power that is at work within us,
to him be glory in the church and in Christ Jesus,
throughout all generations, for ever and ever!

---

*Deut. 2:7; 15:7; 2 Chron. 31:10; Luke 22:35; Matt.
14:20; 2 Cor. 3:4; 9:8; 12:9; Ruth 2:14; Eph. 3:20-21.*

feb/15

If you fear the Lord and serve and obey him and do not rebel against his commands.—"May your God, whom you serve continually, rescue you!" . . . "Daniel, servant of the living God, has your God, whom you serve continually, been able to rescue you from the lions?" Daniel answered, "O king, live forever! My God sent his angel, and he shut the mouths of the lions."—If you obey my commands, you will remain in my love.— Strengthening the disciples and encouraging them to remain true to the faith. . . . But I have had God's help to this very day, and so I stand here and testify to small and great alike.—Continue in your faith, established and firm, not moved from the hope held out in the gospel.—As for you, continue in what you have learned and have become convinced of.—Let us continually offer to God a sacrifice of praise.—To those who by persistence in doing good seek glory, honor and immortality, he will give eternal life.—"If you hold to my teaching, you are really my disciples. Then you will know the truth, and the truth will set you free."—The cheerful heart has a continual feast.—Then they worshiped him and returned to Jerusalem with great joy. And they stayed continually at the temple, praising God.

---

1 Sam. 12:14; Dan. 6:16, 20-22; John 15:10; Acts 14:22; 26:22; Col. 1:23; 2 Tim. 3:14; Heb. 13:15; Rom. 2:7; John 8:31-32; Prov. 15:15; Luke 24:52-53.

feb/16

The chief priests and the Pharisees went to Pilate. "Sir," they said, "we remember that while he was still alive that deceiver said, 'After three days I will rise again.'"—[Jesus] took the twelve disciples aside and said to them, "We are going up to Jerusalem, and the Son of Man will be betrayed to the chief priests and the teachers of the law. They will condemn him to death. . . . On the third day he will be raised to life!" . . . "But after I have risen, I will go ahead of you into Galilee." . . . "'He has risen from the dead and is going ahead of you into Galilee.'"—"Why should any of you consider it incredible that God raises the dead?"—If Christ has not been raised, our preaching is useless and so is your faith. . . . But Christ has indeed been raised from the dead, the firstfruits of those who have fallen asleep.—If we have been united with him in his death, we will certainly also be united with him in his resurrection.—I want to know Christ and the power of his resurrection and the fellowship of sharing in his sufferings, becoming like him in his death, and so, somehow, to attain to the resurrection from the dead.—I am the Living One; I was dead, and behold I am alive for ever and ever! And I hold the keys of death and Hades.

Matt. 27:62-63; 20:17-19; 26:32; 28:7; Acts 26:8; 1 Cor 15:14, 20; Rom. 6:5; Phil. 3:10-11; Rev. 1:18.

feb/17

Now faith is being sure of what we hope for and certain of what we do not see. This is what the ancients were commended for. . . . Without faith it is impossible to please God.—Faith comes from hearing the message, and the message is heard through the word of Christ. . . . We maintain that a man is justified by faith apart from observing the law.—For it is by grace you have been saved, through faith—and this not of yourselves, it is the gift of God.—The apostles said to the Lord, "Increase our faith!"—For in the gospel a righteousness from God is revealed, a righteousness that is by faith from first to last, just as it is written: "The righteous will live by faith."—Let us fix our eyes on Jesus, the author and perfecter of our faith.—You, who through faith are shielded by God's power until the coming of the salvation that is ready to be revealed in the last time. . . . Trials . . . have come so that your faith—of greater worth than gold, which perishes even though refined by fire—may be proved genuine and may result in praise, glory and honor when Jesus Christ is revealed.—Then Jesus said, "Did I not tell you that if you believed, you would see the glory of God?"

Heb. 11:1, 2, 6; Rom. 10:17; 3:28; Eph. 2:8; Luke 17:5; Rom. 1:17; Heb. 12:2; 1 Peter 1:5-7; John 11:40.

feb/18

I have no refuge; no one cares for my life.—Cast all your anxiety on him because he cares for you.—The worries of this life, the deceitfulness of wealth and the desires for other things come in and choke the word.—The disciples woke him and said to him, "Teacher, don't you care if we drown?" He got up, rebuked the wind and said to the waves, "Quiet! Be still!"—"Martha, Martha," the Lord answered, "you are worried and upset about many things, but only one thing is needed. Mary has chosen what is better." . . . "Be careful, or your hearts will be weighed down with . . . the anxieties of life, and that day will close on you unexpectedly like a trap.—I would like you to be free from concern. . . . That you may live in a right way in undivided devotion to the Lord.—Besides everything else, I face daily the pressure of my concern for all the churches.—Do not be anxious about anything, but in everything, by prayer and petition, with thanksgiving, present your requests to God.—Do not worry about your life, what you will eat or drink; or about your body, what you will wear. Is not life more important than food, and the body more important than clothes? Who of you by worrying can add a single hour to his life?

Ps. 142:4; 1 Peter 5:7; Mark 4:19, 38-39; Luke 10:41-42; 21:34; 1 Cor. 7:32, 35; 2 Cor. 11:28; Phil. 4:6; Matt. 6:25, 27.

feb /19

Because he is at my right hand, I will not be shaken.—Love the Lord your God and keep his requirements, his decrees, his laws and his commands always. . . . Be careful to do what the Lord your God has commanded you; do not turn aside to the right or to the left.—I walk in the way of righteousness, along the paths of justice.—But thanks be to God, who always leads us in triumphal procession in Christ and through us spreads everywhere the fragrance of the knowledge of him.—He who began a good work in you will carry it on to completion until the day of Christ Jesus. . . . Continue to work out your salvation with fear and trembling, for it is God who works in you.—God . . . is my witness how constantly I remember you in my prayers at all times.—"The one who sent me is with me; he has not left me alone, for I always do what pleases him."—Be joyful always; pray continually. . . . Always try to be kind to each other.—I thank God, whom I serve, as my forefathers did, with a clear conscience, as night and day I constantly remember you in my prayers.—I will make every effort to see that after my departure you will always be able to remember these things. . . . Make your calling and election sure.

Ps. 16:8; Deut. 11:1; 5:32; Prov. 8:20; 2 Cor. 2:14; Phil. 1:6; 2:12; Rom. 1:9; John 8:29; 1 Thess. 5:16-17, 15; 2 Tim. 1:3; 2 Peter 1:15, 10.

feb/20

I have heard your prayer and seen your tears; I will add fifteen years to your life.—Keep my commands in your heart, for they will prolong your life many years and bring you prosperity. . . . The blessing of the Lord brings wealth, and he adds no trouble to it. . . . Do not add to his words, or he will rebuke you and prove you a liar.—"May the Lord your God multiply the troops a hundred times over, and may the eyes of my lord the king see it. But why does my lord the king want to do such a thing?"—"You said, 'Woe to me! The Lord has added sorrow to my pain; I am worn out with groaning and find no rest.'"—Do not add to what I command you and do not subtract from it, but keep the commands of the Lord your God that I give you.—"Who of you by worrying can add a single hour to his life? . . . Seek first his kingdom and his righteousness, and all these things will be given to you as well."—All the believers were together and had everything in common. . . . And the Lord added to their number daily those who were being saved.—I warn every one who hears the words of the prophecy of this book: If anyone adds anything to them, God will add to him the plagues described in this book.

Isa. 38:5; Prov. 3:1, 2; 10:22; 30:6; 2 Sam. 24:3; Jer. 45:3; Deut. 4:2; Matt. 6:27, 33; Acts 2:44, 47; Rev. 22:18.

feb/21

"For I know the plans I have for you, . . . plans to prosper you and not to harm you, plans to give you hope and a future."—Knowing their thoughts, Jesus said, "Why do you entertain evil thoughts in your hearts." . . . "What do you think about the Christ? Whose Son is he?"—They kept looking for Jesus and . . . asked one another, "What do you think? Isn't he coming to the Feast at all?"—For by the grace given me I say to every one of you: Do not think of yourself more highly than you ought, but rather think of yourself with sober judgment.—The man who thinks he knows something does not yet know as he ought to know.—If you think you are standing firm, be careful that you don't fall!—I appeal to you, brothers, in the name of our Lord Jesus Christ, that all of you agree with one another so that . . . you may be perfectly united in mind and thought. . . . "Who has known the mind of the Lord that he may instruct him?" But we have the mind of Christ.—Now to him who is able to do immeasurably more than all we ask or imagine.—Finally, brothers, whatever is true, whatever is noble, whatever is right, whatever is pure, whatever is lovely, whatever is admirable—if anything is excellent or praiseworthy—think about such things.

Jer. 29:11; Matt. 9:4; 22:42; John 11:56; Rom. 12:3; 1 Cor. 8:2; 10:12; 1:10; 2:16; Eph. 3:20; Phil. 4:8.

feb /22

"I thank and praise you, O God of my fathers:
You have given me wisdom and power." . . .
Three times a day [Daniel] got down on his knees
and prayed, giving thanks to his God.—Enter his
gates with thanksgiving and his courts with
praise; give thanks to him and praise his
name.—At the sight of [the brothers] Paul
thanked God and was encouraged.—I thank my
God every time I remember you.—He who eats
meat, eats to the Lord, for he gives thanks to God;
and he who abstains, does so to the Lord and
gives thanks to God.—Thanks be to God! He gives
us the victory through our Lord Jesus
Christ.—Thanks be to God for his indescribable
gift! —Always giving thanks to God the Father for
everything, in the name of our Lord Jesus
Christ.—Whenever the living creatures give
glory, honor and thanks to him who sits on the
throne and who lives for ever and ever, the
twenty-four elders fall down before him who sits
on the throne, and worship him who lives for ever
and ever.—"Now, our God, we give you thanks,
and praise your glorious name."—The trumpeters
and singers joined in unison, as with one voice, to
give praise and thanks to the Lord.—Jesus said, "I
praise you, Father, Lord of heaven and earth."

Dan. 2:23; 6:10; Ps. 100:4; Acts 28:15; Phil. 1:3;
Rom. 14:6; 1 Cor. 15:57; 2 Cor. 9:15; Eph. 5:20; Rev.
4:9-10; 1 Chron. 29:13; 2 Chron 5:13; Matt. 11:25.

feb /23

"Be strong and courageous. Do not be afraid or terrified because of them, for the Lord your God goes with you; he will never leave you nor forsake you."—"Be strong and let us fight bravely for our people and the cities of our God. The Lord will do what is good in his sight."—"Act with courage, and may the Lord be with those who do well." —Be strong and very courageous. Be careful to obey all the law.—At the sight of these [brothers] Paul thanked God and was encouraged.—You, dear children, are from God and have overcome them, because the one who is in you is greater than the one who is in the world.—Even if you should suffer for what is right, you are blessed. "Do not fear what they fear; do not be frightened." But in your hearts set apart Christ as Lord.—"You must go to everyone I send you to and say whatever I command you. Do not be afraid of them, for I am with you and will rescue you," declares the Lord.—For rulers hold no terror for those who do right, but for those who do wrong. Do you want to be free from fear of the one in authority? Then do what is right and he will commend you.—Wait for the Lord; be strong and take heart. . . . I will not fear the tens of thousands drawn up against me on every side.

Deut. 31:6; 1 Chron. 19:13; 2 Chron. 19:11, Josh. 1:7; Acts 28:15; 1 John 4:4; 1 Peter 3:14-15; Jer. 1:7, 8; Rom. 13:3; Pss. 27:14; 3:6.

feb/24

The Lord your God has blessed you in all the work of your hands. He has watched over your journey through this vast desert. These forty years the Lord your God has been with you, and you have not lacked anything.—The Lord is my shepherd, I shall lack nothing.—"Your Father knows what you need before you ask him. . . . Seek first his kingdom and his righteousness, and all these things will be given you as well."—He welcomed [the crowds] and spoke to them about the kingdom of God, and healed those who needed healing. "He is not served by human hands, as if he needed anything, because he himself gives all men life and breath and everything else."—I know what it is to be in need, and I know what it is to have plenty. I have learned the secret of being content in any and every situation, whether well fed or hungry, whether living in plenty or in want. . . . My God will meet all your needs according to his glorious riches in Christ Jesus.—Let us then approach the throne of grace with confidence, so that we may receive mercy and find grace to help us in our time of need.—If anyone has material possessions and sees his brother in need but has no pity on him, how can the love of God be in him?

Deut. 2:7; Ps. 23:1; Matt. 6:8, 33; Luke 9:11; Acts 17:25; Phil. 4:12, 19; Heb. 4:16; 1 John 3:17.

feb /25

The Lord knows the thoughts of man, he knows that they are futile.—"What you are doing is not right. Shouldn't you walk in the fear of our God to avoid the reproach of our Gentile enemies?"—"What do you think? If a man owns a hundred sheep, and one of them wanders away, will he not leave the ninety-nine on the hills and go to look for the one that wandered off?"—"As John was completing his work, he said, 'Who do you think I am? I am not that one. No, but he is coming after me, whose sandals I am not worthy to untie.'"—Be transformed by the renewing of your mind. Then you will be able to test and approve what God's will is—his good, pleasing and perfect will.—"For my thoughts are not your thoughts, neither are your ways my ways," declares the Lord. "As the heavens are higher than the earth, so are my ways higher than your ways and my thoughts than your thoughts."—Knowing their thoughts, Jesus said, "Why do you entertain evil thoughts in your hearts?"—"Why are you troubled, and why do doubts rise in your minds?"—We demolish arguments and every pretension that sets itself up against the knowledge of God, and we take captive every thought to make it obedient to Christ.

Ps. 94:11; Neh. 5:9; Matt. 18:12; Acts 13:25; Rom. 12:2; Isa. 55:8-9; Matt. 9:4; Luke 24:38; 2 Cor. 10:4-5.

feb/26

Better a dry crust with peace and quiet than a
house full of feasting, with strife.—Better one
handful with tranquillity than two handfuls with
toil and chasing after the wind.—"In repentance
and rest is your salvation, in quietness and trust is
your strength." . . . The fruit of righteousness will
be peace; the effect of righteousness will be
quietness and confidence forever.—If he remains
silent, who can condemn him?—Make it your
ambition to lead a quiet life, to mind your own
business and to work with your hands, . . . so that
your daily life may win respect of outsiders and so
that you will not be dependent on anybody.
—Your beauty should not come from outward
adornment . . . Instead, it should be that of your
inner self, the unfading beauty of a gentle and
quiet spirit, which is of great worth in God's
sight.—He stilled the storm to a whisper; the
waves of the sea were hushed. They were glad
when it grew calm, and he guided them to their
desired haven.—He replied, "You of little faith,
why are you so afraid?" Then he got up and
rebuked the winds and the waves, and it was
completely calm. The men were amazed and
asked, "What kind of man is this? Even the winds
and the waves obey him!"

*Prov. 17:1; Eccl. 4:6; Isa. 30:15; 32:17; Job 34:29; 1
Thess. 4:11-12; 1 Peter 3:3-4; Ps. 107:29-30; Matt.
8:26-27.*

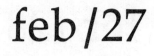

feb /27

Place me like a seal over your heart, like a seal over your arm.—"The Son of Man . . . on him God the Father has placed his seal of approval."—Even though I may not be an apostle to others, surely I am to you! For you are the seal of my apostleship in the Lord.—Stand firm in Christ. He anointed us, set his seal of ownership on us, and put his Spirit in our hearts as a deposit, guaranteeing what is to come.—You also were included in Christ when you heard the word of truth, the gospel of your salvation. Having believed, you were marked in him with a seal, the promised Holy Spirit. . . . Do not grieve the Holy Spirit of God, with whom you were sealed for the day of redemption.—Then I saw in the right hand of him who sat on the throne a scroll with writing on both sides and sealed with seven seals. . . . "The Lion of the tribe of Judah, the Root of David, has triumphed. He is able to open the scroll and its seven seals." They sang a new song: "You are worthy to take the scroll and to open its seals, because you were slain, and with your blood you purchased men for God." . . . "Do not harm the land or the sea or the trees until we put a seal on the foreheads of the servants of our God." . . . "Do not seal up the words of the prophecy of this book, because the time is near."

Song of Songs 8:6; John 6:27; 1 Cor. 9:2; 2 Cor. 1:21-22; Eph. 1:13; 4:30; Rev. 5:1, 5, 9; 7:3; 22:10.

feb /28

"This is the one I esteem: he who is humble and contrite in spirit, and trembles at my word."—He holds victory in store for the upright, he is a shield to those whose walk is blameless. . . . He who pursues righteousness and love finds life, prosperity, and honor.—Jesus answered, "If you want to be perfect, go, sell your possessions and give to the poor, and you will have treasure in heaven. Then come, follow me." . . . "The kingdom of heaven is like treasure hidden in a field. When a man found it, he hid it again, and then in his joy went and sold all he had and bought the field."—"Provide purses for yourselves that will not wear out, a treasure in heaven that will not be exhausted. . . . For where your treasure is, there your heart will be also. . . . Do not set your heart on what you will eat or drink; do not worry about it. . . . But seek his kingdom, and these things will be given you as well."—[Moses] regarded disgrace for the sake of Christ as of greater value than the treasures of Egypt, because he was looking ahead to his reward.—We have this treasure in jars of clay to show that this all-surpassing power is from God and not from us.—Since, then, you have been raised with Christ, set your hearts on things above.

Isa. 66:2; Prov. 2:7; 21:21; Matt. 19:21; 13:44; Luke 12:33-34, 29, 31; Heb. 11:26; 2 Cor. 4:7; Col. 3:1.

feb /29

For the sake of his great name the Lord will not reject his people, because the Lord was pleased to make you his own.—"How great you are, O Sovereign Lord! There is no one like you, and there is no God but you, as we have heard with our own ears."—He performs wonders that cannot be fathomed, miracles that cannot be counted. . . . God's voice thunders in marvelous ways; he does great things beyond our understanding.—Your righteousness reaches to the skies, O God, you who have done great things. Who, O God, is like you? . . . Great are the works of the Lord; they are pondered by all who delight in them. Glorious and majestic are his deeds. —Should you then seek great things for yourself? Seek them not.—The Mighty One has done great things for me—holy is his name. . . . "Who is this? He commands even the winds and the water, and they obey him."—"I tell you the truth, anyone who has faith in me will do what I have been doing. He will do even greater things than these, because I am going to the Father." —Great and marvelous are your deeds, Lord God Almighty. Just and true are your ways, King of the ages."—Great is the Lord, and most worthy of praise, in the city of our God, his holy mountain.

1 Sam. 12:22; 2 Sam. 7:22; Job 5:9; 37:5; Pss. 71:19; 111:2-3; Jer. 45:5; Luke 1:49; 8:25; John 14:12; Rev. 15:3; Ps. 48:1.

John Thornberg

*If we walk in the light, . . . we
have fellowship with one another.*

mar/1

Those who feared the Lord talked with each other, and the Lord listened and heard. A scroll of remembrance was written in his presence concerning those who feared the Lord and honored his name.—We proclaim to you what we have seen and heard, so that you also may have fellowship with us. And our fellowship is with the Father and with his Son, Jesus Christ. . . . If we claim to have fellowship with him yet walk in the darkness, we lie and do not live by the truth. But if we walk in the light, as he is in the light, we have fellowship with one another.—God, who has called you into fellowship with his Son Jesus Christ our Lord, is faithful.—Do not be yoked together with unbelievers. . . . What fellowship can light have with darkness?—I always pray with joy because of your partnership in the gospel . . . If [you have] any fellowship with the Spirit, if any tenderness and compassion, then make my joy complete by being like-minded, having the same love, being one in spirit and purpose.—All the believers were together and had everything in common. . . . Every day they continued to meet together in the temple courts. They broke bread in their homes and ate together with glad and sincere hearts.—You are all one in Christ Jesus.

Mal. 3:16; 1 John 1:3, 6-7; 1 Cor. 1:9; 2 Cor. 6:14; Phil. 1:4-5; 2:1, 2; Acts 2:44, 46; Gal. 3:28.

mar /2

He who dwells in the shelter of the Most High will rest in the shadow of the Almighty.—The glorious riches of this mystery, which is Christ in you, the hope of glory.—"Remain in me, and I will remain in you. . . . If a man remains in me and I in him, he will bear much fruit, apart from me you can do nothing. . . . If you remain in me and my words remain in you, ask whatever you wish, and it will be given you. . . . If you obey my commands, you will remain in my love, just as I obeyed my Father's commands and remain in his love."—Whoever claims to live in him, must walk as Jesus did. . . . No one who lives in him keeps on sinning. No one who continues to sin has either seen him or known him. . . . Those who obey his commands live in him, and he in them. And this is how we know that he lives in us: We know it by the Spirit he gave us.—In Christ we who are many form one body, and each member belongs to all the others.—Praise be to the God and Father of our Lord Jesus Christ, who has blessed us in the heavenly realms with every spiritual blessing in Christ.—We know that the one who raised the Lord Jesus from the dead will also raise us with Jesus and present us with you in his presence.—We will be with the Lord forever.

Ps. 91:1; Col. 1:27; John 15:4-5, 7, 10; 1 John 2:6; 3:6, 24; Rom. 12:5; Eph. 1:3; 2 Cor. 4:14; 1 Thess. 4:17.

mar /3

"But you, . . . whom I have chosen, you descendants of Abraham my friend."—The Lord would speak to Moses face to face, as a man speaks with his friend.—A friend loves at all times, and a brother is born for adversity. . . . A man of many companions may come to ruin, but there is a friend who sticks closer than a brother. . . . The kisses of an enemy may be profuse, but faithful are the wounds of a friend. . . . As iron sharpens iron, so one man sharpens another.—"I tell you, my friends, do not be afraid of those who kill the body and after that can do no more."—Judas said, "Greetings, Rabbi!" and kissed him. Jesus replied, "Friend, do what you came for." —"Abraham believed God, and it was credited to him as righteousness," and he was called God's friend. . . . Don't you know that friendship with the world is hatred toward God? Anyone who chooses to be a friend of the world becomes an enemy of God.—"Greater love has no one than this, that one lay down his life for his friends. You are my friends if you do what I command. I no longer call you servants, because a servant does not know his master's business. Instead, I have called you friends, for everything I learned from my Father I have made known unto you."

Isa. 41:8; Exod. 33:11; Prov. 17:17; 18:24; 27:6, 17; Luke 12:4; Matt. 26:49-50; James 2:23; 4:4; John 15:13-15.

mar/4

The Lord hates . . . haughty eyes . . . To fear the Lord is to hate evil; I hate pride and arrogance, evil behavior and perverse speech. . . . Pride goes before destruction, a haughty spirit before a fall. Better to be lowly in spirit and among the oppressed than to share plunder with the proud. . . . Haughty eyes and a proud heart, the lamp of the wicked, are sin!—"He has scattered those who are proud in their inmost thoughts. He has brought down rulers from their thrones but has lifted up the humble." . . . For everyone who exalts himself will be humbled, and he who humbles himself will be exalted.—"For from within, out of men's hearts, come . . . arrogance and folly."—"God opposes the proud but gives grace to the humble."—Everything in the world—the cravings of sinful man, the lust of his eyes and the boasting of what he has and does —comes not from the Father but from the world. —"Though you soar like the eagle and make your nest among the stars, from there I will bring you down," declares the Lord.—"Should you then seek great things for yourself? Seek them not."— Seek first his kingdom and his righteousness. —Learn from me, for I am gentle and humble in heart, and you will find rest for your souls.

Prov. 6:16-17; 8:13; 16:18-19; 21:4; Luke 1:51-52; 14:11; Mark 7:21-22; 1 Peter 5:5; 1 John 2:16; Obad. 4; Jer. 45:5; Matt. 6:33; 11:29.

mar/5

Hate what is evil; cling to what is good.—
Hating even the clothing stained by corrupted
flesh.—You have this in your favor: You hate the
practices of the Nicolaitans, which I also
hate.—The righteous hate what is false.
—They do all kinds of detestable things the Lord
hates.—[The wicked man] boasts of the cravings
of his heart; he blesses the greedy and reviles the
Lord.—The man who loves his life will lose it,
while the man who hates his life in this world will
keep it for eternal life.—Do not be surprised, my
brothers, if the world hates you. We know that we
have passed from death to life, because we love
our brothers. Anyone who does not love remains
in death.—"You have loved righteousness and
hated wickedness, therefore God, your God, has
set you above your companions by anointing you
with the oil of joy."—"If the world hates you,
keep in mind that it hated me first. If you
belonged to the world, it would love you as its
own. As it is, you do not belong to the world, but I
have chosen you out of the world. That is why the
world hates you. . . . They have seen these
miracles, and yet they have hated both me and my
Father. But this is to fulfill what is written in their
Law: 'They hated me without a reason.'"

Rom. 12:9; Jude 23; Rev. 2:6; Prov. 13:5; Deut.
12:31; Ps. 10:3; John 12:25; 1 John 3:13-14; Heb. 1:9;
John 15:18-19, 24-25.

mar/6

I, Daniel, was the only one who saw the vision; the men with me did not see it, but such horror overwhelmed them that they fled and hid themselves. So I was left alone, gazing at this great vision.—"I have trodden the winepress alone; from the nations no one was with me."—"Israel will live in safety alone; Jacob's spring is secure in a land of grain and new wine, where the heavens drop dew."—Very early in the morning, while it was still dark, Jesus got up, left the house and went off to a solitary place, where he prayed. —Jesus, knowing that they intended to come and make him king by force, withdrew again into the hills by himself. . . . Each man went to his own home. But Jesus went to the Mount of Olives. . . . "A time is coming, and has come, when you will be scattered, each to his own home. You will leave me all alone. Yet I am not alone, for my Father is with me."—No one came to my support, but everyone deserted me. . . . But the Lord stood at my side and gave me strength, so that through me the message might be fully proclaimed and all the Gentiles might hear it.—"I tell you the truth," Jesus replied, "no one who has left home or brothers or sisters or mother or father or children or fields for me and the gospel will fail to receive . . . in the age to come, eternal life."

Dan. 10:7-8; Isa. 63:3; Deut. 33:28; Mark 1:35; John 6:15; 7:53—8:1; 16:32; 2 Tim. 4:16-17; Mark 10:29-30.

mar/7

"**H**ere is my servant, whom I uphold, my chosen one in whom I delight." . . . "If you call the Sabbath a delight . . . then you will find your joy in the Lord." . . . You will be called Hephzibah [meaning "my delight is in her"], . . . for the Lord will take delight in you.—The Lord disciplines those he loves, as a father the son he delights in. . . . The Lord abhors dishonest scales, but accurate weights are his delight. . . . The Lord detests men of perverse heart but he delights in those whose ways are blameless.—The Lord delights in the way of the man whose steps he has made firm.—He brought me out into a spacious place; he rescued me because he delighted in me.—Praise be the Lord your God, who has delighted in you.—"I am the Lord, who exercises kindness, justice and righteousness on earth, for in these I delight."—In my inner being I delight in God's law.—"Yours will be a delightful land," says the Lord Almighty.—Delight yourself in the Lord and he will give you the desires of your heart.—The Lord detests the sacrifice of the wicked, but the prayer of the upright pleases him.—I was filled with delight day after day, rejoicing always in his presence, rejoicing in his whole world and delighting in mankind.

Isa. 42:1; 58:13-14; 62:4; Prov. 3:12; 11:1, 20; Ps. 37:23; 2 Sam. 22:20; 1 Kings 10:9; Jer. 9:24; Rom. 7:22; Mal. 3:12; Ps. 37:4; Prov. 15:8; 8:30-31.

mar/8

Through him all things were made; without him nothing was made that has been made.—"I am the Lord, who has made all things."—"You are worthy, our Lord and God, to receive glory and honor and power, for you created all things." —God placed all things under his feet.—"All things have been committed to me by my Father."—"With God all things are possible."—"The Holy Spirit, whom the Father will send in my name, will teach you all things."—We know that in all things God works for the good of those who love him. . . . In all these things we are more than conquerors through him who loved us. . . . For from him and through him and to him are all things.—The Spirit searches all things, even the deep things of God. . . . The Father, from whom all things came and for whom we live; and there is but one Lord, Jesus Christ, through whom all things came and through whom we live.—God is able to make all grace abound to you, so that in all things at all times, having all you need, you will abound in every good work.—[God purposed] to bring all things in heaven and on earth together under one head, even Christ.—Sustaining all things by his powerful word.

John 1:3; Isa. 44:24; Rev. 4:11; Eph. 1:22; Luke 10:22; Matt. 19:26; John 14:26; Rom. 8:28, 37; 11:36; 1 Cor. 2:10; 8:6; 2 Cor. 9:8; Eph. 1:10; Heb. 1:3.

mar/9

Let us draw near to God with a sincere heart in full assurance of faith. . . . A better hope is introduced, by which we draw near to God.—Come near to God and he will come near to you.—But now in Christ Jesus you who once were far away have been brought near through the blood of Christ.—You who are near, acknowledge my power! . . . He who vindicates me is near. Who then will bring charges against me? . . . Seek the Lord while he may be found; call on him while he is near. . . . "Peace, peace to those far and near," says the Lord. "And I will heal them." —The Lord is close to the brokenhearted. . . . But as for me, it is good to be near God. . . . You are near, O Lord.— "Surely the Lord is in this place, and I was not aware of it."—"'My son, . . . you are always with me, and everything I have is yours.'"—The Lord is near to all who call on him, to all who call on him in truth.—Who shall separate us from the love of Christ? . . . I am convinced that neither death nor life, neither angels nor demons, neither the present nor the future, nor any powers, neither height nor depth, nor anything else in all creation, will be able to separate us from the love of God that is in Christ Jesus our Lord.

Heb. 10:22; 7:19; James 4:8; Eph. 2:13; Isa. 33:13; 50:8; 55:6; 57:19; Pss. 34:18; 73:28; 119:151; Gen. 28:16; Luke 15:31; Ps. 145:18; Rom. 8:35, 38-39.

mar/10

[Abraham] was looking forward to the city with foundations, whose architect and builder is God. . . . Therefore God is not ashamed to be called their God, for he has prepared a city for them. . . . They were longing for a better country—a heavenly one.—"In my father's house are many rooms; if it were not so, I would have told you. I am going there to prepare a place for you. And if I go and prepare a place for you, I will come back and take you to be with me that you also may be where I am. You know the way to the place where I am going."—"As I looked, thrones were set in place, and the Ancient of Days took his seat. His clothing was as white as snow; the hair of his head was white like wool. His throne was flaming with fire, and its wheels were all ablaze. A river of fire was flowing, coming out from before him. Thousands upon thousands attended him; ten thousand times ten thousand stood before him."—After this I looked and there before me was a great multitude that no man could count, from every nation, tribe, people and language, standing before the throne and in front of the Lamb.—Your eyes will see the king in his beauty and view a land that stretches afar.—I desire to depart and be with Christ, which is better by far.

Heb. 11:10, 16; John 14:2-4; Dan. 7:9-10; Rev. 7:9; Isa. 33:17; Phil. 1:23.

mar/11

He has made everything beautiful in its time.
—In that day the Branch of the Lord will be
beautiful. . . . In that day the Lord Almighty will
be a glorious crown, a beautiful wreath for the
remnant of his people. . . . Your eyes will see the
king in his beauty and view a land that stretches
afar.—They will sparkle in his land like jewels in a
crown. How attractive and beautiful they will
be.—How beautiful on the mountains are the feet
of those who bring good news, who proclaim
peace, bring good tidings, who proclaim
salvation.—Worship the Lord in the splendor of
his holiness.—Your beauty should not come from
outward adornment. . . . It should be that of your
inner self, the unfading beauty of a gentle and
quiet spirit, which is of great worth in God's
sight.—This is what I seek: that I may dwell in the
house of the Lord all the days of my life, to gaze
upon the beauty of the Lord and to seek him in his
temple. . . . The king is enthralled by your
beauty; honor him, for he is your lord.—"'You
became very beautiful and rose to be a queen. And
your fame spread among the nations on account of
your beauty, because the splendor I had given you
made your beauty perfect, declares the Sovereign
Lord. But you trusted in your beauty.'"

*Eccl. 3:11; Isa. 4:2; 28:5; 33:17; Zech. 9:16-17; Isa.
52:7; 1 Chron. 16:29; 1 Peter 3:3-4; Pss. 27:4; 45:11;
Ezek. 16:13-15.*

mar/12

Yet, O Lord, you are our Father. . . . He will be called . . . Everlasting Father.—A father to the fatherless, . . . is God in his holy dwelling. . . . As a father has compassion on his children, so the Lord has compassion on those who fear him.—"It is my Father who gives you the true bread from heaven." . . . "No man can come to me unless the Father has enabled him." . . . "I give [my sheep] eternal life, and they shall never perish; no one can snatch them out of my hand. My Father, who has given them to me, is greater than all; no one can snatch them out of my Father's hand. I and the Father are one." . . . "This is to my Father's glory, that you bear much fruit. . . . The Father will give you whatever you ask in my name."—"Your Father knows what you need before you ask him. . . . Be perfect, therefore, as your heavenly Father is perfect."—"Be merciful, just as your Father is merciful."—"Pray to your Father, who is unseen. Then your Father, who sees what is done in secret, will reward you. . . . 'Our Father in heaven, hallowed be your name.'" . . . "Shall I not drink the cup the Father has given me?" . . . "'I am returning to my Father and your Father, to my God and your God.'"—"Father, into your hands I commit my spirit."

Isa. 64:8; 9:6; Pss. 68:5; 103:13; John 6:32, 65; 10:28-30; 15:8, 16; Matt. 6:8; 5:48; Luke 6:36; Matt. 6:6, 9; John 18:11; 20:17; Luke 23:46.

mar / 13

He gives strength to the weary and increases the power of the weak.—He who oppresses the poor to increase his wealth and he who gives gifts to the rich—both come to poverty.—The increase from the land is taken by all. . . . As goods increase, so do those who consume them.—The apostles said to the Lord, "Increase our faith!" He replied, "If you have faith as small as a mustard seed, you can say to this mulberry tree, 'Be uprooted and planted in the sea,' and it will obey you."—May the Lord make your love increase and overflow for each other and for everyone else, just as ours does for you.—Now he who supplies seed to the sower and bread for food will also supply and increase your store of seed and will enlarge the harvest of your righteousness.—Though your riches increase, do not set your heart on them. . . . He will bless those who fear the Lord—small and great alike. May the Lord make you increase, both you and your children.—Live a life worthy of the Lord and . . . please him in every way: bearing fruit in every good work, growing in the knowledge of God.—Where there are no oxen, the manger is empty, but from the strength of an ox comes an abundant harvest.—Of the increase of his government and peace there will be no end.

Isa. 40:29; Prov. 22:16; Eccl. 5:9, 11; Luke 17:5-6; 1 Thess. 3:12; 2 Cor. 9:10; Pss. 62:10; 115:13-14; Col. 1:10; Prov. 14:4; Isa. 9:7.

mar/14

The Lord will be your confidence and will keep your foot from being snared.—It is better to take refuge in the Lord than to trust in man.—"If I have put my trust in gold or said to pure gold, 'You are my security,' . . . I would have been unfaithful to God on high.—Therefore we are always confident and know that as long as we are at home in the body we are away from the Lord. . . . We are confident, I say, and would prefer to be away from the body and at home with the Lord.—We who worship by the Spirit of God, who glory in Christ Jesus, and who put no confidence in the flesh.—In him and through faith in him we may approach God with freedom and confidence.—We have come to share in Christ if we hold firmly till the end the confidence we had at first. . . . So do not throw away your confidence; it will be richly rewarded. You need to persevere so that when you have done the will of God, you will receive what he has promised.—And now, dear children, continue in him, so that when he appears we may be confident and unashamed before him at his coming. . . . Dear friends, if our hearts do not condemn us, we have confidence before God and receive from him anything we ask, because we obey his commands and do what pleases him.

Prov. 3:26; Ps. 118:8; Job 31:24, 28; 2 Cor. 5:6, 8; Phil. 3:3; Eph. 3:12; Heb. 3:14; 10:35-36; 1 John 2:28; 3:21-22.

mar/15

"**H**ear my prayer, O Lord, listen to my cry for help; be not deaf to my weeping." . . . My tears have been my food day and night, while men say to me all day long, "Where is your God?" . . . You have fed them with the bread of tears; you have made them drink tears by the bowlful.—If you do not listen, I will weep in secret because of your pride.—"'Let my eyes overflow with tears night and day without ceasing; for . . . my people.'" —As [Jesus] approached Jerusalem and saw the city, he wept over it.—This is what the Lord says: "Restrain your voice from weeping and your eyes from tears, for your work will be rewarded." —During the days of Jesus' life on earth, he offered up prayers and petitions with loud cries and tears to the one who could save him from death, and he was heard because of his reverent submission.—I served the Lord with great humility and with tears. . . . Remember that for three years I never stopped warning each of you night and day with tears.—Weeping may remain for a night, but rejoicing comes in the morning.—"God will wipe away every tear from their eyes." . . . "There will be no more death or mourning or crying or pain, for the old order of things has passed away."

Pss. 39:12; 42:3; 80:5; Jer. 13:17; 14:17; Luke 19:41; Jer. 31:16; Heb. 5:7; Acts 20:19, 31; Ps. 30:5; Rev. 7:17; 21:4.

mar/16

"When [Christ] ascended on high, he led captives in his train and gave gifts to men." —God's gifts and his call are irrevocable. . . . We have different gifts, according to the grace given us.—There are different kinds of gifts, but the same Spirit. There are different kinds of service, but the same Lord. . . . God has appointed . . . those having gifts of healing, those able to help others, those with gifts of administration. . . . But eagerly desire the greater gifts. . . . Each man has his own gift from God; one has this gift, another has that.—God also testified to [the great salvation] by signs, wonders, and various miracles, and gifts of the Holy Spirit distributed according to his will.—"If you, then, though you are evil, know how to give good gifts to your children, how much more will your Father in heaven give good gifts to those who ask him!"—For this reason I remind you to fan into flame the gift of God. . . . God did not give us a spirit of timidity, but a spirit of power, of love and of self-discipline. . . . Do not neglect your gift.—Those who receive God's abundant provision of grace and of the gift of righteousness reign in life through the one man, Jesus Christ. —Thanks be to God for his indescribable gift!

Eph. 4:8; Rom. 11:29; 12:6; 1 Cor. 12:4, 5, 28, 31; 7:7; Heb. 2:4; Matt. 7:11; 2 Tim. 1:6-7; 1 Tim. 4:14; Rom. 5:17; 2 Cor. 9:15.

mar/17

[David] was shaken. He went up to the room over the gateway and wept. As he went, he said: "O my son Absalom! My son, my son Absalom! If only I had died instead of you—O Absalom, my son, my son!"—"Woe to you, O Jerusalem! How long will you be unclean?"—"O Jerusalem, Jerusalem, you who kill the prophets and stone those sent to you, how often I have longed to gather your children together, as a hen gathers her chicks under her wings, but you were not willing." . . . "Woe to you, Korazin! Woe to you, Bethsaida! If the miracles that were performed in you had been performed in Tyre and Sidon, they would have repented long ago in sackcloth and ashes. But I tell you, it will be more bearable for Tyre and Sidon on the day of Judgment than for you."—[Saul] fell to the ground and heard a voice say to him, "Saul, Saul, why do you persecute me?" "Who are you, Lord?" Saul asked. "I am Jesus, whom you are persecuting," he replied.—Woe to me if I do not preach the gospel!—"Woe to me!" I cried. "I am ruined! For I am a man of unclean lips, and I live among a people of unclean lips, and my eyes have seen the King, the Lord Almighty."—Then Job replied: . . . "If only I knew where to find him; if only I could go to his dwelling!"

2 Sam. 18:33; Jer. 13:27; Matt. 23:37; 11:21-22; Acts 9:4-5; 1 Cor. 9:16; Isa. 6:5; Job 23:1, 3.

mar/18

My cup overflows. . . . Lord, you have assigned me my portion and my cup; you have made my lot secure. . . . I will lift up the cup of salvation and call on the name of the Lord.—Your Sovereign Lord says, . . . "See, I have taken out of your hand the cup that made you stagger; from that cup, the goblet of my wrath, you will never drink again."—Jesus commanded Peter, "Put your sword away! Shall I not drink the cup the Father has given me?"—"My Father, if it is possible, may this cup be taken from me. Yet not as I will, but as you will." . . . [Jesus said,] "Can you drink the cup I am going to drink? . . . You will indeed drink from my cup."—After the supper he took the cup, saying, "This cup is the new covenant in my blood, which is poured out for you." . . . "Do this, whenever you drink it, in remembrance of me."—Is not the cup of thanksgiving for which we give thanks a participation in the blood of Christ? . . . You cannot drink the cup of the Lord and the cup of demons too.—"If anyone gives a cup of cold water to one of these little ones because he is my disciple, I tell you the truth, he will certainly not lose his reward."—"He, too, will drink of the wine of God's fury, which has been poured full strength into the cup of his wrath."

Pss. 23:5; 16:5; 116:13; Isa. 51:22; John 18:11; Matt. 26:39; 20:22-23; Luke 22:20; 1 Cor. 11:25; 10:16, 21; Matt. 10:42; Rev. 14:10.

mar /19

"Do not fear, for I am with you. . . . I myself will help you," declares the Lord, your Redeemer, the Holy One of Israel. . . . Because the Sovereign Lord helps me, I will not be disgraced. . . . Woe to those who go down to Egypt for help, . . . but do not look to the Holy One of Israel, or seek help from the Lord.—The woman came and knelt before him. "Lord, help me!" she said.—The Spirit helps us in our weakness.—On him we have set our hope that he will continue to deliver us, as you help us by your prayers.—In the church God has appointed . . . those able to help others. —We may say with confidence, "The Lord is my helper; I will not be afraid. What can man do unto me?" . . . Let us then approach the throne of grace with confidence, so that we may receive mercy and find grace to help us in our time of need.—Samuel took a stone and set it up between Mizpah and Shen. He named it Ebenezer, saying, "Thus far has the Lord helped us."—O my Strength, come quickly to help me. . . . You are the helper of the fatherless. . . . "Hear, O Lord, and be merciful unto me; O Lord, be my help." . . . Surely God is my help; the Lord is the one who sustains me. . . . He will deliver the needy who cry out, the afflicted who have no one to help.

Isa. 41:10, 14; 50:7; 31:1; Matt. 15:25; Rom. 8:26; 2 Cor. 1:10-11; 1 Cor. 12:28; Heb. 13:6; 4:16; 1 Sam. 7:12; Pss. 22:19; 10:14; 30:10; 54:4; 72:12.

mar/20

"See, the former things have taken place, and new things I declare; before they spring into being I announce them to you." Sing to the Lord a new song, his praise from the ends of the earth. . . . "From now on I will tell you of new things, of hidden things unknown to you." . . . "See, I am doing a new thing! Now it springs up; do you not perceive it? I am making a way in the desert." . . . You will be called by a new name that the mouth of the Lord will bestow.—"I will write on him the name of my God, . . . my new name." . . . They sang a new song before the throne and before the four living creatures and the elders.—He put a new song in my mouth.—"A new commandment I give unto you: Love one another."—If anyone is in Christ, he is a new creation.—His purpose was to create in himself one new man out of the two, thus making peace.—We have confidence to enter the Most Holy Place by the blood of Jesus, by a new and living way opened for us through the curtain, that is, his body.—He who was seated on the throne said, "I am making everything new!"—"Behold, I will create new heavens and a new earth. The former things will not be remembered, nor will they come into mind."

Isa. 42:9-10; 48:6; 43:19; 62:2; Rev. 3:12; 14:3; Ps. 40:3; John 13:34; 2 Cor. 5:17; Eph. 2:15; Heb. 10:19-20; Rev. 21:5; Isa. 65:17.

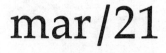

mar/21

"For I am the Lord your God, who takes hold of your right hand and says to you, Do not fear; I will help you." . . . "I, the Lord, have called you in righteousness; I will take hold of your hand." . . . You will be a crown of splendor in the Lord's hand, a royal diadem in the hand of your God. . . . Yet, O Lord, you are our Father. We are the clay, you are the potter; we are all the work of your hand.—The king's heart is in the hand of the Lord; he directs it like a watercourse wherever he pleases.—"The Lord your God brought you out of [Egypt] with a mighty hand and an outstretched arm."—"I give [my sheep] eternal life, and they shall never perish; no one can snatch them out of my hand. My Father, who has given them to me, is greater than all; no one can snatch them out of my Father's hand." . . . The Father loves the Son and has placed everything in his hands.—No one can hold back his hand or say to him: "What have you done?" . . . You did not honor the God who holds in his hand your life and all your ways.—In your hands are strength and power to exalt and give strength to all.—I will put you in a cleft in the rock and cover you with my hand.—Humble yourselves, therefore, under God's mighty hand, that he may lift you up in due time.

Isa. 41:13; 42:6; 62:3; 64:8; Prov. 21:1; Deut. 5:15; John 10:28-29; 3:35; Dan. 4:35; 5:23; 1 Chron 29:12; Exod. 33:22; 1 Peter 5:6.

mar/22

Return to your fortress, O prisoners of hope; even now I announce that I will restore twice as much to you.—I know that when I come to you, I will come in the full measure of the blessing of Christ.—Now to him who is able to do immeasurably more than all we ask or imagine, according to his power that is at work within us.—Be at rest once more, O my soul, for the Lord has been good to you. . . . How precious to me are your thoughts, O God! How vast is the sum of them!—God is able to make all grace abound to you, so that in all things at all times, having all that you need, you will abound in every good work.—"Everyone who has left houses or brothers or sisters or father or mother or children or fields for my sake will receive a hundred times as much and will inherit eternal life."—From this one man . . . came descendants as numerous as the stars in the sky and as countless as the sand on the seashore.—After this I looked and there before me was a great multitude that no one could count, from every nation, tribe, people and language, standing before the throne and in front of the Lamb.—"Give, and it will be given to you. A good measure, pressed down, shaken together and running over, will be poured into your lap."

Zech. 9:12; Rom. 15:29; Eph. 3:20; Pss. 116:7; 139:17; 2 Cor. 9:8; Matt. 19:29; Heb. 11:12; Rev. 7:9; Luke 6:38.

mar/23

The hand of the Mighty One of Jacob, because of the Shepherd, the Rock of Israel.—"I saw all Israel scattered on the hills like sheep without a shepherd."—He tends his flock like a shepherd: He gathers the lambs in his arms and carries them close to his heart.—The words of the wise are like goads, their collected sayings like firmly embedded nails—given by one Shepherd.—Hear us, O Shepherd of Israel, you who lead Joseph like a flock. . . . The Lord is my shepherd, I shall lack nothing.—You were like sheep going astray, but now you have returned to the Shepherd and Overseer of your souls.—"Awake, O sword, against my shepherd."—"I am the good shepherd. The good shepherd lays down his life for the sheep. . . . I am the good shepherd; I know my sheep and my sheep know me. . . . There shall be one flock and one shepherd."—That great Shepherd of the sheep.—When the Chief Shepherd appears, you will receive the crown of glory that will never fade away. . . . Be shepherds of God's flock that is under your care.—These are they who have come out of the great tribulation. . . . The Lamb at the center of the throne will be their shepherd; he will lead them to springs of living water.

Gen. 49:24; 1 Kings 22:17; Isa. 40:11; Eccl. 12:11; Pss. 80:1; 23:1; 1 Peter 2:25; Zech. 13:7; John 10:11, 14, 16; Heb. 13:20; 1 Peter 5:4, 2; Rev. 7:14, 17.

mar/24

"Do whatever seems best . . . in accordance with the will of your God."—"Whoever does God's will is my brother and sister and mother."—"Your will be done on earth as it is in heaven."—He who searches our hearts knows the mind of the Spirit, because the Spirit intercedes for the saints in accordance with God's will. . . . Test and approve what God's will is—his good, pleasing and perfect will.—They gave themselves first to the Lord and then to us in keeping with God's will.—The Lord Jesus Christ, who gave himself for our sins to rescue us from the present evil age, according to the will of our God and Father, to whom be glory for ever and ever.—Doing the will of God from your heart. Serve wholeheartedly.—It is God's will that you should be holy.—Then he said, "Here I am, I have come to do your will."—Those who suffer according to God's will should commit themselves to their faithful Creator and continue to do good.—The world and its desires pass away, but the man who does the will of God lives forever.—You need to persevere so that when you have done the will of God, you will receive what he has promised.—Adopted as his sons through Jesus Christ, in accordance with his pleasure and will.

Ezra 7:18; Mark 3:35; Matt. 6:10; Rom. 8:27; 12:2; 2 Cor. 8:5; Gal. 1:3-5; Eph. 6:6-7; 1 Thess. 4:3; Heb. 10:9; 1 Peter 4:19; 1 John 2:17; Heb. 10:36; Eph. 1:5.

mar/25

I form the light and create darkness, I bring prosperity and create disaster; I, the Lord, do all these things.—"Am I only a God nearby, . . . and not a God far away? Can anyone hide in secret places so that I cannot see him?" declares the Lord.—You know the grace of our Lord Jesus Christ, that though he was rich, yet for your sakes he became poor, so that you through his poverty might become rich.—Consider therefore the kindness and sternness of God: sternness to those who fell, but kindness to you, provided that you continue in his kindness.—I saw the Lord seated on a throne, high and exalted, and the train of his robe filled the temple.—I am gentle and humble in heart.—"Jacob I loved, but Esau I hated." What then shall we say? Is God unjust? Not at all! For he says to Moses, "I will have mercy on whom I have mercy, and I will have compassion on whom I have compassion."—The sea is his, for he made it.—That the Scripture would be fulfilled, Jesus said, "I am thirsty."—His appearance was so disfigured beyond that of any man and his form marred beyond human likeness—Beyond all question, the mystery of godliness is great: [God] appeared in a body.—"I am the bread of life. He who comes to me will never go hungry."

Isa. 45:7; Jer. 23:23, 24; 2 Cor. 8:9; Rom. 11:22; Isa. 6:1; Matt. 11:29; Rom. 9:13-15; Ps. 95:5; John 19:28; Isa. 52:14; 1 Tim. 3:16; John 6:35.

mar/26

Praise be to the Lord: for he showed his wonderful love to me when I was in a besieged city.—The Lord your God . . . is gracious and compassionate, slow to anger and abounding in love.—I will tell of the kindnesses of the Lord, the deeds for which he is to be praised . . . according to his compassion and many kindnesses. . . . "In a surge of anger I hid my face from you for a moment, but with everlasting kindness I will have compassion on you," says the Lord your Redeemer.—"But love your enemies, do good to them . . . and you will be sons of the Most High, because he is kind to the ungrateful and wicked."—Love is patient, love is kind.—As servants of God we commend ourselves in . . . patience and kindness.—The incomparable riches of his grace, expressed in his kindness to us in Christ Jesus. . . . Be kind and compassionate to one another.—When the kindness and love of God our Savior appeared, he saved us, not because of righteous things we had done, but because of his mercy—Clothe yourselves with compassion, kindness, humility, gentleness and patience.—Make every effort to add to your faith . . . godliness; and to godliness, brotherly kindness; and to brotherly kindness, love.

Ps. 31:21; Joel 2:13; Isa. 63:7; 54:8; Luke 6:35; 1 Cor. 13:4; 2 Cor. 6:4; Eph. 2:7; 4:32; Titus 3:4-5; Col. 3:12; 2 Peter 1:5-7.

mar/27

God said, "Let there be light," and there was light.—In him was life, and that life was the light of men. . . . The true light that gives light to every man was coming into the world.—"Arise, shine, for your light has come, and the glory of the Lord rises upon you. . . . The Lord will be your everlasting light." . . . "I will also make you a light for the Gentiles."—"I am the light of the world. Whoever follows me will never walk in darkness, but will have the light of life." . . . "While I am in the world, I am the light of the world."—Declare the praises of him who called you out of darkness into his wonderful light.— The path of the righteous is like the first gleam of dawn, shining ever brighter till the full light of day.—"You are the light of the world. . . . Let your light shine before men, that they may see your good deeds and praise your Father in heaven."—You are all sons of the light and sons of the day.—Whoever loves his brother lives in the light, and there is nothing in him to make him stumble.—The city does not need the sun or the moon to shine on it, for the glory of God gives it light, and the Lamb is its lamp. The nations will walk by its light. . . . There will be no night there.

Gen. 1:3; John 1:4, 9; Isa. 60:1, 19-20; 49:6; John 8:12; 9:5; 1 Peter 2:9; Prov. 4:18; Matt. 5:14, 16; 1 Thess. 5:5; 1 John 2:10; Rev. 21:23-25.

mar/28

All the holy ones are in your hand. At your feet they all bow down, and from you receive instruction.—They have pierced my hands and my feet.—[The] clouds are the dust of his feet.—"I will glorify the place of my feet."—On that day his feet will stand on the Mount of Olives.—As [the woman] stood behind him at his feet weeping, she began to wet his feet with her tears. Then she wiped them with her hair, kissed them and poured perfume on them. . . . "You did not put oil on my head, but she has poured perfume on my feet."—Mary took about a pint of pure nard, an expensive perfume; she poured it on Jesus' feet and wiped his feet with her hair. And the house was filled with the fragrance.—She had a sister called Mary, who sat at the Lord's feet listening to what he said.—He must reign until he has put all his enemies under his feet.—God placed all things under his feet and appointed him to be head over everything for the church, which is his body, the fullness of him who fills everything in every way.—His feet were like bronze glowing in a furnace. . . . "These are the words of the Son of God, whose eyes are like blazing fire and whose feet are like burnished bronze."

Deut. 33:3; Ps. 22:16; Nahum 1:3; Isa. 60:13; Zech. 14:4; Luke 7:38, 46; John 12:3; Luke 10:39; 1 Cor. 15:25; Eph. 1:22-23; Rev. 1:15; 2:18.

mar/29

You are a people holy to the Lord your God. The Lord your God has chosen you out of all the peoples on the face of the earth to be his people, his treasured possession. The Lord did not set his affection on you and choose you because you were more numerous than other peoples, for you were the fewest of all peoples. But it was because the Lord loved you.—"The Christ of God, the Chosen One."—"Many are invited, but few are chosen."—[Jesus] called his disciples to him and chose twelve of them, whom he designated apostles.—"I know those I have chosen." . . . "You did not choose me, but I chose you to go and bear fruit—fruit that will last. . . . I have chosen you out of the world."—He chose us in him before the creation of the world to be holy and blameless in his sight.—God chose the weak things of the world to shame the strong. He chose the lowly things of this world and the despised things—and the things that are not—to nullify the things that are.—From the beginning God chose you to be saved through the sanctifying work of the Spirit and through belief in the truth.—"With him will be his called, chosen and faithful followers." —You are a chosen people, . . . a people belonging to God.

Deut 7:6-8; Luke 23:35; Matt. 22:14; Luke 6:13; John 13:18; 15:16, 19; Eph. 1:4; 1 Cor. 1:27-28; 2 Thess. 2:13; Rev. 17:14; 1 Peter 2:9.

mar/30

In the past God overlooked such ignorance, but now he commands all people everywhere to repent.—"I have not come to call the righteous, but sinners to repentance." . . . "Repentance and forgiveness of sins will be preached in his name."—God's kindness leads you toward repentance.—God exalted him to his own right hand as Prince and Savior that he might give repentance and forgiveness of sins.—The men of Nineveh will stand up at the judgment with this generation and condemn it; for they repented at the preaching of Jonah, and now one greater than Jonah is here.—No one repents of his wickedness, saying, "What have I done?"—"Produce fruit in keeping with repentance." . . . "There is rejoicing in the presence of the angels of God over one sinner who repents than over ninety-nine righteous persons who do not need to repent." . . . "Unless you repent, you too will all perish."—"Repent and do the things you did at first. If you do not repent, I will come to you and remove your lampstand from its place. . . . Repent therefore!"—"I knew that you are a gracious and compassionate God, . . . who relents from sending calamity."

Acts 17:30; Luke 5:32; 24:47; Rom. 2:4; Acts 5:31; Matt. 12:41; Jer. 8:6; Luke 3:8; 15:10, 7; 13:3, 5; Rev. 2:5, 16; Jonah 4:2.

mar/31

The heart is deceitful above all things and beyond cure. Who can understand it? "I the Lord search the heart."—Listen, my son, and be wise, and keep your heart on the right path. . . . My son, give me your heart and let your eyes keep to my ways.—"Hear me, you who know what is right, you people who have my law in your hearts."—Where your treasure is, there your heart will be also.—It is with your heart that you believe and are justified.—"Blessed are the pure in heart, for they will see God."—A heart at peace gives life to the body.—Dear friends, if our hearts do not condemn us, we have confidence before God and receive from him anything we ask, because we obey his commands and do what pleases him.—What does the Lord your God ask of you but to fear [him], to walk in all his ways, to love him, to serve [him] with all your heart and with all your soul.—I will praise you, O Lord, with all my heart.—Light is shed upon the righteous and joy on the upright in heart.—Pursue righteousness, faith, love and peace, along with those who call on the Lord out of a pure heart.—Create in me a pure heart, O God, and renew a steadfast spirit within me.

Jer. 17:9-10; Prov. 23:19, 26; Isa. 51:7; Matt. 6:21; Rom. 10:10; Matt. 5:8; Prov. 14:30; 1 John 3:21-22; Deut. 10:12; Pss. 9:1; 97:11; 2 Tim. 2:22; Ps. 51:10.

"This is my Son, whom I love."

apr/1

A voice from heaven said, "This is my Son, whom I love; with him I am well pleased."—My lover is . . . outstanding among ten thousand. . . . He is altogether lovely.—You are the most excellent of men and your lips have been anointed with grace, since God has blessed you forever. . . . The Lord says to my Lord: "Sit at my right hand until I make your enemies a footstool for your feet."—His Son, whom he appointed heir of all things, and through whom he made the universe. The Son is the radiance of God's glory and the exact representation of his being, sustaining all things by his powerful word. . . . He became as much superior to the angels as the name he has inherited is superior to theirs. For to which of the angels did God ever say, "You are my Son; today I have become your Father?" . . . When God brings his firstborn into the world, he says, "Let all God's angels worship him."—For God was pleased to have all his fullness dwell in him, and through him to reconcile to himself all things, whether things on earth or things in heaven, by making peace through his blood, shed on the cross.—God exalted him to the highest place and gave him the name that is above every name, that at the name of Jesus every knee should bow, in heaven and on earth and under the earth.

Matt. 3:17; Song of Songs 5:10, 16; Pss. 45:2; 110:1; Heb. 1:2-6; Col. 1:19-20; Phil. 2:9-10.

apr/2

For the Lord your God is God of gods and Lord of lords, the great God, mighty and awesome, who shows no partiality and accepts no bribes.—For great is the Lord and most worthy of praise; he is to be feared above all gods.—"The temple I am going to build will be great, because our God is greater than all other gods."—"How great you are, O Sovereign Lord! There is no one like you, and there is no God but you."—"O great and powerful God, whose name is the Lord Almighty, great are your purposes and mighty your deeds." . . . "'I swear by my great name,' says the Lord."—"Shout aloud and sing for joy, people of Zion, for great is the Holy One of Israel among you."—"The Queen of the South . . . came from the ends of the earth to listen to Solomon's wisdom, and now one greater than Solomon is here."—How great is your goodness, which you have stored up for those who fear you. . . . For you are great, and do marvelous deeds; you alone are God.—We wait for the blessed hope—the glorious appearing of our great God and Savior, Jesus Christ.—"Whoever practices and teaches these commands will be called great in the kingdom of heaven."—The one who is in you is greater than the one who is in the world.

Deut. 10:17; 1 Chron. 16:25; 2 Chron. 2:5; 2 Sam. 7:22; Jer. 32:18-19; 44:26; Isa. 12:6; Matt. 12:42; Pss. 31:19; 86:10; Titus 2:13; Matt. 5:19; 1 John 4:4.

apr /3

A little child will lead them.—[Jesus] called a
little child and had him stand among them. And
he said: "I tell you the truth, unless you change
and become like little children, you will never
enter the kingdom of heaven. . . . And whoever
welcomes a little child like this in my name
welcomes me."—Anyone who will not receive the
kingdom of God like a little child will never enter
it." And he took the children in his arms, put his
hands on them and blessed them.—The little you
had before I came has increased greatly.—[A
captive young girl] said to [Naaman's wife], "If
only my master would see the prophet who is in
Samaria! He would cure him of his leprosy." . . .
[Naaman's] flesh was restored and became clean
like that of a young boy. —Samuel said [to Saul],
"Although you were once small in your own eyes,
did you not become the head of the tribes of
Israel?"—Who despises the day of small
things?—"But you, Bethlehem Ephrathah, though
you are small among the clans of Judah, out of you
will come for me one who will be ruler over Israel,
whose origins are from of old, from ancient
times."—"Here is a boy with five small barley
loaves and two small fish, but how far will they go
among so many?" . . . They all had enough to eat.

*Isa. 11:6; Matt. 18:2-3, 5; Mark 10:15-16; Gen.
30:30; 2 Kings 5:3, 14; 1 Sam. 15:17; Zech. 4:10;
Micah 5:2; John 6:9, 12.*

apr/4

"I have found the Book of the Law in the temple of the Lord."—I love those who love me, and those who seek me find me.—"He who seeks finds." . . . "If a man owns a hundred sheep, and one of them wanders away, will he not leave the ninety-nine on the hills and go to look for the one that wandered off? And if he finds it, . . . he is happier about that one sheep than about the ninety-nine that did not wander off."—"'Rejoice with me; I have found my lost coin.' In the same way, I tell you, there is rejoicing in the presence of the angels of God over one sinner who repents." . . . "'This son of mine was lost . . . lost and is found.' So they began to celebrate."—"I was found by those who did not seek me."—[Jesus said,] "I have not lost one of those you gave me."—God did this so that men would seek him and perhaps reach out for him and find him, though he is not far from each one of us.—He who seeks good finds good will, but evil comes to him who searches for it.—"Whoever loses his life for me will find it."—"You will seek me and find me when you seek me with all your heart."—"'I will search for the lost and bring back the strays. I will bind up the injured and strengthen the weak.'"

2 Kings 22:8; Prov. 8:17; Matt. 7:8; 18:12-13; Luke 15:9-10, 24; Rom. 10:20; John 18:9; Acts 17:27; Prov. 11:27; Matt. 16:25; Jer. 29:13; Ezek. 34:16.

apr/5

You open your hand and satisfy the desires of every living thing.—Jesus said to [his disciples], "Come and have breakfast." . . . [He] took the bread and gave it to them, and did the same with the fish.—On this mountain the Lord Almighty will prepare a feast of rich food for all peoples.—It will be good for those servants whose master finds them watching when he comes. . . . He will dress himself to serve, will have them recline at the table and will come and wait on them.—The God who has been my shepherd all my life to this day. —David shepherded them with integrity of heart. . . . "You would be fed with the finest of wheat; with honey from the rock I would satisfy you."—"Give us today our daily bread." —"Consider the ravens: They do not sow or reap, they have no storeroom or barn; yet God feeds them."—You have fed them with the bread of tears; you have made them drink tears by the bowlful.—While they were eating, Jesus took bread, gave thanks and broke it, and gave to his disciples, saying, "Take and eat; this is my body."—"These are they who have . . . washed their robes and made them white in the blood of the Lamb. . . . Never again will they hunger. . . . For the Lamb . . . will be their shepherd."

Ps. 145:16; John 21:12-13; Isa. 25:6; Luke 12:37; Gen. 48:15; Pss. 78:72; 81:16; Matt. 6:11; Luke 12:24; Ps. 80:5; Matt. 26:26; Rev. 7:14, 16-17.

apr/6

Your strength will equal your days. . . . Write [these words of mine] on the door frames of your houses and on your gates, so that your days and the days of your children may be . . . as many as the days that the heavens are above the earth. —Surely goodness and love will follow me all the days of my life.—Nothing is better for a man under the sun than to eat and drink and be glad. Then joy will accompany him in his work all the days of the life God has given him under the sun.—My years have been few and difficult.—As the days of a tree, so will be the days of my people; my chosen ones will long enjoy the works of their hands.—"My days are swifter than a weaver's shuttle." . . . Our days on earth are but a shadow. . . . "Is not wisdom found among the aged? Does not long life bring understanding?" —Serve him without fear in holiness and righteousness before him all our days.—The days of the blameless are known to the Lord. . . . My days are like the evening shadow. . . . "Show me, O Lord, my life's end and the number of my days. . . . You have made my days a mere handbreadth; the span of my years is as nothing before you." . . . Teach us to number our days aright, that we may gain a heart of wisdom.

Deut. 33:25; 11:20-21; Ps. 23:6; Eccl. 8:15; Gen. 47:9; Isa. 65:22; Job 7:6; 8:9; 12:12; Luke 1:74-75; Pss. 37:18; 102:11; 39:4-5; 90:12.

apr/7

He spreads out the northern skies, over empty space; he suspends the earth over nothing. —Before him all the nations are as nothing; they are regarded by him as worthless and less than nothing.—All the peoples of the earth are regarded as nothing.—"[I will] gather all nations and tongues, and they will come and see my glory."—The sluggard craves and gets nothing, but the desires of the diligent are fully satisfied. . . . One man pretends to be rich, yet has nothing; another pretends to be poor, yet has great wealth.—Poor, yet making many rich; having nothing, and yet possessing everything.—If anyone thinks he is something when he is nothing, he deceives himself.—We brought nothing into the world, and we can take nothing out of it.—"I have given you authority . . . to overcome all the power of the enemy; nothing will harm you."—"I do nothing on my own but speak just what the Father has taught me." . . . "Apart from me you can do nothing."—"For forty years you sustained them in the desert; they lacked nothing, their clothes did not wear out nor did their feet become swollen."—If I . . . have not love, I gain nothing.

Job 26:7; Isa. 40:17; Dan. 4:35; Isa. 66:18; Prov. 13:4, 7; 2 Cor. 6:10; Gal. 6:3; 1 Tim. 6:7; Luke 10:19; John 8:28; 15:5; Neh. 9:21; 1 Cor. 13:3.

apr/8

Do not plant two kinds of seed in your
vineyard; if you do, not only the crops you plant
but also the fruit of the vineyard will be defiled.
—"Do not plant your field with two kinds of
seed."—"Those who plow evil and those who
sow trouble reap it."—"They sow the wind and
reap the whirlwind." . . . Sow for yourselves
righteousness, reap the fruit of unfailing love.
—Do not be deceived: God cannot be mocked.
A man reaps what he sows. The one who sows
to please his sinful nature, from that nature will
reap destruction; the one who sows to please the
Spirit, from the Spirit will reap eternal life. . . .
The fruit of the Spirit is love, joy, peace.—
Whoever sows sparingly will also reap sparingly,
and whoever sows generously will also reap
generously. . . . He who supplies seed to the
sower and bread for food will also supply and
increase your store of seed and will enlarge the
harvest of your righteousness.—"Other seed fell
on good soil. It came up, grew and produced a
crop, multiplying thirty, sixty, or even a hundred
times."—Those who sow in tears will reap with
songs of joy. He who goes out weeping, carrying
seed to sow, will return with songs of joy, carrying
sheaves with him.

*Deut. 22:9; Lev. 19:19; Job 4:8; Hos. 8:7; 10:12; Gal.
6:7-8; 5:22; 1 Cor. 9:6, 10; Mark 4:8; Ps. 126:5.*

apr/9

Those who belong to Christ Jesus have crucified the sinful nature with its passions and desires. Since we live by the Spirit, let us keep in step with the Spirit. . . . Live by the Spirit, and you will not gratify the desires of the sinful nature. For the sinful nature desires what is contrary to the Spirit, and the Spirit what is contrary to the sinful nature.—Those controlled by the sinful nature cannot please God.—Can both fresh water and salt water flow from the same spring? . . . Neither can a salt spring produce fresh water.—"No one can serve two masters. Either he will hate the one and love the other, or he will be devoted to the one and despise the other. You cannot serve both God and Money.—What does a believer have in common with an unbeliever? . . . "Therefore come out from them and be separate, says the Lord. Touch no unclean thing, and I will receive you."—Do not love the world or anything in the world. If anyone loves the world, the love of the Father is not in him.—Your iniquities have separated you and your God; your sins have hidden his face from you, so that he will not hear.—"'You are to be holy to me because I, the Lord, am holy, and I have set you apart from the nations to be my own.'"

Gal. 5:24-25, 16-17; Rom. 8:8; James 3:11-12; Matt. 6:24; 2 Cor. 6:15, 17; 1 John 2:15; Isa. 59:2; Lev. 20:26.

apr/10

[Moses] persevered because he saw him who is invisible.—Though you have not seen him, . . . you believe in him and are filled with an inexpressible and glorious joy.—Truly you are a God who hides himself, O God and Savior of Israel.—"You cannot see my face, for no one may see me and live."—Now to the King eternal, immortal, invisible, the only God.—No one has seen the Father except the one who is from God; only he has seen the Father. . . . Jesus told him, "Because you have seen me, you have believed; blessed are those who have not seen and yet have believed."—Suddenly a light from heaven flashed around him. He fell to the ground and heard a voice say to him, "Saul, Saul, why do you persecute me?" . . . The men traveling with Saul stood there speechless; they heard the sound but did not see anyone.—If he hides his face, who can see him? . . . When he is at work in the north, I do not see him; when he turns to the south, I catch no glimpse of him. . . . When he passes me, I cannot see him; when he goes by, I cannot perceive him.—[The Son] is the image of the invisible God, the first born over all creation. For by him all things were created . . . in heaven and on earth, visble and invisible.—But we see Jesus.

Heb. 11:27; 1 Peter 1:8; Isa. 45:15; Exod. 33:20; 1 Tim. 1:17; John 6:46; 20:29; Acts 9:3-4, 7; Job 34:29; 23:9; 9:11; Col. 1:15-16; Heb. 2:9.

apr/11

Let us acknowledge the Lord; let us press on to acknowledge him. As surely as the sun rises, he will appear.—What we will be has not yet been made known. But we know that when he appears, we shall be like him, for we shall see him as he is.—"Israel cries out to me, 'O our God, we acknowledge you!'"—We know that we have come to know him is we obey his commands. . . . This is how we know we are in him: Whoever claims to live in him must walk as Jesus did. . . . We know that we have passed from death to life, because we love our brothers. . . . We know that he lives in us: We know it by the Spirit he gave us. . . . If we know that he hears us—whatever we ask—we know that we have what we asked of him. . . . We know that anyone born of God does not continue to sin. . . . We know that we are children of God. We know also that the Son of God has come and has given us understanding, so that we may know him who is true.—We know that in all things God works for the good of those who love him.—Now I know in part; then I shall know fully, even as I am fully known.—We know that if the earthly tent we live in is destroyed, we have a building from God, an eternal house in heaven, not built by human hands.

Hos. 6:3; 1 John 3:2; Hos. 8:2; 1 John 2:3, 5-6; 3:14, 24; 5:15, 18-20; Rom. 8:28; 1 Cor. 13:12; 2 Cor. 5:1.

apr/12

"This is what the Lord, the God of Israel, says; 'I brought Israel up out of Egypt, and I delivered you from the power of Egypt and all the kingdoms that oppressed you.' But you have now rejected your God, who saves you out of all your calamities and distresses."—"As surely as the Lord lives, who has delivered me out of every trouble."
—Although the Lord gives you the bread of adversity and the water of affliction. . . . Your ears will hear a voice behind you, saying, "This is the way; walk in it."—A friend loves at all times, and a brother is born for adversity. . . . If you falter in times of trouble, how small is your strength!—When times are good, be happy; but when times are bad, consider: God has made the one as well as the other.—Remember those in prison as if you were their fellow prisoners, and those who are mistreated as if you yourselves were suffering.
—"Nothing will shake me; I'll always be happy and never have trouble." . . . I will be glad and rejoice in your love, for you saw my affliction. . . . Blessed is the man you discipline, O Lord . . . grant him relief from days of trouble.—"My son, do not make light of the Lord's discipline, and do not lose heart when he rebukes you, because the Lord disciplines those he loves."

---

1 Sam. 10:18-19; 2 Sam. 4:9; Isa. 30:20-21; Prov. 17:17; 24:10; Eccl. 7:14; Heb. 13:3; Pss. 10:6; 31:7; 94:12-13; Heb. 12:5-6.

apr/13

If you then, though you are evil, know how to give good gifts to your children, how much more will your Father in heaven give the Holy Spirit to those who ask him!" . . . "Do not worry about how you will defend yourselves or what you will say, for the Holy Spirit will teach you at that time what you should say." . . . "I am going to send you what my Father has promised; but stay in the city until you have been clothed with power from on high."—On the last and greatest day of the Feast, Jesus stood and said in a loud voice, "If a man is thirsty, let him come to me and drink. Whoever believes in me, as the Scripture has said, streams of living water will flow from within him." By this he meant the Spirit, whom those who believed in him were later to receive. . . . "I will ask the Father, and he will give you another Counselor to be with you forever—the Spirit of truth." . . . "The Holy Spirit, whom the Father will send in my name, will teach you all things and remind you of everything I have said to you." —"You will receive power when the Holy Spirit comes on you; and you will be my witnesses." . . . All of them were filled with the Holy Spirit.—[Christ] anointed us, set his seal of ownership on us, and put his Spirit in our hearts as a deposit, guaranteeing what is to come.

Luke 11:13; 12:11-12; 24:49; John 7:37-39; 14:16-17, 26; Acts 1:8; 2:4; 2 Cor. 1:22.

apr/14

Saul also went to his home in Gibeah,
accompanied by valiant men whose hearts God
had touched.—"Woe to me! . . . For I am a man of
unclean lips." . . . Then one of the seraphs flew to
me with a live coal in his hands, which he had
taken with tongs from the altar. With it he touched
my mouth and said, "See, this has touched your
lips; your guilt is taken away and your sin atoned
for."—While [Gabriel] was speaking to me, I was
in a deep sleep, with my face to the ground. Then
he touched me and raised me to my feet. . . . A
hand touched me and set me trembling on my
hands and knees. . . . Then one who looked like a
man touched my lips, and I opened my mouth and
began to speak. . . . Again the one who looked
like a man touched me and gave me strength.
—Filled with compassion, Jesus reached out his
hand and touched the man. . . . Immediately the
leprosy left him and he was cured.—Then [Jesus]
went up and touched the coffin, and those
carrying it stood still. He said, "Young man, I say
unto you, get up!" The dead man sat up and began
to talk. . . . People were also bringing babies to
Jesus to have him touch them. . . . One of them
struck the servant of the high priest, cutting off his
right ear. But Jesus answered, "No more of this!"
And he touched the man's ear and healed him.

*1 Sam. 10:26; Isa. 6:5-7; Dan. 8:18; 10:10, 16, 18;
Mark 1:41-42; Luke 7:14-15; 18:15; 22:50-51.*

apr/15

The Lord our God is merciful and forgiving, even though we have rebelled against him.—With you there is forgiveness; therefore you are feared.—The sins of those who dwell [in Zion] will be forgiven.—You are kind and forgiving, O Lord, abounding in love to all who call to you. —"The Son of Man has authority on earth to forgive sins." . . . "I tell you, her many sins have been forgiven—for she loved much. But he who has been forgiven little loves little." . . . "Father, forgive them, for they do not know what they are doing." . . . Repentance and forgiveness of sins will be preached in his name to all nations.— "Everyone who believes in him receives forgiveness of sins through his name."—"Blessed are they whose transgressions are forgiven, whose sins are covered."—Be kind and compassionate to one another, forgiving each other, just as in Christ God forgave you.—God made you alive with Christ. He forgave us all our sins.—I write to you, dear children, because your sins have been forgiven on account of his name. . . . If we confess our sins, he is faithful and just and will forgive us our sins and purify us from all unrighteousness.—"'Forgive us our debts, as we also have forgiven our debtors.'"

Dan. 9:9; Ps. 130:4; Isa. 33:24; Ps. 86:5; Luke 5:24; 7:47; 23:34; 24:47; Acts 10:43; Rom. 4:7; Eph. 4:32; Col. 2:13; 1 John 2:12; 1:9; Matt. 6:12.

apr/16

[Jesus said,] "Be on your guard against all kinds of greed; a man's life does not consist in the abundance of his possessions." . . . "No servant can serve two masters. Either he will hate the one and love the other, or he will be devoted to the one and despise the other. You cannot serve both God and Money." The Pharisees, who loved money, heard all this and were sneering at Jesus.—I would not have known what it was to covet if the law had not said, "Do not covet." But sin, seizing the opportunity afforded by the commandment, produced in me every kind of covetous desire. —No . . . greedy person . . . has any inheritance in the kingdom of Christ and of God.—Put to death, therefore, whatever belongs to your earthly nature: . . . evil desires and greed, which is idolatry.—Keep your lives free from the love of money and be content with what you have, because God has said, "Never will I leave you; never will I forsake you."—If anyone loves the world, the love of the Father is not in him. For everything in the world—the cravings of sinful man, the lust of his eyes and the boasting of what he has and does—comes not from the Father but from the world. The world and its desires pass away, but the man who does the will of God lives forever.

Luke 12:15; 16:13-14; Rom. 7:7-8; Eph. 5:5; Col. 3:5; Heb. 13:5; 1 John 2:15-17.

apr/17

I will sing of the love of the Lord forever.—The Lord your God is a merciful God.—You are a gracious and compassionate God.—The Lord our God is merciful and forgiving, even though we have rebelled against him.—Be merciful, just as your Father is merciful. . . . "'God, have mercy on me, a sinner.'"—Glorify God for his mercy. . . . In view of God's mercy, . . . offer your bodies as living sacrifices, holy and pleasing to God—which is your spiritual worship.—Because of the Lord's great love we are not consumed, for his compassions never fail.—Praise be to the God and Father of our Lord Jesus Christ! In his great mercy he has given us new birth into a living hope through the resurrection of Jesus Christ from the dead. . . . Once you were not a people, but now you are the people of God; once you had not received mercy, but now you have received mercy.—His love endures forever. . . . Your compassion is great, O Lord.—God, who is rich in mercy, made us alive with Christ even when we were dead in transgressions.—We have different gifts, according to the grace given us. . . . If it is showing mercy, let him do it cheerfully.

Ps. 89:1; Deut. 4:31; Jonah 4:3; Dan. 9:9; Luke 6:36; 18:13; Rom. 15:9; 12:1; Lam. 3:22; 1 Peter 1:3; 2:10; Pss. 100:5; 119:156; Eph. 2:4-5; Rom. 12:6, 8.

apr/18

His compassions never fail. They are new every morning; great is your faithfulness.—Know therefore that the Lord your God is God; he is the faithful God, keeping his covenant of love to a thousand generations of those who love him and keep his commands.—Righteousness will be his belt and faithfulness the sash around his waist. . . . I will exalt you and praise your name, for in perfect faithfulness you have done marvelous things, things planned long ago.—You are mighty, O Lord, and your faithfulness surrounds you. . . . Your love, O Lord, reaches to the heavens.—God, who has called you into fellowship with his Son Jesus Christ our Lord, is faithful.—May your whole spirit, soul and body be kept blameless at the coming of our Lord Jesus Christ. The one who calls you is faithful and he will do it.—If we are faithless, he will remain faithful, for he cannot disown himself.—He who promised is faithful.—Before me was a white horse, whose rider is called Faithful and True. . . . Jesus Christ, who is the faithful witness, the firstborn from the dead, and the ruler of the kings of the earth.—Those who suffer according to God's will should commit themselves to their faithful Creator and continue to do good.

Lam. 3:22-23; Deut. 7:9; Isa. 11:5; 25:1; Pss. 89:8; 36:5; 1 Cor. 1:9; 1 Thess. 5:23-24; 2 Tim. 2:13; Heb. 10:23; Rev. 19:11; 1:5; 1 Peter 4:19.

apr/19

"Because of . . . the groaning of the needy, I will now arise," says the Lord. . . . My life is consumed by anguish and my years by groaning.—"You said, 'Woe to me! The Lord has added sorrow to my pain; I am worn out with groaning and find no rest.'"—The roads to Zion mourn. . . . Her priests groan. . . . [Jerusalem] herself groans. . . . "People have heard my groaning, but there is no one to comfort me. . . . My groans are many and my heart is faint." —[Jesus] looked up to heaven and with a deep sigh said to him, "*Ephphatha!*" (which means, "Be opened!"). At this, the man's ears were opened, his tongue was loosened and he began to speak plainly. . . . The Pharisees came and began to question Jesus. To test him, they asked him for a sign from heaven. He sighed deeply and said, "Why does this generation ask for a miraculous sign? I tell you the truth, no sign will be given to it."—Gladness and joy will overtake them, and sorrow and sighing will flee away.—Meanwhile we groan, longing to be clothed with our heavenly dwelling. . . . For while we are in this tent, we groan and are burdened, because we do not wish to be unclothed but to be clothed with our heavenly dwelling.

Ps. 12:5; 31:10; Jer. 45:3; Lam. 1:4, 8, 21-22; Mark 7:34; 8:11-12; Isa. 35:10; 2 Cor. 5:2, 4.

apr/20

Jesus took bread, gave thanks and broke it, and gave it to his disciples, saying, "Take and eat; this is my body." Then he took the cup, gave thanks and offered it to them, saying, "Drink from it, all of you. This is my blood of the covenant, which is poured out for many for the forgiveness of sins. I tell you, I will not drink of this fruit of the vine from now on until that day when I drink it anew with you in my Father's kingdom."—"Do this in remembrance of me."—You cannot drink the cup of the Lord and the cup of demons too; you cannot have a part in both the Lord's table and the table of demons. . . . Is not the cup of thanksgiving for which we give thanks a participation in the blood of Christ? And is not the bread that we break a participation in the body of Christ? Because there is one loaf, we, who are many, are one body, for we all partake of the one loaf.—Whenever you eat this bread and drink this cup, you proclaim the Lord's death until he comes. Therefore, whoever eats the bread or drinks the cup of the Lord in an unworthy manner will be guilty of sinning against the body and blood of the Lord. A man ought to examine himself before he eats of the bread and drinks of the cup. For anyone who eats and drinks without recognizing the body of the Lord eats and drinks judgment on himself.

Matt. 26:26-29; Luke 22:19; 1 Cor. 10:21, 16-17; 11:26-29.

apr/21

Before him all the nations are as nothing; they are regarded by him as worthless and less than nothing. To whom, then, will you compare God? What image will you compare him to? . . . To whom will you compare me or count me equal? To whom will you liken me that we may be compared?—Who in the skies above can compare with the Lord? Who is like the Lord among the heavenly beings? . . . O Lord God Almighty, who is like you? You are mighty, O Lord. . . . Your righteousness reaches to the skies, O God, you who have done great things. Who, O God, is like you?—"There is no one holy like the Lord; there is no one besides you; there is no Rock like our God."—"Who among the gods is like you, O Lord? Who is like you—majestic in holiness, awesome in glory, working wonders?"—He sits enthroned above the circle of the earth, and its people are like grasshoppers. He stretches out the heavens like a canopy, and spreads them out like a tent to live in. . . . O Lord, our God, other lords besides you have ruled over us, but your name alone do we honor.—"'The Lord our God, the Lord is one. Love the Lord your God with all your heart and with all your soul and with all your mind and with all your strength.'"

Isa. 40:17-18; 46:5; Pss. 89:6, 8; 71:19; 1 Sam. 2:2; Exod. 15:11; Isa. 40:22; 26:13; Mark 12:29-30.

apr/22

In the day of Midian's defeat, you have
shattered the yoke that burdens them, the bar
across their shoulders. . . . In that day their
burden will be lifted from your shoulders, their
yoke from your neck; the yoke will be broken. . . .
"Is not this the kind of fasting I have chosen: to
loose the chains of injustice and untie the cords of
the yoke, to set the oppressed free and break every
yoke?"—"I led them with cords of human
kindness, with ties of love; I lifted the yoke from
their neck and bent down to feed them"—It is for
freedom that Christ has set us free. Stand firm,
then, and do not let yourselves be burdened again
by a yoke of slavery.—Do not be yoked together
with unbelievers. For what do righteousness and
wickedness have in common? Or what fellowship
can light have with darkness?—I [Paul] ask you,
loyal yokefellow, help these women who have
contended at my side in the cause of the
gospel.—"Come to me, all you who are weary and
burdened, and I will give you rest. Take my yoke
upon you and learn from me, for I am gentle and
humble in heart, and you will find rest for your
souls. For my yoke is easy and my burden is
light."—It is good for a man to bear the yoke
while he is young.

Isa. 9:4; 10:27; 58:6; Hos. 11:4; Gal. 5:1; 2 Cor. 6:14;
Phil. 4:3; Matt. 11:28-30; Lam. 3:27.

apr/23

No man can redeem the life of another or give to God a ransom for him—the ransom for a life is costly, no payment is ever enough. . . . Put your hope in the Lord, for with the Lord is unfailing love and with him is full redemption. . . . Give thanks to the Lord, for he is good; His love endures forever. Let the redeemed of the Lord say this—those he redeemed from the hand of the foe.—You were redeemed . . . with the precious blood of Christ, a lamb without blemish or defect.—"Fear not, for I have redeemed you; I have called you by name; you are mine." . . . All mankind will know that I, the Lord, am your Savior, your Redeemer, the Mighty One of Jacob." . . . In his love and mercy he redeemed them.—Justified freely by his grace through the redemption that came by Christ Jesus. —In him we have redemption through his blood, the forgiveness of sins. . . . Do not grieve the Holy Spirit of God, with whom you were sealed for the day of redemption.—He entered the Most Holy Place once for all by his own blood, having obtained eternal redemption.—"Stand up and lift up your heads, because your redemption is drawing near."—Their Redeemer is strong; the Lord Almighty is his name.

Pss. 49:8; 130:7; 107:1-2; 1 Peter 1:18-19; Isa. 43:1; 49:26; 63:9; Rom. 3:24; Eph. 1:7; 4:30; Heb. 9:12; Luke 21:28; Jer. 50:34.

apr/24

Honor your father and your mother, as the Lord your God has commanded you."—"'Rise up in the presence of the aged, show respect for the elderly and revere your God. I am the Lord.'" —Honor the Lord with your wealth, with the firstfruits of all your crops; then your barns will be filled to overflowing.—"These people come near to me with their mouth and honor me with their lips, but their hearts are far from me." . . . If you honor [the Lord's holy day] by not going your own way and not doing as you please or speaking idle words, then you will find your joy in the Lord.—Show proper respect to everyone: Love the brotherhood of believers, fear God, honor the king.—Honor one another above yourselves. —[The Lord Jesus Christ] received honor and glory from God the Father when the voice came to him from the Majestic Glory, saying, "This is my Son, whom I love; with him I am well pleased."—Whenever the living creatures give glory, honor and thanks to him who sits on the throne and who lives for ever and ever, the twenty-four elders fall down before him who sits on the throne . . . and say, "You are worthy, our Lord and God, to receive glory and honor and power."

Deut. 5:16; Lev. 19:32; Prov. 3:9-10; Isa. 29:13; 58:13-14; 1 Peter 2:17; Rom. 12:10; 2 Peter 1:17; Rev. 4:9-11.

apr/25

[Christ] is the head of the body, the church; he is the beginning and the firstborn from among the dead, so that in everything he might have the supremacy. For God was pleased to have all his fullness dwell in him, and through him to reconcile to himself all things, whether things on earth or things in heaven, by making peace through his blood, shed on the cross. Once you were alienated from God and were enemies in your minds because of your evil behavior. But now he has reconciled you by Christ's physical body through death to present you holy in his sight, without blemish and free from accusation.—If anyone is in Christ, he is a new creation; the old has gone, the new has come! All this is from God, who reconciled us to himself through Christ and gave us the ministry of reconciliation: that God was reconciling the world to himself in Christ, not counting men's sins against them. And he has committed to us the message of reconciliation. We are therefore Christ's ambassadors, as though God were making his appeal through us. We implore you on Christ's behalf: Be reconciled to God.—He himself is our peace. . . . His purpose was to create in himself one new man out of the two, thus making peace, and in this one body to reconcile both of them to God through the cross.

Col. 1:18-22; 2 Cor. 5:17-20; Eph. 2:14-16.

apr/26

A bruised reed he will not break, and a smoldering wick he will not snuff out. . . . When you pass through the waters, I will be with you; and when you pass through the rivers, they will not sweep over you. When you walk through the fire, you will not be burned.—Because of the Lord's great love we are not consumed, for his compassions never fail.—God is faithful; he will not let you be tempted beyond what you can bear. But when you are tempted, he will also provide a way out so that you can stand up under it.—"I will spare them, just as in compassion a man spares his own son who serves him."—David said to Gad, "I am in deep distress. Let us fall into the hands of the Lord, for his mercy is great; but do not let me fall into the hands of men."—"'I am with you and will save you,' declares the Lord. 'Though I completely destroy all the nations. . . , I will not completely destroy you. I will discipline you but only with justice; I will not let you go entirely unpunished.'" . . . [The people] said to Jeremiah, "Whether it is favorable or unfavorable, we will obey the Lord our God."—He does not treat us as our sins deserve or repay us according to our iniquities. . . . The Lord is compassionate and gracious. . . . He knows how we are formed, he remembers that we are dust.

Isa. 42:3; 43:2; Lam. 3:22; 1 Cor. 10:13; Mal. 3:17; 2 Sam. 24:14; Jer. 30:11; 42:5-6; Ps. 103:10, 14.

apr/27

At that time Jesus said, "I praise you, Father, Lord of heaven and earth, because you have hidden these from the wise and learned, and revealed them to little children. Yes, Father, for this was your good pleasure." . . . He went up into the hills by himself to pray. . . . Little children were brought to Jesus for him to place his hands on them and pray for them. . . . Then Jesus went with his disciples to a place called Gethsemane, and he said to them, "Sit here while I go over there and pray."—Very early in the morning, while it was still dark, Jesus got up, left the house and went off to a solitary place, where he prayed.—As he was praying, heaven was opened and the Holy Spirit descended on him in bodily form like a dove. . . . Jesus often withdrew to lonely places and prayed. . . . One of those days Jesus went out into the hills to pray, and spent the night praying to God. . . . He . . . went up onto a mountain to pray. As he was praying, the appearance of his face changed. . . . "I have prayed for you, Simon, that your faith may not fail."—During the days of Jesus' life on earth, he offered up prayers and petitions . . . and he was heard because of his reverent submission. . . . He always lives to intercede.

Matt. 11:25-26; 14:23; 19:13; 26:36; Mark 1:25; Luke 3:21; 5:16; 6:12; 9:28-29; 22:32; Heb. 5:7; 7:25.

apr/28

Above all else, guard your heart, for it is the wellspring of life.—Blessed are the pure in heart, for they will see God.—Create in me a pure heart, O God.—The Lord your God commands you this day to follow these decrees and laws; carefully observe them with all your heart.—Trust in the Lord with all your heart and lean not on your own understanding. . . . Keep my commands in your heart. . . . Write them on the tablet of your heart.—The good man brings good things out of the good stored up in his heart, and the evil man brings evil things out of the evil stored up in his heart. For out of the overflow of his heart his mouth speaks.—Doing the will of God from your heart. Serve wholeheartedly.—Each heart knows its own bitterness, and no one else can share its joy. . . . A heart at peace gives life to the body, but envy rots the bones. . . . Apply your heart to instruction and your ears to words of knowledge. . . . My son, give me your heart and let your eyes keep to my ways.—"Man looks at the outward appearance, but the Lord looks at the heart."—Let us draw near to God with a sincere heart in full assurance of faith.—Say to those with fearful hearts, "Be strong, do not fear; your God will come."

Prov. 4:23; Matt. 5:8; Ps. 51:10; Deut. 26:16; Prov. 3:5, 2-3; Luke 6:45; Eph. 6:6-7; Prov. 14:10, 30; 23:12, 26; 1 Sam. 16:7; Heb. 10:22; Isa. 35:4.

apr/29

How beautiful your sandaled feet, O prince's daughter!—How beautiful on the mountains are the feet of those who bring good news. . . . The Lord spoke through Isaiah son of Amoz. He said to him, "Take off the sackcloth from your body and the sandals from your feet." And he did so, going around stripped and barefoot. Then the Lord said, "Just as my servant Isaiah has gone stripped and barefoot for three years, as a sign and portent against Egypt and Cush, so the king of Assyria will lead away stripped and barefoot the Egyptian captives.—Stand firm then, . . . with your feet fitted with the readiness that comes from the gospel of peace.—"Upon Edom I toss my sandal; over Philistia I shout in triumph."—"As John [the Baptist] was completing his work, he said: . . . '[One] is coming after me, whose sandals I am not worthy to untie.'"—The commander of the Lord's army replied [to Joshua], "Take off your sandals, for the place where you are standing is holy." And Joshua did so.—During the forty years that I led you through the desert, your clothes did not wear out, nor did the sandals on your feet.—"The father said to his servants, 'Quick! Bring the best robe and put it on him. Put a ring on his finger and sandals on his feet.'"

Song of Songs 7:1; Isa. 52:7; 20:2-4; Eph. 6:14-15; Ps. 108:9; Acts 13:25; Josh. 5:15; Deut. 29:5; Luke 15:22.

apr/30

May the Lord make you increase, both you and
your children. . . . I will praise you more and
more.—The path of the righteous is like the first
gleam of dawn, shining ever brighter till the full
light of day.—Now they sin more and more; they
make for themselves from their silver, cleverly
fashioned images.—How much more shall we be
saved from God's wrath through [Christ]! . . .
How much more, having been reconciled, shall we
be saved through his life! . . . Where sin
increased, grace increased all the more.—If the
ministry that condemns men is glorious, how
much more glorious is the ministry that brings
righteousness! . . . If what was fading away came
with glory, how much greater is the glory of that
which lasts!—This is my prayer: that your love
may abound more and more.—We instructed you
how to live in order to please God, as in fact you
are living. Now we ask you and urge you in the
Lord Jesus to do this more and more.—Let us
encourage one another—and all the more as you
see the Day approaching.—More and more men
and women believed in the Lord and were added
to their number.—Whoever has will be given
more, and he will have an abundance.— "The
Lord can give you much more than that."

---

*Pss. 115:14; 71:14; Prov. 4:18; Hos. 13:2; Rom.
5:9-10, 20; 2 Cor. 3:9, 11; Phil. 1:9; 1 Thess. 4:1;
Heb. 10:25; Acts 5:14; Matt. 13:12; 2 Chron. 25:9.*

may /1

A faith, . . . which God, who does not lie, promised before the beginning of time.—It is impossible for God to lie.—All your words are true; all your righteous laws are eternal.—Sanctify them by the truth; your word is truth.—He who promised is faithful.—Being fully persuaded that God had power to do what he had promised.—For no matter how many promises God has made, they are "Yes" in Christ. And so through him the "Amen" is spoken by us to the glory of God.—The statutes you have laid down are righteous; they are fully trustworthy.—"What I have said, that I will bring about; what I have planned, that will I do."—"'The days are coming,' declares the Lord, 'when I will fulfill the gracious promise I made to the house of Israel and to the house of Judah.'"
—It is the Spirit who testifies, because the Spirit is truth. . . . That we may know him who is true.—When you received the word of God, which you heard from us, you accepted it not as the word of men, but as it actually is, the word of God, which is at work in you who believe.—I tell you that Christ has become a servant of the Jews on behalf of God's truth, to confirm the promises made to the patriarchs.

Titus 1:2; Heb. 6:18; Ps. 119:160; John 17:17; Heb. 10:23; Rom. 4:21; 2 Cor. 1:20; Ps. 119:138; Isa. 46:11; Jer. 33:14;1 John 5:6, 20; 1 Thess. 2:13; Rom. 15:8.

John Thornberg

He set my feet on a rock
and gave me a firm place to stand.

Light to Live By   ◖

may /2

The Lord is my rock, . . . in whom I take
refuge. . . . He is my mighty rock, my refuge.
—[Jeshurun] abandoned the God who made him
and rejected the Rock His Savior. . . . You
deserted the Rock, who fathered you. . . . How
could one man chase a thousand, or two put ten
thousand to flight, unless their Rock had sold
them, unless the Lord had given them up? . . .
"Now where are their gods, the rock they took
refuge in?"—You have forgotten God your Savior;
you have not remembered the Rock, your
fortress. . . . Each man will be like . . . the
shadow of a great rock in a thirsty land.—He lifted
me out of the slimy pit, . . . he set my feet on a
rock. . . . Be my rock of refuge.—It is written:
"See, I lay in Zion a stone that causes men to
stumble and a rock that makes them fall, and the
one who trusts in him will never be put to
shame."—They drank from the spiritual rock that
accompanied them, and that rock was Christ.—I
tell you that you are Peter, and on this rock I will
build my church, and the gates of Hades will not
overcome it.—The living Stone—rejected by men
but chosen by God and precious to him—you
also, like living stones, are being built into a
spiritual house.

*Pss. 18:2; 62:7; Deut. 32:15, 18, 30, 38; Isa. 17:10;
32:2; Pss. 40:2; 31:2; Rom. 9:33; 1 Cor. 10:4; Matt.
16:18; 1 Peter 2:4-5.*

may /3

No one has ever seen God, but God the only Son, who is at the Father's side, has made him known.—Jacob was left alone, and a man wrestled with him. . . . Jacob called the place Peniel, saying, "It is because I saw God face to face, and yet my life was spared." —Moses said, "Now show me your glory." . . . [God] said, "You cannot see my face, for no one may see me and live."—The Father who sent me has himself testified concerning me. You have never heard his voice nor seen his form. . . . "Anyone who has seen me has seen the Father." . . . "Blessed are those who have not seen and yet have believed."—[God] appeared in a body, was vindicated by the Spirit. . . . [God] lives in unapproachable light, whom no one has seen or can see.—[Christ] is the image of the invisible God, the firstborn over all creation.—No one has ever seen God; but if we love each other, God lives in us and his love is made complete in us.—[Moses] persevered because he saw him who is invisible. . . . Faith is being sure of what we hope for and certain of what we do not see.—For since the creation of the world God's invisible qualities—his eternal power and divine nature—have been clearly seen, being understood from what has been made.

John 1:18; Gen. 32:24, 30; Exod. 33:18, 20; John 5:37; 14:9; 20:29; 1 Tim. 3:16; 6:16; Col. 1:15; 1 John 4:12; Heb. 11:27, 1; Rom. 1:20.

may /4

[The seed] became a low, spreading vine. Its branches turned toward him, but its roots remained under it. So it became a vine and produced branches.—Judah and Israel . . . lived in safety, each man under his own vine.—Every man will sit under his own vine and . . . no one will make them afraid.—The blossoming vines spread their fragrance. . . . Catch for us the foxes, the little foxes that ruin the vineyards, our vineyards that are in bloom.—"'In that day each of you will invite his neighbor to sit under his vine and fig tree,' declares the Lord." . . . "The seed will grow well, the vine will yield its fruit, the ground will produce its crops, and the heavens will drop their dew."—"I am the true vine and my Father is the gardener. He cuts off every branch in me that bears no fruit, while every branch that does bear fruit he trims clean so that it will be even more fruitful. . . . No branch can bear fruit by itself; it must remain in the vine. Neither can you bear fruit unless you remain in me. I am the vine, you are the branches. If a man remains in me and I in him, he will bear much fruit; apart from me you can do nothing. . . . This is to my Father's glory, that you bear much fruit, showing yourselves to be my disciples. . . . You did not choose me, but I chose you to go and bear fruit—fruit that will last.

Ezek. 17:6; 1 Kings 4:25; Mic. 4:4; Song of Songs 2:13, 15; Zech. 3:10; 8:12; John 15:1-2, 4-5, 8, 16.

may /5

Who are loved by God and called to be saints.—Sing to the Lord you saints of his; praise his holy name. . . . Love the Lord, all his saints! . . . Fear the Lord, you his saints, for those who fear him lack nothing.—The Spirit intercedes for the saints in accordance with God's will. . . . I ask you to receive [Phoebe] in the Lord in a way worthy of the saints and to give her any help she may need from you.—I pray also that the eyes of your heart may be enlightened in order that you may know the hope to which he has called you, the riches of his glorious inheritance in the saints.—Giving thanks to the Father, who has qualified you to share in the inheritance of the saints in the kingdom of light.—Your love for all the saints. . . . Your love has given me great joy and encouragement, because you, brother, have refreshed the hearts of the saints.—Each one had a harp and they were holding golden bowls full of incense, which are the prayers of the saints. . . . "Let us rejoice and be glad and give him glory! For the wedding of the Lamb has come, and his bride has made herself ready. Fine linen, bright and clean, was given her to wear."—Precious in the sight of the Lord is the death of his saints.

Rom. 1:7; Pss. 30:4; 31:23; 34:9; Rom. 8:27; 16:2; Eph. 1:18; Col 1:12; Philem. 5, 7; Rev. 5:8; 19:8; Ps. 116:15.

may/6

My steps have held to your paths; my feet have not slipped. . . . If I rise on the wings of the dawn, and settle on the far side of the sea, even there your hand will guide me, your right hand will hold me fast.—"For I am the Lord, your God, who takes hold of your right hand and says to you, Do not fear; I will help you." . . . "I, the Lord, have called you in righteousness; I will take hold of your hand."—Christ is faithful as a son over God's house. And we are his house, if we hold on to our courage and the hope of which we boast. . . . We have come to share in Christ if we hold firmly till the end the confidence we had at first. . . . Therefore, since we have a great high priest who was gone through the heavens, Jesus the Son of God, let us hold firmly to the faith we profess.—Holding on to faith and a good conscience.—He must hold firmly to the trustworthy message as it has been taught, so that he can encourage others by sound doctrine and refute those who oppose it.—Test everything. Hold on to the good. Avoid every kind of evil.—I am coming soon. Hold on to what you have, so that no one will take your crown.—The righteous will hold to their ways, and those with clean hands will grow stronger.

Pss. 17:5; 139:9-10; Isa. 41:13; 42:6; Heb. 3:6, 14; 4:14; 1 Tim. 1:19; Titus 1:9; 1 Thess. 5:21-22; Rev. 3:11; Job 17:9.

may /7

Know then in your heart that as a man disciplines his son, so the Lord your God disciplines you.—The Lord has chastened me severely, but he has not given me over to death.—"I have surely heard Ephraim's moaning: 'You disciplined me like an unruly calf, and I have been disciplined. Restore me, and I will return, because you are the Lord my God.'"—"Blessed is the man whom God corrects; so do not despise the discipline of the Almighty.—When we are judged by the Lord, we are being disciplined so that we will not be condemned with the world.—Endure hardship as discipline; God is treating you as sons. For what son is not disciplined by his father? If you are not disciplined (and every one undergoes discipline), then you are illegitimate children and not true sons. Moreover, we have all had human fathers who disciplined us and we respected them for it. . . . Our fathers disciplined us for a little while as they thought best; but God disciplines us for our good, that we may share in his holiness.—"Those whom I love I rebuke and discipline. So be earnest, and repent.—Although [Jesus] was a son, he learned obedience from what he suffered.

Deut. 8:5; Ps. 118:18; Jer. 31:18; Job 5:17; 1 Cor. 11:32; Heb. 12:7-10; Rev. 3:19; Heb. 5:8.

may /8

Even in death the righteous have a refuge.
—Precious in the sight of the Lord is the death of
his saints. . . . Though I walk through the valley
of the shadow of death, I will fear no evil, for you
are with me; your rod and your staff, they comfort
me.—I am convinced that neither death nor
life . . . will be able to separate us from the love of
God that is in Christ Jesus our Lord.—He will
swallow up death forever. The Sovereign Lord will
wipe away the tears from all faces.—"I will
ransom them from the power of the grave; I will
redeem them from death. Where, O death, are
your plagues? Where, O grave, is your
destruction?"—Since the children have flesh and
blood, he too shared in their humanity so that by
his death he might destroy him who holds the
power of death—that is, the devil—and free those
who all their lives were held in slavery by their
fear of death.—The perishable must clothe itself
with the imperishable, and the mortal with
immortality. When the perishable has been
clothed with the imperishable, and the mortal
with immortality, then the saying that is written
will come true: "Death has been swallowed up in
victory."—Consider the blameless, observe the
upright; there is a future for the man of peace.

Prov. 14:32; Pss. 116:15; 23:4; Rom. 8:38-39; Isa.
25:8; Hos. 13:14; Heb. 2:14-15; 1 Cor. 15:53-54; Ps.
37:37.

may /9

To whom, then, will you compare God? What image will you compare him to? . . . "To whom will you liken me that we may be compared?" —As the mountains surround Jerusalem, so the Lord surrounds his people both now and forevermore. . . . As a father has compassion on his children, so the Lord has compassion on those who fear him.—He shielded him and cared for him; he guarded him as the apple of his eye, like an eagle that stirs up the nest and hovers over its young, that spreads its wings to catch them and carries them on its pinions. The Lord alone led him.—How often I have longed to gather your children together, as a hen gathers her chicks under her wings, but you were not willing. . . . "As the lightning comes from the east and flashes to the west, so will be coming the Son of Man." —The breath of the Lord, like a stream of burning sulphur. . . . He was led like a lamb to the slaughter, and as a sheep before her shearers is silent, so he did not open his mouth.—"Is not my word like fire," declares the Lord, "and like a hammer that breaks a rock in pieces?"—"There is no Rock like our God."—The glory of the Lord looked like a consuming fire on top of the mountain.—Your righteousness is like the mighty

Isa. 40:18; 46:5; Pss. 125:2; 103:13; Deut. 32:10-12; Matt. 23:37; 24:27; Isa. 30:33; 53:7; Jer. 23:29; 1 Sam. 2:2; Exod. 24:17.

may/10

"That you may know that the Son of Man has authority on earth to forgive sins. . . ." Then he said to the paralytic, "Get up, take your mat and go home." And the man got up and went home. . . . "The Son of Man will be three days and three nights in the heart of the earth." . . . "The one who sowed the good seed is the Son of Man." . . . "The Son of Man is going to come in his Father's glory with his angels, and then he will reward each person according to what he has done." . . . "The Son of Man is going to be betrayed into the hands of men. They will kill him, and on the third day he will be raised to life.". . ." As the lightning comes from the east and flashes to the west, so will be the coming of the Son of Man."—"The Son of Man came to seek and to save what was lost." . . . "They will see the Son of Man coming in a cloud with power and great glory."—"You shall see heaven open, and the angels of God ascending and descending on the Son of Man." . . . "The Son of Man must be lifted up, that everyone who believes in him may have eternal life."—"Look," [Stephen] said, "I see heaven open and the Son of Man standing at the right hand of God."—"The hour has come for the Son of Man to be glorified."

Matt. 9:6-7; 12:40; 13:37; 16:27; 17:22; 24:27; Luke 19:10; 21:27; John 1:51; 3:14-15; Acts 7:56; John 12:23.

may/11

Rejoice in the Lord always. I will say it again: Rejoice!—"I have told you this so that my joy may be in you and that your joy may be complete." —We rejoice and delight in you.—You have enlarged the nation and increased their joy; they rejoice before you as people rejoice at the harvest, as men rejoice when dividing the plunder. . . . You will go out in joy and be led forth in peace; the mountains and hills will burst into song before you. . . . I delight greatly in the Lord; my soul rejoices in my God. . . . My servants will rejoice.—In this you greatly rejoice, though now for a little while you may have had to suffer grief in all kinds of trials. . . . Though you have not seen him, you love him; and even though you do not see him now, you believe in him and are filled with an inexpressible and glorious joy.—We rejoice in the hope of the glory of God. Not only so, but we also rejoice in our sufferings, because we know that suffering produces perseverance; perseverance, character; and character, hope. And hope does not disappoint us, because God has poured out his love into our hearts by the Holy Spirit, whom he has given us. . . . Not only is this so, but we also rejoice in God through our Lord Jesus Christ, through whom we have now received reconciliation.

Phil. 4:4; John 15:11; Song of Songs 1:4; Isa. 9:3; 41:16; 55:12; 65:13; 1 Peter 1:6, 8; Rom. 5:2-5, 11.

may / 12

"**H**allelujah! For our Lord God Almighty
reigns." . . . On his robe and on his thigh he has
this name written: KING OF KINGS AND LORD OF
LORDS.—"I know that you can do all things."—He
does as he pleases with the powers of heaven and
the peoples of the earth. No one can hold back his
hand or say to him: "What have you done?" . . .
"The Lord our God is righteous in everything he
does."—"I am the Lord, and there is no other;
apart from me there is no God."—I know that
everything God does will endure forever; nothing
can be added to it and nothing taken from it. God
does it, and men will revere him.—"With God all
things are possible."—"Glorify your Son, that
your Son may glorify you. For you granted him
authority over all people that he might give eternal
life to all those you have given him."—Now to
him who is able to do immeasurably more than all
we ask or imagine, according to his power that is
at work within us.—Being fully persuaded that
God had power to do what he had promised.
—Yours, O Lord, is the greatness and the power
and the glory and the majesty and the splendor,
for everything in heaven and earth is yours.
Yours, O Lord, is the kingdom; you are exalted as
head over all. . . . You are the ruler of all things.

Rev. 19:6, 16; Job 42:2; Dan. 4:35; 9:14; Isa. 45:5;
Eccl. 3:14; Matt. 19:26; John 17:1-2; Eph. 3:20; Rom.
4:21; 1 Chron. 29:11-12.

may /13

"Your Father knows what you need before you ask him. . . . Ask and it will be given to you. . . . Everyone who asks receives. . . . If you, then, though you are evil, know how to give good gifts to your children, how much more will your Father in heaven give good gifts to those who ask him!"—If we ask anything according to his will, he hears us. And if we know that he hears us—whatever we ask—we know that we have what we asked of him. . . . We . . . receive from him anything we ask, because we obey his commands and do what pleases him.—If any of you lacks wisdom, he should ask God, who gives generously to all without finding fault, and it will be given to him. But when he asks, he must believe and not doubt.—"You may ask me for anything in my name, and I will do it." . . . "Ask and you will receive, and your joy will be complete."—"If you believe, you will receive whatever you ask for in prayer."—You do not have, because you do not ask God. When you ask, you do nostt receive, because you ask with wrong motives.—"I revealed myself to those who did not ask me; I was found by those who did not seek me."—They asked, and he brought them quail and satisfied them with the bread of heaven.

Matt. 6:8; 7:7-8, 11; 1 John 5:14-15; 3:22; James 1:5-6; John 14:14; 16:24; Matt. 21:22; James 4:2-3; Isa. 65:1; Ps. 105:40.

may/14

He will be called Wonderful Counselor, Mighty God.—Your love for me was wonderful, more wonderful than that of women.—Jesus of Nazareth was a man accredited by God to you by miracles, wonders and signs.—How great are his signs, how mighty his wonders!—To him who alone does great wonders, *His love endures forever.*—In perfect faithfulness you have done marvelous things. . . . All this also comes from the Lord Almighty, wonderful in counsel and magnificent in wisdom. . . . Once more I will astound these people with wonder upon wonder.—"Surely I spoke of things I did not understand, things too wonderful for me to know."—Your statutes are wonderful; therefore I obey them.—When the chief priests and the teachers of the law saw the wonderful things he did and the children shouting in the temple area, "Hosanna."—Praise be to the Lord God, the God of Israel, who alone does marvelous deeds.—You are a chosen people, a royal priesthood, a holy nation, a people belonging to God, that you may declare the praises of him who called you out of darkness into his wonderful light.—Let me understand the teaching of your precepts; then will I meditate on your wonders.

Isa. 9:6; 2 Sam. 1:26; Acts 2:22; Dan. 4:3; Ps. 136:4; Isa. 25:1; 28:29; 29:14; Job 42:3; Ps. 119:129; Matt. 21:15; Pss. 72:18; 1 Peter 2:9; Ps. 119:27.

may/15

Let God be true, and every man a liar.—We are in him who is true—even in his Son Jesus Christ. He is the true God and eternal life.—O Sovereign Lord, you are God! Your words are trustworthy. —"These are the true words of God." . . . The angel said to me, "These words are trustworthy and true."—"May the Lord be a true and faithful witness against us if we do not act in accordance with everything the Lord your God sends you to tell us."—"Yes, Lord God Almighty, true and just are your judgments." . . . I saw heaven standing open and there before me was a white horse, whose rider is called Faithful and True.—They came to [Jesus] and said, "Teacher, we know you are a man of integrity."—[Jesus] the true light that gives light to every man was coming into the world. . . . Jesus said to them, "I tell you the truth, it is not Moses who has given you the bread from heaven, but it is my Father who gives you the true bread from heaven." . . . "He who sent me is true. . . . I know him because I am from him and he sent me." . . . "I am the true vine and my Father is the gardener. . . . The Spirit of truth who goes out from the Father, he will testify about me."—Whatever is true, whatever is noble, . . . think about such things.

Rom. 3:4; 1 John 5:20; 2 Sam. 7:28; Rev. 19:9; 22:6; Jer. 42:5; Rev. 16:7; 19:11; Mark 12:14; John 1:9; 6:32; 7:28-29; 15:1, 26; Phil. 4:8.

may/16

Every house is built by someone, but God is the builder of everything.—Unless the Lord builds the house, its builders labor in vain.—"On this rock I will build my church, and the gates of Hades will not overcome it."—The city with foundations, whose architect and builder is God.—You also, like living stones, are being built into a spiritual house to be a holy priesthood. . . . "The stone the builders rejected has become the capstone."—You are . . . God's building. By the grace God has given me, I laid a foundation as an expert builder, and someone else is building on it. But each one should be careful how he builds. For no one can lay any foundation other than the one already laid, which is Jesus Christ.—Everyone who hears these words of mine and puts them into practice is like a wise man who built his house on the rock. . . . The winds blew and beat against that house; yet it did not fall, because it had its foundation on the rock.—You are . . . members of God's household, built on the foundation of the apostles and prophets, with Christ Jesus himself as the chief cornerstone. In him the whole building is joined together and rises to become a holy temple in the Lord. And in him you too are being built together to become a dwelling in which God lives by His Spirit.

Heb. 3:4; Pss. 127:1; Matt. 16:18; Heb. 11:10; 1 Peter 2:5, 7; 1 Cor. 3:9-11; Matt. 7:24-25; Eph. 2:19-22.

may/17

On his head are many crowns.—Jesus came out
wearing the crown of thorns and the purple
robe.—"You made him a little lower than the
angels; you crowned him with glory and
honor." . . . We see Jesus . . . now crowned with
glory and honor because he suffered death, so that
by the grace of God he might taste death for
everyone.—In that day the Lord Almighty will be
a glorious crown, a beautiful wreath for the
remnant of his people.—Gray hair is a crown of
splendor; it is attained by a righteous life. . . .
Children's children are a crown to the aged.—My
brothers, you whom I love and long for, my joy
and crown.—Everyone who competes in the
games goes into strict training. They do it to get a
crown that will last; but we do it to get a crown
that will last forever.—"Be faithful, even to the
point of death, and I will give you the crown of
life."—Blessed is the man who perseveres under
trial, because when he has stood the test, he will
receive the crown of life that God has promised to
those who love him.—I have kept the faith. Now
there is in store for me the crown of
righteousness.—They lay their crowns before the
throne and say: "You are worthy, our Lord and
God, to receive glory and honor and power."

*Rev. 19:12; John 19:5; Heb. 2:7, 9; Isa. 28:5; Prov.
16:31; 17:6; Phil. 4:1; 1 Cor. 9:25; Rev. 2:10; James
1:12; 2 Tim. 4:7-8; Rev. 4:10.*

may/18

"'The silver is mine and the gold is mine,'
declares the Lord Almighty.''—Jesus sat down
opposite the place where the offerings were put
and watched the crowd putting their money into
the temple treasury. Many rich people threw in
large amounts. But a poor widow came and put in
two very small copper coins, worth only a fraction
of a penny. Calling his disciples to him, Jesus
said, "I tell you the truth, this poor widow has put
more into the treasury than all the others. They all
gave out of their wealth: but she, out of her
poverty, put in everything—all she had to live
on.''—"But who am I, or who are my people, that
we should be able to give as generously as this?
Everything comes from you, and we have given
you only what comes from your hand.''—The law
from your mouth is more precious to me than
thousands of pieces of silver and gold.—The love
of money is a root of all kinds of evil. Some people,
eager for money, have wandered from the faith
and pierced themselves with many griefs.—"They
took the thirty silver coins, the price set on him by
the people of Israel, and they used them to buy the
potter's field, as the Lord commanded me."—You
know that it was not with perishable things such
as silver or gold that you were redeemed, . . . but
with the precious blood of Christ.

Hag. 2:8; Mark 12:41-44; 1 Chron. 29:14; Ps. 119:72;
1 Tim. 6:10; Matt. 27:9-10; 1 Peter 1:18.

may /19

The angel answered [Mary], "The Holy Spirit
will come upon you, and the power of the Most
High will overshadow you. So the holy one to be
born will be called the Son of God."—Those who
were in the boat worshiped him, saying, "Truly
you are the Son of God." . . . The tempter came to
him and said, "If you are the Son of God, tell these
stones to become bread." . . . "Tell us if you are
the Christ, the Son of God." "Yes, it is as you
say," Jesus replied. . . . When the centurion and
those with him who were guarding Jesus saw the
earthquake and all that happened, they were
terrified, and exclaimed, "Surely he was the Son of
God!"—Who through the Spirit of holiness was
declared with power to be the Son of God by his
resurrection from the dead.—The life I live in the
body, I live by faith in the Son of God, who loved
me and gave himself for me.—Since we have a
great high priest who has gone through the
heavens, Jesus the Son of God, let us hold firmly to
the faith we profess. . . . A man deserves to be
punished who has trampled the Son of God under
foot.—The reason the Son of God appeared was to
destroy the devil's work.—These are the words of
the Son of God, whose eyes are like blazing fire
and whose feet are like burnished bronze.

*Luke 1:35; Matt. 14:33; 4:3; 26:63-64; 27:54; Rom.
1:4; Gal. 2:20; Heb. 4:14; 10:29; 1 John 3:8; Rev.
2:18.*

may/20

"I have set my rainbow in the clouds, and it will be the sign of the covenant between me and the earth."—"The clouds pour down their moisture and abundant showers fall on mankind. Who can understand how he spreads out the clouds? . . . Do you know how the clouds hang poised?"—Your faithfulness [reaches] to the skies. . . . He makes the clouds his chariot. . . . He spread out a cloud.—"I will command the clouds not to rain on it." . . . See, the Lord rides on a swift cloud.—There before me was one like a son of man, coming with the clouds of heaven.—They will see the Son of Man coming on the clouds of the sky, with power and great glory.—Look, he is coming with the clouds, and every eye will see him.—Caught up with them in the clouds to meet the Lord in the air. And so we will be with the Lord forever.—Since we are surrounded by such a great cloud of witnesses, let us throw off everything that hinders and the sin that so easily entangles.—They have taken the way of Cain. . . . They are clouds without rain, blown along by the wind; autumn trees, without fruit and uprooted—twice dead.—When a king's face brightens, it means life; his favor is like a rain cloud in spring.

Gen. 9:13; Job 36:27-28; 37:16; Pss. 36:5; 104:3; 105:39; Isa. 5:6; 19:1; Dan. 7:13; Matt. 24:30; Rev. 1:7; 1 Thess. 4:17; Heb. 12:1; Jude 11-12; Prov. 16:15.

may/21

"Sing about a fruitful vineyard: I, the Lord, watch over it; I water it continually. I guard it day and night so that no one may harm it." . . . "Morning is coming, but also the night."—I thank God, whom I serve, as my forefathers did, with a clear conscience, as night and day I constantly remember you in my prayers.—The widow who is really in need and left all alone puts her hope in God and continues night and day to pray and ask God for help.—If I say, "Surely the darkness will hide me and the light become night around me," even the darkness will not be dark to you; the night will shine like the day, for darkness is as light to you. . . . The sun will not harm you by day, nor the moon by night. . . . The day is yours, and yours also the night; you established the sun and moon.—"As long as the earth endures, . . . day and night will never cease."—Will not God bring about justice for his chosen ones, who cry out to him day and night?—On his law he meditates day and night.—By day the Lord went ahead of them in a pillar of cloud to guide them on their way and by night in a pillar of fire to give them light, so they could travel by day or night. Neither the pillar of cloud by day nor the pillar of fire by night left its place in front of the people.

Isa. 27:3; 21:12; 2 Tim. 1:3; 1 Tim. 5:5; Pss. 139;11-12; 121:6; 74:16; Gen. 8:22; Luke 18:7; Ps. 1:2; Exod. 13:21-22.

may /22

I know that everything God does will endure
forever; nothing can be added to it and nothing
taken from it. God does it, so men will revere
him.—God's gifts and his call are irrevocable.
—Every good and perfect gift is from above,
coming down from the Father of the heavenly
lights, who does not change like shifting shadows.
He chose to give us birth through the word of
truth, that we might be a kind of firstfruits of all he
created.—"I give [my sheep] eternal life, and they
shall never perish; no one can snatch them out of
my hand. My Father, who has given them to me,
is greater than all; no one can snatch them out of
my Father's hand. . . . I and the Father are
one."—Israel will be saved by the Lord with an
everlasting salvation. . . . "My salvation will last
forever, my righteousness will never fail. . . . My
righteousness will last forever, my salvation
through all generations."—I know whom I have
believed, and am convinced that he is able to
guard what I have entrusted to him for that
day.—I am convinced that neither death nor life,
neither angels nor demons, neither the present
nor the future, nor any powers, neither height nor
depth, nor anything else in all creation will be able
to separate us from the love of God that is in Christ
Jesus our Lord.

*Eccl. 3:14; Rom. 11:29; James 1:17-18; John 10:28-30;
Isa. 45:17; 51:6, 8; 2 Tim. 1:12; Rom. 8:38-39.*

may/23

Speak to one another with psalms, hymns and spiritual songs. Sing and make music in your heart to the Lord.—Sing psalms, hymns and spiritual songs with gratitude in your hearts to God.—A happy heart makes the face cheerful, but heartache crushes the spirit. . . . A cheerful heart is good medicine, but a crushed spirit dries up the bones.—I will sing with my spirit, but I will also sing with my mind.—I delight greatly in the Lord; my soul rejoices in my God.—He put a new song in my mouth, a hymn of praise to our God. — Is anyone happy? Let him sing songs of praise.—Joyfully giving thanks to the Father, who has qualified you to share in the inheritance of the saints in the kingdom of light.—I have told you this so that my joy may be in you and that your joy may be complete.—It is written: "Therefore I will praise you among the Gentiles; I will sing hymns to your name." . . . "Praise the Lord, all you Gentiles, and sing praises to him, all you peoples."—Joy and gladness will be found in her, thanksgiving and the sound of singing. . . . [The ransomed of the Lord] will enter Zion with singing; everlasting joy will crown their heads. Gladness and joy will overtake them, and sorrow and sighing will flee away.

Eph. 5:19; Col. 3:16; Prov. 15:13; 17:22; 1 Cor. 14:15; Isa. 61:10; Ps. 40:3; James 5:13; Col. 1:11; John 15:11; Rom. 15:9, 11; Isa. 51:3; 35:10.

may/24

In their hunger you gave them bread from heaven.—"Give us today our daily bread."—Go, eat your food with gladness.—"'Man does not live on bread alone, but on every word that comes from the mouth of God.'"—"'He gave them bread from heaven to eat.'" Jesus said to them, "I tell you the truth, it is not Moses who has given you the bread from heaven, but it is my Father who gives you the true bread from heaven. For the bread of God is he who comes down from heaven and gives life to the world. . . . I am the bread of life. He who comes to me will never go hungry. . . . I am the bread of life. Your forefathers ate the manna in the desert, yet they died. . . . I am the living bread that came down from heaven. If a man eats of this bread, he will live forever. This bread is my flesh, which I will give for the life of the world."—Jesus took bread, gave thanks and broke it, and gave it to his disciples, saying, "Take and eat, this is my body."—"Do this in remembrance of me."—Is not the bread that we break a participation in the body of Christ? Because there is one loaf, we, who are many, are one body, for we all partake of the one loaf. . . . Whenever you eat this bread and drink this cup, you proclaim the Lord's death until he comes.

Neh. 9:15; Matt. 6:11; Eccl. 9:7; Matt. 4:4; John 6:31-33, 35, 48-49, 51; Matt. 26:26; Luke 22:19; 1 Cor. 10:16-17; 11:26.

may/25

Whatever your lips utter you must be sure to do, because you made your vow freely to the Lord your God with your own mouth.—"I am a man of unclean lips, and I live among a people of unclean lips, and my eyes have seen the King, the Lord Almighty." Then one of the seraphs flew to me with a live coal in his hand, which he had taken with tongs from the altar. With it he touched my mouth and said, "See, this has touched your lips; your guilt is taken away and your sin atoned for."—Truthful lips endure forever, but a lying tongue lasts only a moment. . . . Lips that speak knowledge are a rare jewel. . . . Listen, for I have worthy things to say; I open my lips to speak what is right. . . . My lips detest wickedness.—May my lips overflow with praise, for you teach me your decrees. May my tongue sing of your word. . . . Save me, O Lord, from lying lips and from deceitful tongues. . . . Set a guard over my mouth, O Lord; keep a watch over the door of my lips.—"'These people honor me with their lips, but their hearts are far from me.'"—I will guide him and restore comfort to him, creating praise on the lips of the mourners in Israel.—Through Jesus, therefore, let us continually offer to God a sacrifice of praise—the fruits of lips that confess his name.

Deut. 23:23; Isa. 6:5-7; Prov. 12:19; 20:15; 8:6-7; Pss. 119:171-172; 120:2; 141:3; Matt. 15:8; Isa. 57:19; Heb. 13:15.

may /26

Enoch walked with God 300 years. . . ; then he was no more, because God took him away. . . . When Abram was ninety-nine years old, the Lord appeared to him and said, "I am God Almighty; walk before me and be blameless."—"My Presence will go with you, and I will give you rest." Then Moses said to him, "If your Presence does not go with us, do not send us up from here."—God is with us.—You have made known to me the path of life; you will fill me with joy in your presence, with eternal pleasures at your right hand.—As they talked and discussed these things with each other, Jesus himself came up and walked along with them. . . . As they approached the village to which they were going, Jesus acted as if he were going father. But they urged him strongly, "Stay with us, for it is nearly evening; the day is almost over." So he went in to stay with them. . . . "Were not our hearts burning within us while he talked with us on the road and opened the Scriptures to us?"— Surely I will be with you always, to the very end of the age."—"Never will I leave you; never will I forsake you."—"You have a few people in Sardis who have not soiled their clothes. They will walk with me, dressed in white, for they are worthy."

Gen. 5:22, 24; 17:1; Exod. 33:14-15; Isa. 8:10; Pss. 16:11; Luke 24:15, 28-29, 32; Matt. 28:20; Heb. 13:5; Rev. 3:4.

may /27

"I will put my laws in their hearts, and I will
write them on their minds."—[False teachers
have] an unhealthy interest in . . . evil suspicions
and constant friction between men of corrupt
mind, who have been robbed of the truth and who
think that godliness is a means to financial
gain.—In my inner being I delight in God's law;
but I see another law at work in the members of
my body, waging war against the law of my mind
and making me a prisoner of the law of sin at work
within my members.—Their minds were made
dull, for to this day the same veil remains when
the old covenant is read. It has not been removed,
because only in Christ is it taken away.
—Therefore, prepare your minds for action;
be self-controlled; set your hope fully on the grace
to be given you when Jesus Christ is revealed.
—The god of this age has blinded the
minds of unbelievers, so that they cannot see the
light of the gospel of the glory of Christ, who is the
image of God.—To the pure, all things are pure,
but to those who are corrupted and do not believe,
nothing is pure. In fact, both their minds and
consciences are corrupted.—"For who has known
the mind of the Lord that he may instruct him?"
But we have the mind of Christ.

*Heb. 10:15; 1 Tim. 6:3-5; Rom. 7:22-23; 2 Cor. 3:14;
1 Peter 1:13; 2 Cor. 4:4; Titus 1:15; 1 Cor. 2:16.*

may /28

God said, "Let there be light," and there was light. God saw that the light was good, and he separated the light from the darkness.—God is light; in him there is no darkness at all. . . . If we walk in the light, as he is in the light, we have fellowship with one another, and the blood of Jesus, his Son, purifies us from every sin.—When Jesus spoke again to the people, he said, "I am the light of the world. Whoever follows me will never walk in darkness, but will have the light of life." . . . "While I am in the world, I am the light of the world." . . . "Put your trust in the light while you have it, so that you may become sons of light."—You were once darkness, but now you are light in the Lord. Live as children of light.—Children of God without fault in a crooked and depraved generation, in which you shine like stars in the universe.—Giving thanks to the Father, who has qualified you to share in the inheritance of the saints in the kingdom of light.—"You are the light of the world. . . . Let your light shine before men, that they may see your good deeds and praise your Father in heaven."—The city does not need the sun or the moon to shine on it, for the glory of God gives it light, and the Lamb is its lamp. The nations will walk by its light.

Gen. 1:3-4; 1 John 1:5, 7; John 8:12; 9:5; 12:36; Eph. 5:8; Phil. 2:15; Col. 1:12; Matt. 5:14, 16; Rev. 21:23.

may/29

God said, "Ask for whatever you want me to give you."—"Go in peace, and may the God of Israel grant you what you have asked of him." —They will ask the way to Zion and turn their faces toward it.—"I tell you that if two of you on earth agree about anything you ask for, it will be done for you by my Father in heaven."—"Which of you fathers, if your son asks for a fish, will give him a snake instead? . . . If you then, though you are evil, know how to give good gifts to your children, how much more will your Father in heaven give the Holy Spirit to those who ask him!"—"The Father will give you whatever you ask in my name. . . . If you remain in me and my words remain in you, ask whatever you wish, and it will be given you." . . . "In that day you will no longer ask me anything. I tell you the truth, my Father will give you whatever you ask in my name. . . . Ask and you will receive, and your joy will be complete."—This is the assurance we have in approaching God: that if we ask anything according to his will, he hears us. And if we know that he hears us—whatever we ask—we know that we have what we asked of him.—"Ask and it will be given to you; seek and you will find; knock and the door will be opened to you."

1 Kings 3:5; 1 Sam. 1:17; Jer. 50:5; Matt. 18:19; Luke 11:11, 13; John 15:16, 7; 16:23-24; 1 John 5:14-15; Luke 11:9.

may/30

"**B**lessed are the pure in heart, for they will see God."—To the pure, all things are pure, but to those who are corrupted and do not believe, nothing is pure.—The Lord detests the thoughts of the wicked, but those of the pure are pleasing to him.—Jesus Christ, who gave himself for us to redeem us from all wickedness and to purify for himself a people that are his very own, eager to do what is good.—Set an example for the believers . . . in purity.—"To the faithful you show yourself faithful, to the blameless you show yourself blameless, to the pure you show yourself pure.—Finally, brothers, whatever is true, whatever is noble, whatever is right, whatever is pure, whatever is lovely, whatever is admirable . . . think about such things.—Now that you have purified yourselves by obeying the truth so that you have sincere love for your brothers, love one another deeply, from the heart.—We know that when he appears, we shall be like him, for we shall see him as he is. Everyone who has this hope in him purifies himself, just as he is pure.—Religion that God our Father accepts as pure and faultless is this: to look after orphans and widows in their distress and to keep oneself from being polluted by the world.

Matt. 5:8; Titus 1:15; Prov. 15:26; Titus 2:13-14, 1 Tim. 4:12; 2 Sam. 22:26-27; Phil. 4:8; 1 Peter 1:22; 1 John 3:2-3; James 1:27.

may /31

The house of Judah will take root below and bear fruit above.—A man cannot be established through wickedness, but the righteous cannot be uprooted. . . . The root of the righteous flourishes.—Their roots will decay . . . for they have rejected the law of the Lord Almighty. . . . A shoot will come up from the stump of Jesse; from his roots a Branch will bear fruit.—Isaiah says, "The Root of Jesse will spring up, one who will arise to rule over nations; the Gentiles will hope in him."—"See, the Lion of the tribe of Judah, the Root of David, has triumphed." . . . "I am the Root and the Offspring of David, and the bright Morning Star."—In days to come Jacob will take root, Israel will bud and blossom and fill all the world with fruit.—The love of money is a root of all kinds of evil.—The sun came up, the plants were scorched, and they withered because they had no root. . . . They saw the fig tree withered from the roots.—I pray that you, being rooted and established in love, may have power, together with all the saints, to grasp how wide and long and high and deep is the love of Christ.—Continue to live in him, rooted and built up in him, strengthened in the faith as you were taught, and overflow with thankfulness.

---

2 Kings 19:30; Prov. 12:3, 12; Isa. 5:24; 11:1; Romans 15:12; Rev. 5:5; 22:16; Isa. 27:6; 1 Tim. 6:10; Mark 4:6; 11:20; Eph. 3:17-19; Col. 2:7.

June /1

He is your praise; he is your God.—"Save us, O God our Savior; . . . that we may give thanks to your holy name, that we may glory in your praise."—It is fitting for the upright to praise him. . . . His praise will always be on my lips. . . . He who sacrifices thank offerings honors me. . . . My mouth is filled with your praise, declaring your splendor all day long. . . . Praise the Lord. How good it is to sing praises to our God, how pleasant and fitting to praise him! . . . Let them praise the name of the Lord, for his name alone is exalted; his splendor is above the earth and the heavens.—Sing to the Lord a new song, his praise from the ends of the earth. . . . My chosen, the people I formed for myself that they may proclaim my praise. . . . You will call your walls Salvation and your gates Praise.—Save me and I will be saved, for you are the one I praise.—" 'From the lips of children and infants you have ordained praise.' "—[The Pharisees] loved praise from men more than praise from God.—To the praise of his glorious grace, which he has freely given us in the One he loves.—You are . . . a people belonging to God, that you may declare the praises of him who called you out of darkness into his wonderful light.

Deut. 10:21; 1 Chron. 16:35; Pss. 33:1; 34:1; 50:23; 71:8; 147:1; 148:13; Isa. 42:10; 43:21; 60:18; Jer. 17:14; Matt. 21:16; John 12:43; Eph. 1:6; 1 Peter 2:9.

Dave Koechel

May I never boast except in the cross of our Lord Jesus Christ.

june/2

Carrying his own cross, [Jesus] went out to The Place of the Skull (which in Aramaic is called Golgotha). Here they crucified him. . . . Pilate had a notice prepared and fastened to the cross. It read, JESUS OF NAZARETH, THE KING OF THE JEWS. . . . Near the cross of Jesus stood his mother.—Christ did not send me to baptize, but to preach the gospel—not with words of human wisdom, lest the cross of Christ be emptied of its power. For the message of the cross is foolishness to those who are perishing, but to us who are being saved it is the power of God.—Brothers, if I am still preaching circumcision, why am I still being persecuted? In that case the offense of the cross has been abolished. . . . The only reason they do this is to avoid being persecuted for the cross of Christ. . . . May I never boast except in the cross of our Lord Jesus Christ, through which the world has been crucified to me, and I to the world.—His purpose was to create in himself one new man out of the two, . . . and in this one body to reconcile both of them to God through the cross.—He humbled himself and became obedient to death—even death on a cross! . . . Many live as enemies of the cross of Christ.—Making peace through his blood, shed on the cross.

John 19:17-19, 25; 1 Cor. 1:17-18; Gal. 5:11; 6:12, 14; Eph. 2:15-16; Phil. 2:8; 3:18; Col. 1:20.

June/3

On the Day of Atonement sound the trumpet
throughout your land.—Hezekiah gave the order
to sacrifice the burnt offering on the altar. As the
offering began, singing to the Lord began also,
accompanied by trumpets and the instruments of
David king of Israel. The whole assembly bowed
in worship, while the singers sang and the
trumpeters played.—The Spirit of the Lord came
upon Gideon, and he blew a trumpet.—The seven
priests carrying the seven trumpets went forward
marching before the ark of the Lord and blowing
the trumpets.—"Put the trumpet to your lips! An
eagle is over the house of the Lord because the
people have broken my covenant.—The Sovereign
Lord will sound the trumpet; he will march in the
storms of the south, and the Lord Almighty will
shield them.—Listen, I tell you a mystery: We
shall not all sleep, but we will all be changed—in a
flash, in the twinkling of an eye, at the last
trumpet. For the trumpet will sound, the dead will
be raised imperishable, and we will be
changed.—For the Lord himself will come down
from heaven, with a loud command, with the
voice of the archangel and with the trumpet call of
God.—If the trumpet does not sound a clear call,
who will get ready for battle?

*Lev. 25:9; 2 Chron. 29:27-28; Judg. 6:34; Josh. 6:13;
Hos. 8:1; Zech. 9:14; 1 Cor. 15:51-52; 1 Thess. 4:16; 1
Cor. 14:8.*

june /4

"**I**, even I, am he who blots out your transgressions, for my own sake, and remembers your sins no more.—A righteous man will be remembered forever.—After I looked things over, I stood up and said to the nobles, and officials and the rest of the people, "Don't be afraid of them. Remember the Lord, who is great and awesome, and fight."—A scroll of remembrance was written in his presence concerning those who feared the Lord and honored his name.—Be on your guard! Remember that for three years I never stopped warning each of you night and day with tears.—Remember Jesus Christ, raised from the dead, descended from David. This is my gospel, for which I am suffering even to the point of being chained like a criminal.—I want you to recall the words spoken in the past by the holy prophets and the command given by our Lord and Savior through your apostles.—The Holy Spirit, whom the Father will send in my name, will teach you all things and will remind you of everything I have said to you. . . ."Remember the words I spoke to you: 'No servant is greater than his master.'" —[Jesus] took bread, gave thanks and broke it, and gave it to them, saying, "This is my body given for you; do this in remembrance of me."

Isa. 43:25; Ps. 112:6; Neh. 4:14; Mal. 3:16; Acts 20:31; 2 Tim. 2:8-9; 2 Peter 3:2; John 14:26; 15:20; Luke 22:19.

June/5

Guard yourself in your spirit.—Renew a steadfast spirit within me.—Pride goes before destruction, a haughty spirit before a fall. Better to be lowly in spirit and among the oppressed than to share plunder with the proud. . . . The lamp of the Lord searches the spirit of a man; it searches out his inmost being.—Do not be quickly provoked in your spirit, for anger resides in the lap of fools. . . . The dust returns to the ground it came from, and the spirit returns to God who gave it.—This is what the high and lofty One says . . . "I live in a high and holy place, but also with him who is contrite and lowly in spirit."—Mary said: "My soul praises the Lord and my spirit rejoices in God my Savior."—While they were stoning him, Stephen prayed, "Lord Jesus, receive my spirit."—The unfading beauty of a gentle and quiet spirit, which is of great worth in God's sight.—We have all had human fathers who disciplined us and we respected them for it. How much more should we submit to the Father of our spirits and live! . . . You have come to God, the judge of all men, to the spirits of righteous men made perfect.—"Father, into your hands I commit my spirit."—The Lord be with your spirit. Grace be with you.

Mal. 2:16; Ps. 51:10; Prov. 16:18-19; 20:27; Eccl. 7:9; 12:7; Isa. 57:15; Luke 1:46-47; Acts 7:59; 1 Peter 3:4, Heb. 12:9, 23; Luke 23:46; 2 Tim. 4:22.

june/6

O Lord, . . . Your eyes are too pure to look on evil; you cannot tolerate wrong.—"They will look on me, the one they have pierced, and mourn for him as one mourns for an only child.—You looked in that day . . . you saw the City of David . . . but you did not look to the One who made it, or have regard for the One who planned it long ago. . . . Woe to those who go down to Egypt for help, . . . but do not look to the Holy One of Israel, or seek help from the Lord. . . . "Look to the rock from which you were cut and to the quarry from which you were hewn."—[Anna] gave thanks to God and spoke about the child to all who were looking forward to the redemption of Jerusalem. . . . The Lord turned and looked straight at Peter. Then Peter remembered the word the Lord had spoken to him.—That which was from the beginning, . . . which we have seen with our eyes, which we have looked at and our hands have touched.—Anyone who listens to the word but does not do what it says is like a man who looks at his face in a mirror and, after looking at himself, goes away and immediately forgets what he looks like.—Since you are looking forward to [the new heaven and a new earth], make every effort to be found spotless, blameless and at peace with him.

Hab. 1:12-13; Zech. 12:10; Isa. 22:8-11; 31:1; 51:1; Luke 2:38; 22:61; 1 John 1:1; James 1:23; 2 Peter 3:14.

june /7

[This law] is to be with him, and he is to read it all the days of his life so that he may learn to revere the Lord his God and follow carefully all the words of this law and these decrees.—"My days are swifter than a weaver's shuttle." . . . All the days of my hard service I will wait for my renewal to come.—Surely goodness and love will follow me all the days of my life. . . . One thing I ask of the Lord, this is what I seek: that I may dwell in the house of the Lord all the days of my life, to gaze upon the beauty of the Lord and to seek him in his temple. . . . Teach us to number our days aright, that we may gain a heart of wisdom.—"Serve him without fear in holiness and righteousness before him all our days."—Be very careful, then, how you live—not as unwise but as wise, making the most of every opportunity, because the days are evil.—"Whoever would love life and see good days must keep his tongue from evil and his lips from deceitful speech."—Bloodthirsty and deceitful men will not live out half their days. . . . The days of the blameless are known to the Lord, and their inheritance will endure forever.—If they obey and serve him, they will spend the rest of their days in prosperity and their years in contentment.

Deut. 17:19; Job 7:6; 14:14; Pss. 23:6; 27:4; 90:12; Luke 1:75; Eph. 5:16; 1 Peter 3:10; Pss. 55:23; 37:18; Job 36:11.

June/8

"'On what are you basing this confidence of yours? . . .'We are depending upon the Lord our God.' "—"Should not your piety be your confidence and your blameless ways your hope?"—I had confidence in all of you, that you would all share my joy. For I wrote you out of great distress and anguish of heart and with many tears, not to grieve you but to let you know the depth of my love for you. . . . We are sending with them our brother who has often proved to us in many ways that he is zealous, and now even more so because of his great confidence in you.—In him and through faith in him we may approach God with freedom and confidence.—We who worship by the Spirit of God, who glory in Christ Jesus, and who put no confidence in the flesh.—We have confidence in the Lord that you are doing and will continue to do the things we command.—We have come to share in Christ if we hold firmly till the end the confidence we had at first. . . . Do not throw away your confidence; it will be richly rewarded.—Continue in him, so that when he appears we may be confident and unashamed before him at his coming. . . . If our hearts do not condemn us, we have confidence before God and receive from him anything we ask.

Isa. 36:4, 7; Job 4:6; 2 Cor. 2:3-4; 8:22; Eph. 3:12; Phil. 3:4; 2 Thess. 3:4; Heb. 3:14; 10:35; 1 John 2:28; 3:21.

june/9

When the woman saw that the fruit of the tree was good for food and pleasing to the eye, and also desirable for gaining wisdom, she took some and ate it. . . . "Don't look back!" . . . But Lot's wife looked back and she became a pillar of salt.—"No one who puts his hand to the plow and looks back is fit for service in the kingdom of God."—"The Lord does not look at the things men look at. Man looks at the outward appearance, but the Lord looks at the heart."—I lift up my eyes to you, to you whose throne is in heaven. As the eyes of slaves look to the hand of their master, as the eyes of a maid look to the hand of her mistress, so our eyes look to the Lord our God, till he shows us mercy. . . . God looks down from heaven upon the sons of men to see if there are any who understand, any who seek God. . . . Those who look to him are radiant; their faces are never covered with shame.—Let your eyes look straight ahead, fix your gaze directly before you.—Each of you should look not only to your own interests, but also to the interests of others. —"They will look on the one they have pierced."—Let us fix our eyes on Jesus, the author and perfecter of our faith.—I looked, and there before me was a door standing open in heaven.

Gen. 3:6; 19:17, 26; Luke 9:62; 1 Sam. 16:7; Pss. 123:1-2; 53:2; 34:5; Prov. 4:25; Phil. 2:4; John 19:37; Heb. 12:2; Rev. 4:1.

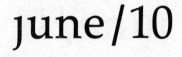

june/10

God tested Abraham. He said to him, . . . "Take your son, your only son Isaac, whom you love, and go to the region of Moriah. Sacrifice him there as a burnt offering. . . . When they had reached the place God had told him about, Abraham . . . bound his son Isaac and laid him on the altar.—[Esther said,] "I will go to the king, even though it is against the law. And if I perish, I perish."—Ruth replied, "Don't urge me to leave you or to turn back from you. Where you go I will go, and where you stay I will stay. Your people will be my people and your God my God. Where you die I will die, and there I will be buried. —Reaching into his bag and taking out a stone, [David] slung it and struck the Philistine on the forehead. The stone sank into his forehead, and he fell facedown on the ground. So David triumphed over the Philistine with a sling and a stone.—They brought Daniel and threw him into the lions' den. The king said to Daniel, "May your God, whom you serve continually, rescue you!"—When he had received the drink, Jesus said, "It is finished." With that, he bowed his head and gave up his spirit.—When they saw the courage of Peter and John and realized that they were unschooled, ordinary men, they were astonished and they took note that these men had been with Jesus.

Gen. 22:1-2, 9; Esth. 4:16; Ruth 1:16-17; 1 Sam. 17:49-50; Dan. 6:16; John 19:30; Acts 4:13.

june/11

So perishes the hope of the godless. What he trusts in is fragile; what he relies on is a spider's web.—Why are you downcast, O my soul? Why so disturbed within me? Put your hope in God, for I will yet praise him. . . . Blessed is he whose help is the God of Jacob, whose hope is in the Lord his God.—The prospect of the righteous is joy, but the hopes of the wicked come to nothing.—"I stand on trial because of my hope in the resurrection of the dead."—Against all hope, Abraham in hope believed and so became the father of many nations. . . . Hope does not disappoint us, because God has poured out his love into our hearts by the Holy Spirit, whom he has given us.—By faith we eagerly await through the Spirit the righteousness for which we hope.—I pray also that the eyes of your heart may be enlightened in order that you may know the hope to which he has called you, the riches of his glorious inheritance in the saints.—We wait for the blessed hope—the glorious appearing of our great God and Savior, Jesus Christ.—May the God of hope fill you with all joy and peace as you trust in him, so that you may overflow with hope by the power of the Holy Spirit.

Job 8:13-14; Pss. 42:5; 146:5; Prov. 10:28; Acts 23:6; Rom. 4:18; 5:5; Gal. 5:5; Eph. 1:18; Titus 2:13; Rom. 15:13.

june /12

The Lord said, "I will cause all my goodness to pass in front of you, and I will proclaim my name, the Lord, said in your presence."—Surely goodness and love will follow me all the days of my life. . . . I am still confident of this: I will see the goodness of the Lord in the land of the living. . . . How great is your goodness, which you have stored up for those who fear you.—They ate to the full and were well-nourished; they reveled in your great goodness. . . . Even while they were in their kingdom, enjoying your great goodness to them in the spacious and fertile land you gave them, they did not serve you or turn from their evil ways.—The fruit of the light consists in all goodness, righteousness and truth.—"They will come and shout with joy on the heights of Zion; they will rejoice in the bounty of the Lord. . . . I will satisfy the priests with abundance, and my people will be filled with my bounty."—They will tell of the power of your awesome works, and I will proclaim your great deeds. They will celebrate your abundant goodness and joyfully sing of your righteousness.—"May your priests, O Lord God, be clothed with salvation, may your saints rejoice in your goodness."

Exod. 33:19; Pss. 23:6; 27:13; 31:19; Neh. 9:25, 35; Eph. 5:9; Jer. 31:12, 14; Ps. 145:6-7; 2 Chron. 6:41.

june/13

They mounted the onyx stones in gold filigree settings and engraved them like a seal with the names of the sons of Israel. Then they fastened them on the shoulder pieces of the ephod as memorial stones for the sons of Israel, as the Lord commanded Moses.—"I will also give him a white stone with a new name written on it, known only to him who receives it."—"Build the altar of the Lord your God with fieldstones. . . . Write very clearly all the words of this law on these stones you have set up."—"I tell you that out of these stones God can raise up children for Abraham." . . . "He who falls on this stone will be broken to pieces, but he on whom it falls will be crushed." . . . They went and made the tomb secure by putting a seal on the stone. . . . An angel of the Lord came down from heaven and, going to the tomb, rolled back the stone and sat on it.—The devil said to [Jesus], "If you are the Son of God, tell this stone to become bread." Jesus answered, "It is written: 'Man does not live on bread alone.'"—As you come to him, the living Stone—rejected by men but chosen by God and precious to him—you also, like living stones, are being built into a spiritual house to be a holy priesthood, offering spiritual sacrifices acceptable to God through Jesus Christ.

Exod. 39:6-7; Rev. 2:17; Deut. 27:6-8; Matt. 3:9; 21:44; 27:66; 28:2; Luke 4:3-4; 1 Peter 2:4-5.

june/14

"Men like you, . . . each one with the bearing of a prince."—Then God said, "Let us make man in our image, in our likeness." . . . So God created man in his own image, in the image of God he created him. . . . "Whoever sheds the blood of man, by man shall his blood be shed; for in the image of God has God made man."—Although they claimed to be wise, they became fools and exchanged the glory of the immortal God for images made to look like mortal man and birds and animals and reptiles.—Every man who prays or prophesies with his head covered dishonors his head. . . . A man ought not to cover his head, since he is the image and glory of God.—We, who with unveiled faces all reflect the Lord's glory, are being transformed into his likeness with every-increasing glory, which comes from the Lord, who is the Spirit. . . . The god of this age has blinded the minds of unbelievers, so that they cannot see the light of the gospel of the glory of Christ, who is the image of God.—Put on the new self, which is being renewed in knowledge in the image of its Creator.—The Son is the radiance of God's glory and the exact representation of his being, sustaining all things by his powerful word.—There is no rest day or night for those who worship the beast and his image.

Judg. 8:18; Gen. 1:26-27; 9:6; Rom. 1:23; 1 Cor. 11:4, 7; 2 Cor. 3:18; 4:4; Col. 3:10; Heb. 1:3; Rev. 14:11.

june/15

When you walk, your steps will not be
hampered; when you run, you will not
stumble. . . . The name of the Lord is a strong
tower; the righteous run to it and are safe.—They
will soar on wings like eagles; they will run and
not grow weary, they will walk and not be
faint.—The sun, which is like a bridegroom
coming forth from his pavilion, like a champion
rejoicing to run his course. . . . I will run in the
path of your commands, for you have set my heart
free. . . . He sends his command to the earth; his
word runs swiftly.—Do you not know that in a
race all the runners run, but only one gets the
prize? Run in such a way as to get the prize. . . .
Therefore I do not run . . . aimlessly.—You were
running a good race. Who cut in on you and kept
you from obeying the truth?—Children of God
without fault in a crooked and depraved
generation, in which you shine like stars in the
universe as you hold out the word of life—in order
that I may boast on the day of Christ that I did not
run or labor for nothing.—Therefore, since we are
surrounded by such a great cloud of witnesses, let
us throw off everything that hinders and the sin
that so easily entangles, and let us run with
perseverance the race marked out for us.

*Prov. 4:12; 18:10; Isa. 40:31; Pss. 19:4-5; 119:32;
147:15; 1 Cor. 9:24, 26; Gal. 5:7; Phil. 2:15-16; Heb.
12:1.*

june/16

Surely I spoke of things I did not understand,
things too wonderful for me to know.—He will be
called Wonderful Counselor, Mighty God,
Everlasting Father, Prince of Peace. Of the
increase of his government and peace there will be
no end. . . . O Lord, you are my God; I will exalt
you and praise your name, for in perfect
faithfulness you have done marvelous things,
things planned long ago. . . . All this also comes
from the Lord Almighty, wonderful in counsel and
magnificent in wisdom.—Great is the Lord and
most worthy of praise; his greatness no one can
fathom. . . . Give thanks to the Lord of lords . . .
to him who alone does great wonders. . . . Your
statutes are wonderful; therefore I obey them. . . .
Give thanks to the Lord for his unfailing love and
his wonderful deeds for men.—When the chief
priests and the teachers of the law saw the
wonderful things [Jesus] did and the children
shouting in the temple area, "Hosanna to the Son
of David," they were indignant.—I am the Lord,
and there is no other; apart from me there is no
God. . . . I form the light and create darkness.
—For us there is but one God, the Father, from
whom all things came and for whom we live; and
there is but one Lord, Jesus Christ, through whom
all things came and through whom we live.

Job 42:3; Isa. 9:6-7; 25:1; 28:29; Pss. 145:3; 136:3-4;
119:129; 107:8; Matt. 21:15; Isa. 45:5, 7; 1 Cor. 8:6.

june/17

May his name endure forever; may it continue as long as the sun. . . . His anger lasts only a moment, but his favor lasts a lifetime. . . . But you, O Lord, sit enthroned forever; your renown endures through all generations.—All men will hate you because of me, but he who stands firm to the end will be saved. . . . Because of the increase of wickedness, the love of most will grow cold, but he who stands firm to the end will be saved.—So after waiting patiently, Abraham received what was promised. . . . By faith [Moses] left Egypt, not fearing the king's anger; he persevered because he saw him who is invisible.—You have heard of Job's perseverance and have seen what the Lord finally brought about.—Love is patient, . . . always hopes, always perseveres.—Among God's churches we boast about your perseverance and faith in all the persecutions and trials you are enduring.—Who for the joy set before him endured the cross. . . . Consider him who endured such opposition from sinful men, so that you will not grow weary and lose heart.—Endure hardship with us like a good soldier of Christ Jesus. . . . Therefore I endure everything for the sake of the elect. . . . Keep your head in all situations, endure hardship.

Pss. 72:17; 30:5; 102:12; Matt. 10:22; 24:12-13; Heb. 6:15; 11:27; James 5:11; 1 Cor. 13:4, 7; 2 Thess. 1:4; Heb. 12:2-3; 2 Tim. 2:3, 10; 4:5.

june/18

He grants sleep to those he loves. . . . I lie down and sleep; I awake again, because the Lord sustains me. . . . I will lie down and sleep in peace, for you alone, O Lord, make me dwell in safety.—When you lie down, you will not be afraid; when you lie down, your sleep will be sweet. . . . He who gathers crops in summer is a wise son, but he who sleeps during harvest is a disgraceful son.—The sleep of a laborer is sweet, whether he eats little or much, but the abundance of a rich man permits him no sleep.—While [Gabriel] was speaking to me, I was in a deep sleep, with my face to the ground. Then he touched me and raised me to my feet.—That night the king could not sleep; so he ordered the book of the chronicles, the record of his reign, to be brought in and read to him.—The Lord God caused the man to fall into a deep sleep; and while he was sleeping, he took one of the man's ribs and closed up the place with flesh. Then the Lord God made a woman from the rib he had taken out of the man.—Jesus was in the stern, sleeping on a cushion. The disciples woke him and said to him, "Teacher, don't you care if we drown?"—We will not all sleep, but we will all be changed.

Pss. 127:2; 3:5; 4:8; Prov. 3:24; 10:5; Eccl. 5:12; Dan. 8:18; Esth. 6:1; Gen. 2:21-22; Mark 4:38; 1 Cor. 15:51.

june/19

We are aliens and strangers in your sight, as were all our forefathers. Our days on earth are like a shadow, without hope.—You have been a . . . shelter from the storm and a shade from the heat. . . . In the shadow of his hand he hid me.—The Lord God provided a vine and made it grow up over Jonah to give shade for his head to ease his discomfort, and Jonah was very happy about the vine.—A king will reign in righteousness. . . . Each man will be like . . . the shadow of a great rock in a thirsty land.—Until the day breaks and the shadows flee.—Keep me as the apple of your eye; hide me in the shadow of your wings. . . . Both high and low among men find refuge in the shadow of your wings.—People brought the sick into the streets and laid them on beds and mats so that at least Peter's shadow might fall on some of them as he passed by.—Every good and perfect gift is from above, coming down from the Father of the heavenly lights, who does not change like shifting shadows.—Because you are my help, I sing in the shadow of your wings. . . . He who dwells in the shelter of the Most High will rest in the shadow of the Almighty. . . . I am poor and needy. . . . I fade away like an evening shadow.

1 Chron. 29:15; Isa. 25:4; 49:2; Jonah 4:6; Isa. 32:1-2; Song of Songs 2:17; Pss. 17:8; 36:7; Acts 5:15; James 1:17; Pss. 63:7; 91:1; 109:22-23.

june /20

You are a people holy to the Lord your God. Out of all peoples on the face of the earth, the Lord has chosen you to be his treasured possession.—"In accordance with your great love, forgive the sin of these people, just as you have pardoned them from the time they left Egypt until now."—But I, by your great mercy, will come into your house; in reverence will I bow down toward your holy temple.—[God] says to Moses, "I will have mercy on whom I have mercy, and I will have compassion on whom I have compassion." It does not, therefore, depend on man's desire or effort, but on God's mercy.—Because of his great love for us, God, who is rich in mercy, made us alive with Christ even when we were dead in transgressions—it is by grace you have been saved.—Praise be to the God and Father of our Lord Jesus Christ! In his great mercy he has given us new birth into a living hope through the resurrection of Jesus Christ from the dead. . . . Once you were not a people, but now you are the people of God; once you had not received mercy, but now you have received mercy.—Be merciful, just as your Father is merciful.—Therefore, I urge you, brothers, in view of God's mercy, to offer your bodies as living sacrifices, holy and pleasing to God—which is your spiritual worship.

Deut. 14:2; Num. 14:19; Ps. 5:7; Rom. 9:15-16; Eph. 2:4-5; 1 Peter 1:3; 2:10; Luke 6:36; Rom. 12:1.

june /21

Who in the skies above can compare with the Lord? Who is like the Lord among the heavenly beings? In the council of the holy ones God is greatly feared; he is more awesome than all who surround him. . . . O Lord God Almighty, who is like you? . . . The heavens are yours, and yours also the earth; you founded the world and all that is in it. . . . Among the gods there is none like you, O Lord; no deeds can compare with yours —Moses replied [to Pharaoh], "It will be as you say, so that you may know there is no one like the Lord our God."—"I am God, and there is no other; I am God, and there is none like me. . . . My purpose will stand, and I will do all that I please. . . . To whom, then, will you compare God? What image will you compare him to? . . . He sits enthroned above the circle of the earth.—Now to him who is able to do immeasurably more than all we ask or imagine, according to his power that is at work within us. . . . One God and Father of all, who is over all and through all and in all.—God exalted him to the highest place and gave him the name that is above every name, that at the name of Jesus every knee should bow, in heaven and on earth and under the earth, and every tongue confess that Jesus Christ is Lord, to the glory of God the Father.

Pss. 89:6-8, 11; 86:8; Exod. 8:10; Isa. 46:9-10; 40:18, 22; Eph. 3:20; 4:6; Phil. 2:9-11.

june/22

"Do not be afraid, Abram. I am your shield, your very great reward."—He is your shield and helper and your glorious sword.—"Every word of God is flawless; he is a shield to those who take refuge in him."—For surely, O Lord, you bless the righteous; you surround him with your favor as with a shield. . . . The Lord is my strength and my shield; my heart trusts in him, and I am helped. . . . We wait in hope for the Lord; he is our help and our shield. . . . O Lord our shield. . . . My refuge in times of trouble. . . . Hear my prayer, O Lord God Almighty; listen to me, O God of Jacob. Look upon our shield, O God; look with favor on your anointed one. . . . You give me your shield of victory, and your right hand sustains me; you stooped down to make me great. . . . But you are a shield around me, O Lord, my Glorious One, who lifts up my head. . . . For the Lord God is a sun and shield; the Lord bestows favor and honor; no good thing does he withhold from those whose walk is blameless.—This is the day I have spoken of. Israel will go out and use the weapons for fuel and burn them up—the small and large shields.— In addition to all this, take up the shield of faith, with which you can extinguish all the flaming arrows of the evil one.

Gen. 15:1; Deut. 33:29; Prov. 30:5; Pss. 5:12; 28:7; 33:20; 59:11, 16; 84:8-9; 18:35; 3:3; 89:11; Ezek. 39:9; Eph. 6:16.

june/23

Then the Lord said, "There is a place near me where you may stand on a rock. When my glory passes by, I will put you in a cleft in the rock and cover you with my hand until I have passed by."—He brought you water out of hard rock.—They all ate the same spiritual food and drank the same spiritual drink; for they drank from the spiritual rock that accompanied them, and that rock was Christ.—To you I call, O Lord my Rock; do not turn a deaf ear to me. . . . I say to God my Rock, "Why have you forgotten me?" . . . Lead me to the rock that is higher than I. . . . He alone is my rock and my salvation; he is my fortress, I will not be shaken. . . . Be my rock of refuge, to which I can always go; give the command to save me, for you are my rock and my fortress.—Each man will be like . . . the shadow of a great rock in a thirsty land.—"You are the Christ, the Son of the living God." Jesus replied, . . . "On this rock I will build my church, and the gates of Hades will not overcome it."—Go into the rocks, hide in the ground from the dread of the Lord and the splendor of his majesty!— They called to the mountains and the rocks, "Fall on us and hide us from the face of him who sits on the throne and from the wrath of the Lamb!"

Exod. 33:21-22; Deut. 8:15; 1 Cor. 10:3-4; Pss. 28:1; 42:9; 61:2; 62:2, 6; 71:3; Isa. 32:2; Matt. 16:16-18; Isa. 2:10; Rev. 6:16.

june/24

Comfort, comfort my people, says your God.
. . . The Lord comforts his people and will have
compassion on his afflicted ones. . . . The Lord
will surely comfort Zion. . . . As a mother
comforts her child, so will I comfort you.—I will
turn their mourning into gladness; I will give
them comfort and joy instead of sorrow.—I looked
for sympathy, but there was none, for comforters,
but I found none. . . . You are with me; your rod
and your staff, they comfort me. . . . My comfort
in my suffering is this: Your promise renews my
life.—"Blessed are those who mourn, for they will
be comforted."—Many Jews had come to Martha
and Mary to comfort them in the loss of their
brother.—Praise be to the God and Father of our
Lord Jesus Christ, the Father of compassion and
the God of all comfort, who comforts us in all our
troubles, so that we can comfort those in any
trouble with the comfort we ourselves have
received from God. For just as the sufferings of
Christ flow over into our lives, so also through
Christ our comfort overflows. If we are distressed,
it is for your comfort and salvation; if we are
comforted, it is for your comfort, which produces
in you patient endurance of the same sufferings
we suffer.

---

*Isa. 40:1; 49:13; 51:3; 66:13; Jer. 31:13; Pss. 69:20;
23:4; 119:50; Matt. 5:4; John 11:19; 2 Cor. 1:3-6.*

june/25

May he be enthroned in God's presence forever; appoint your love and faithfulness to protect him. . . . He who dwells in the shelter of the Most High will rest in the shadow of the Almighty. —The Spirit of truth . . . to be with you forever. . . . He lives with you and will be in you. . . . Remain in me, and I will remain in you. No branch can bear fruit by itself; it must remain in the vine. Neither can you bear fruit unless you remain in me. . . . If you remain in me and my words remain in you, ask whatever you wish, and it will be given you.—Those who obey his commands live in him, and he in them. And this is how we know that he lives in us: We know it by the Spirit he gave us. . . . The word of God lives in you, and you have overcome the evil one.— Anyone who runs ahead and does not continue in the teaching of Christ does not have God; whoever continues in the teaching has both the Father and the Son.—As for you, the anointing you received from him remains in you, and you do not need anyone to teach you.—You have never heard his voice nor seen his form, nor does his word dwell in you, for you do not believe the one he sent.—The world and its desires pass away, but the man who does the will of God lives forever.

Pss. 61:7; 91:1; John 14:16-17; 15:4, 7; 1 John 3:24; 2:14; 2 John 9; 1 John 2:27; John 5:37-38; 1 John 2: 17.

june/26

Isaac said, "I am now an old man and don't know the day of my death."—"Let me die the death of the righteous, and may my end be like theirs!"—He will swallow up death forever. The Sovereign Lord will wipe away the tears from all faces.—Even though I walk through the valley of the shadow of death, I will fear no evil, for you are with me. . . . For this God is our God for ever and ever; he will be our guide even to the end.—Now as always Christ will be exalted in my body, whether by life or by death. For to me, to live is Christ and to die is gain. If I am to go on living in the body, this will mean fruitful labor for me. Yet what shall I choose? I do not know! I am torn between the two: I desire to depart and be with Christ, which is better by far; but it is more necessary for you that I remain in the body.—The trumpet will sound, the dead will be raised imperishable, and we shall be changed. For the perishable must clothe itself with the imperishable, and the mortal with immortality. When the perishable has been clothed with the imperishable, and the mortal with immortality, then the saying that is written will come true: "Death has been swallowed up in victory." "Where, O death, is your victory? Where, O death is your sting?"

Gen. 27:2; Num. 23:10; Isa. 25:8; Pss. 23:4; 48:14; Phil. 1:20-24; 1 Cor. 15:52-55.

June /27

[Moses] asked the Lord, "Why have you brought this trouble on your servant? What have I done to displease you that you put the burden of all these people on me?"—He took up our infirmities and carried our sorrows.—"Have I become a burden to you?"—You have shattered the yoke that burdens them. . . . In that day their burden will be lifted from your shoulders, their yoke from your neck. . . . "His yoke will be taken from my people, and his burden removed from their shoulders."—"Come to me, all you who are weary and burdened, and I will give you rest. . . . My yoke is easy and my burden is light."—"You experts in the law, woe to you, because you load people down with burdens they can hardly carry, and you yourselves will not lift one finger to help them."—Carry each other's burdens, and in this way you will fulfill the law of Christ. . . . Each one should carry his own load.—My guilt has overwhelmed me like a burden too heavy to bear. . . . Cast your cares on the Lord, and he will sustain you; he will never let the righteous fall. . . . He says, "I removed the burden from their shoulders. . . . In your distress you called and I rescued you."—"I will not impose any other burden on you."

Num. 11:11; Isa. 53:4; Job 7:20; Isa. 9:4; 10:27; 14:25; Matt. 11:28, 30; Luke 11:46; Gal. 6:2, 5; Pss. 38:4; 55:22; 81:6, 7; Rev. 2:24.

june/28

Three men, firmly tied, fell into the blazing furnace. Then King Nebuchadnezzar leaped to his feet in amazement and asked his advisers, "Wasn't it three men that we tied up and threw into the fire?" They replied, "Certainly, O King." He said, "Look! I see four men walking around in the fire, unbound and unharmed, and the fourth looks like a son of the gods."—The Lord takes his place in court; he rises to judge the people.—The angel of the Lord encamps around those who fear him, and he delivers them. . . . Who will rise up for me against the wicked? Who will take a stand for me against evildoers? Unless the Lord had given me help, I would soon have dwelt in the silence of death. . . . As the mountains surround Jerusalem, so the Lord surrounds his people both now and forevermore.—The Lord stood near Paul and said, "Take courage!"—"Here I am! I stand at the door and knock. If anyone hears my voice and opens the door, I will go in and eat with him, and he with me."—"He trusts in the Lord; let the Lord rescue him. Let him deliver him, since he delights in him."—The Lord stood at my side and gave me strength. . . . I was delivered from the lion's mouth. The Lord will rescue me from every evil attack and will bring me safely to his heavenly kingdom.

Dan. 3:23-25; Isa. 3:13; Pss. 34:7; 94:16-17; 125:2; Acts 23:11; Rev. 3:20; Ps. 22:8; 2 Tim. 4:17-18.

June /29

Moses said to God, "Suppose I go to the Israelites and say to them, 'The God of your fathers has sent me to you,' and they ask me, 'What is his name?' Then what shall I tell them?" God said to Moses, "I am who I am. This is what you are to say to the Israelites, 'I AM has sent me to you.'"—"I am the bread of life." . . . "I am the light of the world." . . . "I am from above. You are of this world: I am not of this world. I told you that you would die in your sins; if you do not believe that I am the one I claim to be, you will indeed die in your sins." . . . "I tell you the truth, . . . before Abraham was born, I am!" . . . "While I am in the world, I am the light of the world." . . . "I tell you the truth, I am the gate for the sheep. All who ever came before me were thieves and robbers, but the sheep did not listen to them. . . . I am the good shepherd. The good shepherd lays down his life for the sheep. . . . "I am the resurrection and the life." . . . "I am the way and the truth and the life." . . . "I am the true vine and my Father is the gardener."—"I, Jesus, have sent my angel to give you this testimony for the churches. I am the Root and the Offspring of David, and the bright Morning Star. . . . I am the Alpha and the Omega, the First and the Last, the Beginning and the End."

Exod. 3:13-14; John 6:35; 8:12, 23-24, 58; 9:5; 10:7-8; 11:25; 14:6; 15:1; Rev. 22:16, 13.

june /30

The men of Israel sampled their provisions but did not inquire of the Lord.—"To God belong wisdom and power; counsel and understanding are his.—You guide me with your counsel, and afterward you will take me into glory. . . . Some sat in darkness and the deepest gloom, prisoners suffering in iron chains, for they had rebelled against the words of God and despised the counsel of the Most High. . . . Your statutes are my delight; they are my counselors.—Have you no king? Has your counselor perished?—"I will ask the Father, and he will give you another Counselor to be with you forever—the Spirit of truth. The world cannot accept [this Counselor], because it neither sees him nor knows him. But you know him, for he lives with you and will be in you. . . . Unless I go away, the Counselor will not come to you; but if I go, I will send him to you.—"I counsel you to buy from me gold refined in the fire, so that you can become rich; . . . and salve to put on your eyes, so you can see."—Oh, the depth of the riches of the wisdom and knowledge of God! How unsearchable his judgments, and his paths beyond tracing out! "Who has known the mind of the Lord? Or who has been his counselor?"

Josh. 9:14; Job. 12:13; Pss. 73:24; 107:10-11; 119:24; Mic. 4:9; John 14:16-17; 16:7; Rev. 3:18; Rom. 11:33-34.

I have learned to be content
whatever the circumstances.

Bob Taylor

july/1

I rejoice greatly in the Lord that at last you have renewed your concern for me. Indeed, you have been concerned, but you had no opportunity to show it. I am not saying this because I am in need, for I have learned to be content whatever the circumstances. I know what it is to be in need, and I know what it is to have plenty. I have learned the secret of being content in any and every situation, whether well fed or hungry, whether living in plenty or in want. I can do everything through him who gives me strength.—But godliness with contentment is great gain. For we brought nothing into the world, and we can take nothing out of it. But if we have food and clothing, we will be content with that. People who want to get rich fall into temptation and a trap and into many foolish and harmful desires that plunge men into ruin and destruction. For the love of money is a root of all kinds of evil. Some people, eager for money, have wandered from the faith and pierced themselves with many griefs.—Keep your lives free from the love of money and be content with what you have, because God has said, "Never will I leave you; never will I forsake you."—"If only we had been content to stay on the other side of the Jordan!" —He replied, "Don't extort money and don't accuse people falsely—be content with your pay."

Phil. 4:10-13; 1 Tim. 6:6-10; Heb. 13:5; Joshua 7:7; Luke 3:14.

july /2

When the dew was gone, thin flakes like frost on the ground appeared on the desert floor. When the Israelites saw it, they said to each other, "What is it?" For they did not know what it was. Moses said to them, "It is the bread the Lord has given you to eat."—He may eat the most holy food of his God, as well as the holy food.—"Our forefathers ate the manna in the desert; as it is written: 'He gave them bread from heaven to eat.'" Jesus said to them, "I tell you the truth, it is not Moses who has given you the bread from heaven, but it is my Father who gives you the true bread from heaven. For the bread of God is he who comes down from heaven and gives life to the world." . . . "I am the bread of life. He who comes to me will never go hungry." . . . "The bread is my flesh, which I will give for the life of the world."—Jesus took bread, gave thanks and broke it, and gave it to his disciples, saying, "Take and eat; this is my body."—Grain must be ground to make bread; so one does not go on threshing it forever.—Is not the cup of thanksgiving for which we give thanks a participation in the blood of Christ? And is not the bread that we break a participation in the body of Christ? Because there is one loaf, we, who are many, are one body, for we all partake of the one loaf.—"From now on give us this bread."

Exod. 16:14-15; Lev. 21:22; John 6:31-33, 35, 51; Matt. 26:26; Isa. 28:28; 1 Cor. 10:16-17; John 6:34.

july /3

The Lord turn his face toward you and give you peace.—He will be named . . . Prince of Peace. Of the increase of his government and peace there will be no end.—"Submit to God and be at peace with him; in this way prosperity will come to you."—Blessed is the man who finds wisdom. . . . Her ways are pleasant ways, and all her paths are peace.—The meek will inherit the land and enjoy great peace. . . . Great peace have they who love your law, and nothing can make them stumble.—"Blessed are the peacemakers, for they will be called sons of God."—"Peace I leave with you; my peace I give you. I do not give to you as the world gives."—Now may the Lord of peace himself give you peace at all times and in every way.—The fruit of the Spirit is . . . peace.—He himself is our peace. . . . His purpose was to create in himself one new man out of two, thus making peace. . . . He came and preached peace to you who were far away and peace to those who were near.—Since we have been justified through faith, we have peace with God through our Lord Jesus Christ, through whom we have gained access by faith into this grace in which we now stand.—Be of one mind, live in peace. And the God of love and peace will be with you.

Num. 6:26; Isa. 9:6-7; Job 22:21; Prov. 3:13, 17; Pss. 37:11; 119:165; Matt. 5:9; John 14:27; 2 Thess. 3:16; Gal. 5:22; Eph. 2:14-15, 17; Rom. 5:1-2; 2 Cor. 13:11.

july /4

I looked up and there before me was a man dressed in linen, with a belt of the finest gold around his waist. His body was like chrysolite, his face like lightning, his eyes like flaming torches, his arms and legs like the gleam of burnished bronze, and his voice like the sound of a multitude.—When I turned I saw seven golden lampstands, and among the lampstands was someone "like a son of man," dressed in a robe reaching down to his feet and with a golden sash around his chest. His head and hair were white like wool, as white as snow, and his eyes were like blazing fire. His feet were like bronze glowing in a furnace, and his voice was like the sound of rushing waters. In his right hand he held seven stars, and out of his mouth came a sharp double-edged sword. His face was like the sun shining in all its brilliance. When I saw him, I fell at his feet as though dead.—We, who with unveiled faces all reflect the Lord's glory, are being transformed into his likeness with ever-increasing glory, which comes from the Lord, who is the Spirit.—From heaven the Lord looks down and sees all mankind; from his dwelling place he watches all who live upon the earth. . . . Those who look to him are radiant; their faces are never covered with shame.

Dan. 10:5-6; Rev. 1:12-17; 2 Cor. 3:18; Pss. 33:13-14; 34:5.

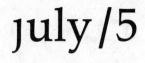

july /5

The Lord had said to Moses, "Tell the Israelites, 'You are a stiffnecked people. If I were to go with you even for a moment, I might destroy you.'"—"What is man that you make so much of him, that you give him so much attention, that you examine him every morning and test him every moment?" . . . "The mirth of the wicked is brief, the joy of the godless lasts but a moment."—"For a brief moment I abandoned you, but with deep compassion I will bring you back. In a surge of anger I hid my face from you for a moment, but with everlasting kindness I will have compassion on you," says the Lord your Redeemer.—Listen, I tell you a mystery: We will not all sleep, but we will all be changed—in a flash, in the twinkling of an eye, at the last trumpet. For the trumpet will sound, the dead will be raised imperishable, and we shall be changed.—Therefore we do not lose heart. Though outwardly we are wasting away, yet inwardly we are being renewed day by day. For our light and momentary troubles are achieving for us an eternal glory that far outweighs them all. So we fix our eyes not on what is seen, but on what is unseen. For what is seen is temporary, but what is unseen is eternal.—"Each of them will tremble every moment for his life."

Exod. 33:5; Job 7:17-18; 20:5; Isa. 54:7-8; 1 Cor. 15:51-52; 2 Cor. 4:16-18; Ezek. 32:10.

July /6

Blessed is the man who listens to me, watching daily at my doors, waiting at my doorway.—For day after day they seek me out; they seem eager to know my ways, as if they were a nation that does what is right and has not forsaken the commands of its God.—The Lord said to Moses, "I will rain down bread from heaven for you. The people are to go out each day and gather enough for that day."—"Father, give us each day our daily bread."—"The bolts of your gates will be iron and bronze, and your strength will equal your days."—Day by day the King gave Jehoiachin a regular allowance as long as he lived.—Praise be to the Lord, to God our Savior, who daily bears our burdens. . . . I will exalt you, my God the King; I will praise your name for ever and ever. Every day I will praise you and extol your name for ever and ever.—Every day they continued to meet together in the temple courts. They broke bread in their homes and ate together with glad and sincere hearts, praising God and enjoying the favor of all the people. . . . They received the message with great eagerness and examined the Scriptures every day to see if what Paul said was true.—I die every day—I mean that, brothers—just as surely as I glory over you in Christ Jesus our Lord.

Prov. 8:34; Isa. 58:2; Exod. 16:4; Luke 11:3; Deut. 33:25; 2 Kings 25:30; Pss. 68:19; 145:1-2; Acts 2:46-47; 17:11; 1 Cor. 15:31.

july/7

When they heard that the Lord was concerned about them and had seen their misery, they bowed down and worshiped.—The Lord had seen how bitterly everyone in Israel, whether slave or free, was suffering . . . [but] he saved them by the hand of Jeroboam.—Though he brings grief, he will show compassion, so great is his unfailing love. For he does not willingly bring affliction or grief to the children of men.—"They will seek my face; in their misery they will earnestly seek me."—Although the Lord gives you the bread of adversity and the water of affliction, your teachers will be hidden no more; with your own eyes you will see them. . . . "See, I have refined you, though not as silver; I have tested you in the furnace of affliction."—Make us glad for as many days as you have afflicted us, for as many years as we have seen trouble. . . . My comfort in my suffering is this: Your promise renews my life. . . . Before I was afflicted I went astray, but now I obey your word.—Jealous of Joseph, they sold him as a slave into Egypt. But God was with him and rescued him from all his troubles.—I rejoice in what was suffered for you, and I fill up in my flesh what is still lacking in regard to Christ's afflictions, for the sake of . . . the church.

Exod. 4:31; 2 Kings 14:26-27; Lam. 3:32-33; Hos. 5:15; Isa. 30:20; 48:10; Pss. 90:15; 119:50, 67; Acts 7:10; Col. 1:24.

july /8

The day before Saul came, the Lord had revealed this to Samuel: "About this time tomorrow I will send you [Saul]."—"I am telling you now before it happens, so that when it does happen you will believe that I am He." . . . "I have told you now before it happens, so that when it does happen you will believe."—"Before they call I will answer; while they are still speaking I will hear."—Righteousness goes before him and prepares the way for his steps.—The word of the Lord came to me, saying, "Before I formed you in the womb I knew you, before you were born I set you apart; I appointed you as a prophet to the nations."—Before a word is on my tongue you know it completely, O Lord. You hem me in, behind and before; you have laid your hand upon me.—"When you pray, do not keep on babbling like pagans, for they think they will be heard because of their many words. Do not be like them, for your Father knows what you need before you ask him."—The prophets . . . searched intently and with the greatest care, trying to find out the time and circumstances to which the Spirit of Christ in them was pointing when he predicted the sufferings of Christ and the glories that would follow.

1 Sam. 9:15-16; John 13:19; 14:29; Isa. 65:24; Ps. 85:13; Jer. 1:4-5; Ps. 139:4-5; Matt. 6:7-8; 1 Peter 1:10-11.

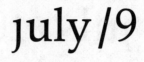

july /9

"I will sing to the Lord, for he is highly exalted. The horse and its rider he has hurled into the sea."—[Eleazar] stood his ground and struck down the Philistines till his hand grew tired and froze to the sword. . . . Shammah took his stand in the middle of the field. He defended it and struck the Philistines down, and the Lord brought about a great victory.—How awesome is the Lord Most High, the great King over all the earth! He subdued nations under us, peoples under our feet. . . . You make me glad by your deeds, O Lord; I sing for joy at the works of your hands. . . . He saved them from the hand of the foe; from the hand of the enemy he redeemed them. The waters covered their adversaries; not one of them survived. Then they believed his promises and sang his praise.—Thanks be to God! He gives us the victory through our Lord Jesus Christ.—Thanks be to God, who always leads us in triumphal procession in Christ and through us spreads everywhere the fragrance of the knowledge of him.—Him who overcomes I will make a pillar in the temple of my God. . . . To him who overcomes, I will give the right to sit with me on my throne, just as I overcame and sat down with my Father on his throne.

Exod. 15:1; 2 Sam. 23:10, 12; Pss. 47:2-3; 92:4; 106:10-12; 1 Cor. 15:57; 2 Cor. 2:14; Rev. 3:12, 21.

July / 10

"[Man] tunnels through the rock; his eyes see all its treasures. He searches the sources of the rivers and brings hidden things to light.—"May the Lord bless his land with the precious dew from heaven above and with the deep waters that lie below; with the best the sun brings forth and the finest the moon can yield."—Blessed is the man who finds wisdom. . . . She is more precious than rubies; nothing you desire can compare with her." . . . Gold there is, and rubies in abundance, but lips that speak knowledge are a rare jewel. —How the gold has lost its luster, the fine gold become dull! The sacred gems are scattered at the head of every street. How the precious sons of Zion, once worth their weight in gold, are now considered as pots of clay.—He has given us his very great and precious promises, so that through them you may participate in the divine nature and escape the corruption in the world caused by evil desires. . . . To those who through the righteousness of our God and Savior Jesus Christ have received a faith as precious as ours.—Precious in the sight of the Lord is the death of his saints. . . . How precious to me are your thoughts, O God! How vast is the sum of them! Were I to count them, they would outnumber the grains of sand.

Job 28:10-11; Deut. 33:13-14; Prov. 3:13, 15; 20:13; Lam. 4:1-2; 2 Peter 1:4, 1; Pss. 116:15; 139:17-18.

july / 11

My son, do not despise the Lord's discipline and do not resent his rebuke, because the Lord disciplines those he loves, as a father the son he delights in. . . . Stern discipline awaits him who leaves the path; he who hates correction will die.—All Scripture is God-breathed and is useful for teaching, rebuking, correcting and training in righteousness.—"My son, do not make light of the Lord's discipline, and do not lose heart when he rebukes you." . . . Endure hardship as discipline; God is treating you as sons. For what son is not disciplined by his father? If you are not disciplined (and everyone undergoes discipline), then you are illegitimate children and not true sons. . . . Our fathers disciplined us for a little while as they thought best; but God disciplines us for our good, that we may share in his holiness.—"Blessed is the man whom God corrects; so do not despise the discipline of the Almighty. For he wounds, but he also binds up; he injures, but his hands also heal."—He does not treat us as our sins deserve or repay us according to our iniquities.—"This is the nation that has not obeyed the Lord its God or responded to correction."—Because of the Lord's great love we are not consumed, for his compassions never fail.

Prov. 3:11-12; 15:10; 2 Tim. 3:16; Heb. 12:5, 7-8, 10;
Job 5:17-18; Ps. 103:10; Jer. 7:28; Lam. 3:22.

july / 12

"Your right hand, O Lord, was majestic in power. Your right hand, O Lord, shattered the enemy. In the greatness of your majesty you threw down those who opposed you."—Who is this, robed in splendor, striding forward in the greatness of his strength? "It is I, speaking in righteousness, mighty to save."—"Yours, O Lord, is the greatness and the power and the glory and the majesty and the splendor, for everything in heaven and earth is yours."—"God is greater than man."—Say to God, "How awesome are your deeds! So great is your power that your enemies cringe before you." . . . What god is so great as our God? You are the God who performs miracles; you display your power among the peoples. —"One greater than Jonah is here. . . . One greater than Solomon is here."—His incomparably great power for us who believe. That power is like the working of his mighty strength, which he exerted in Christ when he raised him from the dead and seated him at his right hand.—"The Mighty One has done great things for me—holy is his name. . . . He has performed mighty deeds with his arm."—"Great and marvelous are your deeds, Lord God Almighty. Just and true are your ways."

Exod. 15:6-7; Isa. 63:1; 1 Chron. 29:11; Job 33:12; Pss. 66:3; 77:13-14; Matt. 12:41-42; Eph. 1:19-20; Luke 1:49, 51; Rev. 15:3.

july /13

The Lord has broken the rod of the wicked. . . .
All the lands are at rest and at peace; they break
into singing. . . . Sing for joy, O heavens, for the
Lord has done this; shout aloud, O earth beneath.
Burst into song, you mountains, you forests and
all your trees, for the Lord has redeemed Jacob, he
displays his glory in Israel.—Hezekiah gave the
order to sacrifice the burnt offering on the altar. As
the offering began, singing to the Lord began also,
accompanied by trumpets and the instruments of
David king of Israel.—When they had sung a
hymn, they went out to the Mount of Olives.—
Paul and Silas were praying and singing hymns to
God, and the other prisoners were listening to
them.—Speak to one another with psalms, hymns
and spiritual songs. Sing and make music in your
heart to the Lord, always giving thanks to God the
Father for everything, in the name of our Lord
Jesus Christ.—I will praise you, O Lord, among
the nations; I will sing of you among the
peoples. . . . I will sing of the love of the Lord
forever; with my mouth I will make your
faithfulness known through all generations . . . .
May the righteous be glad and rejoice before God;
may they be happy and joyful. Sing to God, sing
praise to his name, extol him who rides on the
clouds–his name is the Lord.

*Isa. 14:5, 7; 44:23; 2 Chron. 29:27-28; Matt. 26:30;
Acts 16:25; Eph. 5:19-20; Pss. 57:9; 89:1; 68:3-4.*

July / 14

All the peoples of the earth are regarded as nothing. [The Most High] does as he pleases with the powers of heaven and the peoples of earth.—Her nobles will have nothing there to be called a kingdom. . . . Before him all the nations are as nothing; they are regarded by him as worthless and less than nothing. . . . He brings princes to naught, and reduces the rulers of this world to nothing. . . . "Those who wage war against you will be as nothing at all." . . . "See, they are all false! Their deeds amount to nothing; their images are but wind and confusion."—"We were born only yesterday and know nothing, and our days on the earth are but a shadow." . . . "He spreads out the northern skies over empty space; he suspends the earth over nothing."—"Dust you are and to dust you will return."—If I have a faith that can move mountains, but have not love, I am nothing. If I give all I possess to the poor and surrender my body to the flames, but have not love, I gain nothing.—Sorrowrul, yet always rejoicing; poor, yet making many rich; having nothing, and yet possessing everything. . . . I have made a fool of myself, but you drove me to it. I ought to have been commended by you, for I am not in the least inferior to the "super apostles," even though I am nothing.

Dan. 4:35; Isa. 34:12; 40:17, 23; 41:12, 29; Job 8:9; 26:7; Gen. 3:19; 1 Cor. 13:2-3; 2 Cor. 6:10; 12:11.

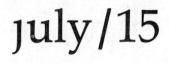

july/15

Let your face shine upon your servant: save me in your unfailing love. . . . One thing I ask of the Lord, this is what I seek: that I may dwell in the house of the Lord all the days of my life, to gaze upon the beauty of the Lord and to seek him in his temple. . . . Look to the Lord and his strength; seek his face always. . . . The face of the Lord is against those who do evil, to cut off the memory of them from the earth.—"If my people, who are called by my name, will humble themselves and pray and seek my face and turn from their wicked ways, then will I hear from heaven and will forgive their sin and will heal their land." . . . "The Lord your God is gracious and compassionate. He will not turn his face from you if you return to him."—As he was praying, the appearance of his face changed, and his clothes became as bright as a flash of lightning.—Christ, who is the image of God . . . who said, "Let light shine out of darkness," made his light shine in our hearts to give us the light of the knowledge of the glory of God in the face of Christ.—His face was like the sun shining in all its brilliance. When I saw him, I fell at his feet as though dead. . . . His servants will serve him. They will see his face, and his name will be on their foreheads.

Pss. 31:16; 27:4; 105:4; 34:16; 2 Chron. 7:14; 30:9; Luke 9:29; 2 Cor. 4:4, 6; Rev. 1:16-17; 22:3-4.

July / 16

"Acknowledge the God of your father, and serve him with wholehearted devotion and with a willing mind."—"To do your will, O my God, is my desire; your law is within my heart." . . . Your troops will be willing on your day of battle. . . . Teach me to do your will, for you are my God.—"Whoever does God's will is my brother and sister and mother."—"I have come down from heaven not to do my will but to do the will of him who sent me. And this is the will of him who sent me, that I shall lose none of all that he has given me, but raise them up at the last day. For my Father's will is that everyone who looks to the Son and believes in him shall have eternal life, and I will raise him up at the last day." . . . "If any one chooses to do God's will, he will find out whether my teaching comes from God or whether I speak on my own."—The Spirit intercedes for the saints in accordance with God's will. . . . By God's will I may come to you with joy and together with you be refreshed.—May . . . our Lord Jesus, that great Shepherd of the sheep, equip you with everything good for doing his will.—This is the assurance we have in approaching God: that if we ask any thing according to his will, he hears us.—Your will be done on earth as it is in heaven."

---

1 Chron. 28:9; Pss. 40:8; 110:3; 143:10; Mark 3:35; John 6:38-40; 7:17; Rom. 8:27; 15:32; Heb. 13:20-21; 1 John 5:14; Matt. 6:10.

july / 17

"**He** changes times and seasons; he sets up kings and deposes them.—It is God who judges: he brings one down, he exalts another. . . . The Lord is on his heavenly throne. He observes the sons of men; his eyes examine them. . . . Righteousness and justice are the foundations of your throne. . . . "His throne [will] endure before me like the sun; it will be established forever like the moon, the faithful witness in the sky." . . . The Lord has established his throne in heaven, and his kingdom rules over all.—The Lord seated on a throne, high and exalted, and the train of his robe filled the temple.—"As I looked, thrones were set in place, and the Ancient of Days took his seat. . . . His throne was flaming with fire, and its wheels were all ablaze."—"By me kings reign and rulers make laws that are just; by me princes govern, and all nobles who rule on earth." . . . Love and faithfulness keep a king safe; through love his throne is made secure.—By him all things were created: things in heaven and on earth, visible and invisible, whether thrones or powers or rulers or authorities.—"To him who overcomes, I will give the right to sit with me on my throne, just as I overcame and sat down with my Father on his throne."

Dan. 2:21; Pss. 75:7; 11:4; 89:14, 36-37; 103:19; Isa. 6:1; Dan. 7:9; Prov. 8:15-16; 20:28; Col. 1:16; Rev. 3:21.

july / 18

You will be called Hephzibah [my delight is in her], and your land Beulah [married]; for the Lord will take delight in you. . . . As a bridegroom rejoices over his bride, so will your God rejoice over you. . . . "Here is my servant, whom I uphold, my chosen one in whom I delight; I will put my Spirit on him and he will bring justice to the nations."—"This is my Son, whom I love; with him I am well-pleased."—In my inner being I delight in God's law.—His delight is in the law of the Lord and on his law he meditates day and night. . . . As for the saints who are in the land, they are the glorious ones in whom is all my delight. . . . The Lord delights in the way of man whose steps he has made firm. . . . Your statutes are my delight; they are my counselors.—I was filled with delight day after day, rejoicing always in his presence, rejoicing in his whole world and delighting in mankind. . . . The Lord abhors dishonest scales, but accurate weights are his delight. . . . Discipline your son, and he will give you peace; he will bring delight to your soul.—I delight to sit in his shade, and his fruit is sweet to my taste.—"He trusts in the Lord; let the Lord rescue him. Let him deliver him, since he delights in him."

Isa. 62:4-5; 42:1; Matt. 3:17; Rom. 7:22; Pss. 1:2; 16:3; 37:23; 119:24; Prov. 8:30-31; 11:1; 29:17; Song of Songs 2:3; Ps. 22:8.

July / 19

"Lord God, keep forever the promise you have made concerning your servant and his house. . . . Then men will say, 'The Lord Almighty is God over Israel.''—Do you not know? Have you not heard? Has it not been told you from the beginning? Have you not understood since the earth was founded? He sits enthroned above the circle of the earth, and its people are like grasshoppers. He stretches out the heavens like a canopy, and spreads them out like a tent to live in. He brings princes to naught, and reduces the rulers of the world to nothing. . . . It pleased the Lord for the sake of his righteousness to make his law great and glorious.—"The Mighty One has done great things for me—holy be his name. . . . He has performed mighty deeds with his arm; he has scattered those who are proud in their inmost thoughts."—The Lord loves righteousness and justice, the earth is full of his unfailing love. By the word of the Lord the heavens were made, their starry host by the breath of his mouth. . . . "The Lord be exalted, who delights in the well-being of his servant." My tongue will speak of your righteousness and of your praises all day long. . . . May all the kings of the earth praise you, O Lord, when they hear the words of your mouth.

2 Sam. 7:25, 26; Isa. 40:21-23; 42:21; Luke 1:49, 51; Pss. 33:5-6; 35:27-28; 138:4.

july /20

The Sovereign Lord is my strength; he makes my feet like the feet of a deer.—He gives strength to the weary and increases the power of the weak. . . . Those who hope in the Lord will renew their strength. . . . My God has been my strength. . . . "In the Lord alone are righteousness and strength." . . . Who is this, robed in splendor, striding forward in the greatness of his strength?—Splendor and majesty are before him, strength and joy in his dwelling place.—I pray that out of his glorious riches he may strengthen you with power through his Spirit in your inner being.—Being strengthened with all power according to his glorious might so that you may have great endurance and patience, and joyfully giving thanks to the Father.—The Lord stood at my side and gave me strength, so that through me the message might be fully proclaimed and all the Gentiles might hear it.—It is God who arms me with strength and makes my way perfect. . . . You armed me with strength for the battle; you made my adversaries bow at my feet. . . . The Lord is the stronghold of my life—of whom shall I be afraid? . . . The Lord is the strength of his people, a fortress of salvation for his anointed one.

Hab. 3:19; Isa. 40:29, 31; 49:5; 45:24; 63:1; 1 Chron. 16:27; Eph. 3:16; Col 1:11-12; 2 Tim. 4:17; Pss. 18:32, 39; 27:1; 28:8.

july /21

Do not boast about tomorrow, for you do not know what a day may bring forth. . . . Through me your days will be many, and years will be added to your life.—"Give us each day our daily bread."—Make it your ambition to lead a quiet life, to mind your own business and to work with your hands, just as we told you, so that your daily life may win the respect of outsiders and so that you will not be dependent on anybody. —Therefore we do not lose heart.—Though outwardly we are wasting away, yet inwardly we are being renewed day by day.—Jerusalem celebrated the Feast of Unleavened Bread for seven days with great rejoicing, while the Levites and priests sang to the Lord every day.—"Your strength will equal your days."—He asked you for life, and you gave it to him—length of days, for ever and ever. . . . The heavens declare the glory of God . . . day after day they pour forth speech; night after night they display knowledge.— "Whoever would love life and see good days must keep his tongue from evil and his lips from deceitful speech."—Be very careful, then, how you live—not as unwise but as wise, making the most of every opportunity, because the days are evil.

Prov. 27:1; 9:11; Luke 11:3; 1 Thess. 4:11-12; 2 Cor. 4:16; 2 Chron. 30:21; Deut. 33:25; Pss. 21:4; 19:1-2; 1 Peter 3:10; Eph. 5:15-16.

july /22

The greatest among you will be your servant. For whoever exalts himself will be humbled, and whoever humbles himself will be exalted.—"He has scattered those who are proud in their inmost thoughts. He has brought down rulers from their thrones but has lifted up the humble."—"The God of our fathers raised Jesus from the dead —whom you had killed by hanging him on a tree. God exalted him to his own right hand as Prince and Savior that he might give repentance and forgiveness of sins to Israel."—Clothe yourselves with humility toward one another, because, "God opposes the proud but gives grace to the humble." Humble yourselves, therefore, under God's mighty hand, that he may lift you up in due time.—O Lord, you are my God; I will exalt you and praise your name.—"The Lord is my strength and my song; he has become my salvation. He is my God, and I will praise him, my father's God, and I will exalt him. I will sing to the Lord for he is highly exalted."—"The lowly will be exalted and the exalted will be brought low."—If anyone thinks he is something when he is nothing, he deceives himself.—You save the humble, but bring low those whose eyes are haughty.

Matt. 23:11-12; Luke 1:51-52; Acts 5:30-31; 1 Peter 5:5-6; Isa. 25:1; Exod. 15:1-2; Ezek. 21:26; Gal. 6:3; Ps. 18:27.

july /23

I will tell of the kindnesses of the Lord, the deeds for which he is to be praised, according to all the Lord has done for us.—"When you enter the land that the Lord will give you as he promised, observe the [Passover] ceremony." —The Levites have no share or inheritance among their brothers; the Lord is their inheritance, as the Lord your God told them.—Remember not the sins of my youth and my rebellious ways, according to your love remember me, for you are good, O Lord.—"God is not a man, that he should lie, nor a son of man, that he should change his mind. Does he speak and then not act? Does he promise and not fulfill?"—Christ died for our sins according to the Scriptures, . . . buried, . . . and raised on the third day according to the Scriptures.—[Abraham] did not waver through unbelief regarding the promise of God, but was strengthened in his faith and gave glory to God, being fully persuaded that God had power to do what he had promised.—In him we were also chosen, having been predestined according to the plan of him who works out everything in conformity with the purpose of his will.—The Lord has brought it about; he has done just as he said he would.

Isa. 63:7; Exod. 12:25; Deut. 10:9; Ps. 25:7; Num. 23:19; 1 Cor. 15:3-4; Rom. 4:20-21; Eph. 1:11; Jer. 40:3.

july /24

Do not let this Book of the Law depart from your mouth; meditate on it day and night, so that you may be careful to obey everything written in it. Then you will be prosperous and successful. —"Were not our hearts burning within us while he talked with us on the road and opened the Scriptures to us?"—Blessed is the man, . . . [whose] delight is in the law of the Lord, and on his law he meditates day and night. . . . "My heart grew hot within me, and as I meditated, the fire burned; then spoke I with my tongue." . . . I will remember the deeds of the Lord; yes, I will remember your miracles of long ago. I will meditate on all your works and consider all your mighty deeds. . . . My eyes stay open through the watches of the night that I may meditate on your promises. . . . You are near, O Lord, and all your commands are true. . . . To all perfection I see a limit; but your commands are boundless. Oh, how I love your law! I meditate on it all day long. . . . I have more insight than all my teachers, for I meditate on your statutes. I have more understanding than the elders, for I obey your precepts.—"A Savior has been born to you; he is Christ the Lord." . . . Mary treasured up all these things and pondered them in her heart.

Josh. 1:8; Luke 24:32; Pss. 1:2; 39:3; 77:11-12; 119:148, 151, 96-97, 99; Luke 2:11, 19.

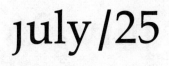

july /25

"I am the Lord your God, who teaches you what is best for you, who directs you in the way you should go."—"Teach me, and I will be quiet; show me where I have been wrong. How painful are honest words!" . . . "'Teach me what I cannot see; if I have done wrong, I will not do so again.'"—"God is exalted in his power. Who is a teacher like him?"—[Nicodemus] came to Jesus by night and said, "Rabbi, we know you are a teacher who has come from God." . . . The Holy Spirit, whom the Father will send in my name, will teach you all things and will remind you of everything I have said to you.—Teach me your way, O Lord; lead me in a straight path because of my oppressors. . . . I will instruct you and teach you in the way you should go; I will counsel you and watch over you. . . . Praise be to you, O Lord; teach me your decrees. . . . Teach me to do your will, for you are my God; may your good Spirit lead me on level ground.—"Lord, teach us to pray."—"Who has known the mind of the Lord that he may instruct him?" But we have the mind of Christ.—Just as you received Christ Jesus as Lord, continue to live in him, rooted and built up in him, strengthened in the faith as you were taught, and overflowing with thankfulness.

Isa. 48:17; Job 6:24-25; 34:32; 36:22; John 3:2; 14:26; Pss. 27:11; 32:8; 119:12; 143:10; Luke 11:1; 1 Cor. 2:16; Col 2:6-7.

July /26

"Multitudes who sleep in the dust of the earth will awake: some to everlasting life, others to shame and everlasting contempt. Those who are wise will shine like the brightness of the heavens, and those who lead many to righteousness, like the stars for ever and ever."—You turn men back to dust, saying, "Return to dust, O mortal man." . . . You sweep men away in the sleep of death; they are like the new grass of the morning—though in the morning it springs up new, by the evening it is dry and withered.—Here we do not have an enduring city, but we are looking for the city that is to come.—"Whoever believes in the Son has eternal life, but whoever rejects the Son will not see life, for God's wrath remains on him." . . . "In my Father's house are many rooms, if it were not so, I would have told you. . . . And if I go and prepare a place for you, I will come back and take you to be with me that you also may be where I am. You know the way to the place where I am going." . . . "Because I live, you also will live."—"I know that my Redeemer lives, and that in the end he will stand upon the earth. And after my skin has been destroyed, yet in my flesh, I will see God. I myself will see him, with my own eyes—I, and not another. How my heart yearns within me!"

Dan. 12:2-3; Ps. 90:3, 5-6; Heb. 13:14; John 3:36; 14:2-4, 19; Job 19:25-27.

july/27

"With everlasting kindness I will have compassion on you," says the Lord your Redeemer. . . . I will tell of the kindnesses of the Lord, the deeds for which he is to be praised, according to all the Lord has done for us—yes, the many good things he has done . . . according to his compassion and many kindnesses.—You are a forgiving God, gracious and compassionate, slow to anger, and abounding in love.—God raised us up with Christ and seated us with him in the heavenly realms in Christ Jesus, in order that in the coming ages he might show the incomparable riches of his grace, expressed in his kindness to us in Christ Jesus.—We lived in malice and envy, being hated and hating one another. But when the kindness and love of God our Savior appeared, he saved us, not because of righteous things we had done, but because of his mercy.—Make every effort to add to your faith . . . godliness, and to godliness, brotherly kindness; and to brotherly kindness, love. For if you possess these qualities in increasing measure, they will keep you from being ineffective and unproductive in your knowledge of our Lord Jesus Christ.—Be kind and compassionate to one another, forgiving each other, just as in Christ God forgave you.—Love is patient, love is kind.

Isa. 58:8; 63:7; Neh. 9:17; Eph. 2:6-7; Titus 3:3-5; 2 Peter 1:5-8; Eph. 4:32; 1 Cor. 13:4.

july/28

Moses turned and went down the mountain with the two tablets of the Testimony in his hands. . . . The tablets were the work of God; the writing was the writing of God, engraved on the tablets.—We are God's workmanship, created in Christ Jesus to do good works, which God prepared in advance for us to do.—"[God] says to the snow, 'Fall on the earth,' and to the rain shower, 'Be a mighty downpour.' So that all men he has made may know his work, he stops every man from his work." . . . "Stop and consider God's wonders. Do you know how God controls the clouds and makes his lightning flash?" —Come and see what God has done, how awesome his works in man's behalf!—As you do not know the path of the wind, or how the body is formed in a mother's womb, so you cannot understand the work of God, the Maker of all things.—The Lord will rise up . . . to do his work, his strange work, and perform his task.—A person is justified by what he does and not by faith alone.—No one can lay any foundation other than the one already laid, which is Jesus Christ. If any man builds on this foundation . . . his work will be shown for what it is, because the Day will bring it to light.

Exod. 32:15-16; Eph. 2:10; Job 37:6-7, 14-15; Ps. 66:5; Eccl. 11:5; Isa. 28:21; James 2:24; 1 Cor. 3:11-13.

july /29

"**My** heart rejoices in the Lord; . . . I delight in your deliverance."—"May your saints rejoice in your goodness."—"Rejoice in that day and leap for joy, because great is your reward in heaven.—We rejoice in hope of the glory of God. Not only so, but we also rejoice in our sufferings, because we know that suffering produces perseverance; perseverance character.—The important thing is that in every way, whether false motives or true, Christ is preached. And because of this I rejoice. Yes, I will continue to rejoice, for I know that through your prayers and the help given by the Spirit of Jesus Christ, what has happened to me will turn out for my deliverance.—Joyfully giving thanks to the Father, who has qualified you to share in the inheritance of the saints in the kingdom of light.—Rejoice in the Lord always. I will say it again: Rejoice! —Sorrowful, yet always rejoicing; poor, yet making many rich.—We will shout for joy when you are victorious and lift up our banners in the name of our God. . . . May the righteous be glad and rejoice before God; may they be happy and joyful! Sing to God, sing praise to his name. . . . I rejoice in your promise like one who finds great spoil. . . . Seven times a day I praise you.

1 Sam. 2:1; 2 Chron. 6:41; Luke 6:23; Rom. 5:2-4; Phil. 1:18-19; Col. 1:11-12; Phil 4:4; 2 Cor. 6:10; Pss. 20:5; 68:3-4; 119:162, 164.

July /30

The people walking in darkness have seen a great light; on those living in the land of the shadow of death a light has dawned. . . . "The former things will not be remembered, nor will they come to mind. Be glad and rejoice forever . . . the sound of weeping and crying will be heard . . . no more."—Though now for a little while you may have had to suffer grief in all kinds of trials. These have come so that your faith—of greater worth than gold, which perishes even though refined by fire—may be proved genuine and may result in praise, glory and honor when Jesus Christ is revealed.—In all our distress and persecution we were encouraged . . . because of your faith. How can we thank God enough for you in return for all the joy we have in the presence of our God because of you?—It is written, "The insults of those who insult you have fallen on me." . . . I glory in Christ Jesus in my service to God. I will not venture to speak of anything except what Christ has accomplished through me in leading the Gentiles to obey God by what I have said and done.—Because you did not serve the Lord your God joyfully and gladly in the time of prosperity, therefore in hunger and thirst, in nakedness and dire poverty, you will serve the enemies the Lord sends against you.

Isa. 9:2; 65:17-19; 1 Peter 1:6-7; 1 Thess. 3:7, 9; Rom. 15:3, 17-18; Deut. 28:47-48.

july /31

Endure hardship with us like a good soldier of Christ Jesus. No one serving as a soldier gets involved in civilian affairs—he wants to please his commanding officer.—"I have made him . . . a leader and commander of the peoples."—"The Lord says to you: 'Do not be afraid or discouraged because of the vast army. For the battle is not yours, but God's."—Who serves as a soldier at his own expense?—Though we live in the world, we do not wage war as the world does. The weapons we fight with are not the weapons of the world. On the contrary, they have divine power to demolish strongholds.—Who through faith, . . . became powerful in battle and routed foreign armies.—Timothy, my son, I give you this instruction in keeping with the prophecies once made about you, so that by following them you may fight the good fight, holding on to faith and a good conscience. . . . Fight the good fight of faith.—Put on the full armor of God so that you can take your stand against the devil's schemes. Put on the full armor of God, so that when the day of evil comes, you may be able to stand your ground, and after you have done everything, to stand.—"Wherever you hear the sound of the trumpet, join us there. Our God will fight for us!"

2 Tim. 2:3-4; Isa. 55:4; 2 Chron. 20:15; 1 Cor. 9:7; 2 Cor. 10:3-4; Heb. 11:33-34; 1 Tim. 1:18-19; 6:12; Eph. 6:11, 13; Neh. 4:20.

A man of sorrows,
and familiar with suffering.

aug/1

"**D**o not be afraid, O worm Jacob, O little Israel, for I myself will help you," declares the Lord, your Redeemer, the Holy One of Israel. "See, I will make you into a threshing sledge, new and sharp, with many teeth. You will thresh the mountains and crush them, and reduce the hills to chaff."—I am a worm and not a man, scorned by men and despised by the people. All who see me mock at me; they hurl insults, shaking their heads: "He trusts in the Lord; . . . let him deliver him."—He had no beauty or majesty to attract us to him, nothing in his appearance that we should desire him. He was despised and rejected by men.—"If even the moon is not bright and the stars are not pure in his eyes, how much less man, who is but a maggot—a son of man, who is only a worm!" . . . "If I say to corruption, 'You are my father,' and to the worm, 'My mother' or 'My sister,' where then is my hope?" . . . "After my skin has been destroyed, yet in my flesh I will see God; I myself will see him, with my own eyes!"—[The nations] will lick the dust like a snake, like creatures that crawl on the ground. . . . they will turn in fear to the Lord our God.—Those who rebelled against me; their worm will not die. . . ."

Isa. 41:14-15; Ps. 22:6-7; Isa. 53:2-3; Job 25:5-6; 17:14-15; 19:26-27; Mic. 7:17; Isa. 66:24.

aug /2

"The blood will be a sign for you on the houses
where you are; and when I see the blood, I will
pass over you. No destructive plague will touch
you when I strike Egypt."—"The life of the
creature is in the blood, and I have given it to you
to make atonement for yourselves on the altar; it is
the blood that makes atonement for one's life."
—[Judas said,] "I have sinned . . . for I have
betrayed innocent blood." . . . [Jesus] took the
cup . . . saying, . . . "This is my blood of the
covenant, which is poured out for many for the
forgiveness of sins."—In him we have
redemption through his blood, the forgiveness of
sins. . . . In Christ Jesus you who once were far
away have been brought near through the blood of
Christ.—Making peace through his blood, shed
on the cross.—He entered the Most Holy Place
once for all by his own blood, having obtained
eternal redemption. . . . Without the shedding of
blood there is no forgiveness. . . . Jesus . . .
suffered outside the city gate to make the people
holy through his own blood.—"These are they
who have come out of the great tribulation; they
have washed their robes and made them white in
the blood of the Lamb," . . . "They overcame him
by the blood of the Lamb."

*Exod. 12:13; Lev. 17:11; Matt. 27:4; 26:27; Eph. 1:7;
2:13; Col. 1:20; Heb. 9:12, 22; 13:12; Rev. 7:14;
12:11.*

aug/3

The blameless will receive a good inheritance.
—"They said to God, :Leave us alone! What can
the Almighty do to us?" Yet it was he who filled
their houses with good things."—No good thing
does he withhold from those whose walk is
blameless. . . . He satisfies my desires with good
things, so that my youth is renewed like the
eagle's.—"You know with all your heart and soul
that not one of all the good promises the Lord your
God gave you has failed."—"If you, then, though
you are evil, know how to give good gifts to your
children, how much more will your Father in
heaven give good gifts to those who ask
him!"—"He has filled the hungry with good
things but has sent the rich away empty." —
Anyone who receives instruction in the word
must share all good things with his instructor.
—When Christ came as high priest of the good
things that are already here, he went through
the greater and more perfect tabernacle that is not
man-made. . . . The law is only a shadow of the
good things that are coming—not the realities
themselves.—I pray that you may be active in
sharing your faith, so that you will have a full
understanding of every good thing we have in
Christ.

---

*Prov. 28:10; Job 22:17-18; Pss. 84:11; 103:5; Josh.
23:14; Matt. 7:11; Luke 1:53; Gal. 6:6; Heb. 9:11;
10:1; Philem. 6.*

aug/4

You who dwell in the dust, wake up and shout for joy. Your dew is like the dew of the morning.—"Does the rain have a father? Who fathers the drops of dew?"—"I will be like the dew to Israel, he will blossom like a lily." . . . "What can I do with you . . . ? Your love is like the morning mist, like the early dew that disappears."—"May God give you of heaven's dew and of earth's richness."—"The ground will produce its crops, and the heavens will drop their dew. I will give all these things as an inheritance to the remnant of this people."—A king's rage is like the roar of a lion, but his favor is like dew on the grass.—Listen, O heavens, and I will speak; hear, O earth the words of my mouth. Let my teaching fall like rain and my words descend like dew, like showers on new grass, like abundant rain on tender plants. . . . "May the Lord bless his land with the precious dew from heaven above and with the deep waters that lie below; with the best the sun brings forth. . . . So Israel will live in safety alone; Jacob's spring is secure in a land of grain and new wine, where the heavens drop dew"—How good and pleasant it is when brothers live together in unity. . . . It is as if the dew of Hermon were falling. . . .

Isa. 26:19; Job 38:28; Hos. 14:5; 6:4; Gen. 27:28; Zech. 8:12; Prov. 19:12; Deut. 32:1-2; 33:13-14, 28; Ps. 133:1, 3.

aug/5

"You shall not covet. . . ."—Turn my heart toward your statutes and not toward selfish gain. Turn my eyes away from worthless things; renew my life according to your word.—I was enraged by his sinful greed; I punished him, and hid my face in anger, yet he kept on in his willful ways. I have seen his ways, but I will heal him.—I would not have known what it was to covet if the law had not said, "Do not covet." But sin, seizing the opportunity afforded by the commandment, produced in me every kind of covetous desire.—But among you there must not be even a hint of . . . greed. No . . . greedy person . . . has any inheritance in the kingdom of Christ and of God.—I have not coveted anyone's silver or gold or clothing.—Eagerly desire the greater gifts.—For the love of money is a root of all kinds of evil. Some people, eager for money, have wandered from the faith and pierced themselves with many griefs. Godliness with contentment is great gain.—Keep your lives free from the love of money and be content with what you have, because God has said, "Never will I leave you; never will I forsake you."—"From the least to the greatest, all are greedy for gain; prophets and priests alike."

Exod. 20:17; Ps. 119:36-37; Isa. 57:17-18; Rom. 7:7-8; Eph. 5:3, 5; Acts 20:33; 1 Cor. 12:31; 1 Tim. 6:10, 6; Heb. 13:5; Jer. 6:13.

aug/6

"[The Lord your God] has endowed you with splendor." Seek the Lord while he may be found; call upon him while he is near. . . . You who are far away, hear what I have done; you who are near, acknowledge my power!—A man of many companions may come to ruin, but there is a friend who sticks closer than a brother.—As they talked and discussed these things with each other, Jesus himself came up and walked along with them.—We give thanks to you, O God, we give thanks, for your Name is near; men tell of your wonderful deeds. . . . He has raised up for his people a horn, the praise of all his saints, of Israel, the people close to his heart.—He who vindicates me is near. Who then will bring charges against me?—"Am I only a God nearby, . . . and not a God far away? Can anyone hide in secret places so that I cannot see him?"—"Peace, peace, to those who are far and near," says the Lord. "And I will heal them."—"May the Lord bless . . . with the best gifts of the earth and its fullness and the favor of him who dwelt in the burning bush."—The Word became flesh and lived for a while among us. We have seen his glory, the glory of the one and only Son, who came from the Father, full of grace and truth.

Isa. 55:5-6; 33:13; Prov. 18:24; Luke 24:15; Pss. 75:1; 148:14; Isa. 50:8; Jer. 23:23-24; Isa. 57:19; Deut. 33:13, 16; John 1:14.

aug/7

You may become blameless and pure, children of God without fault in a crooked and depraved generation, in which you shine like stars in the universe as you hold out the word of life.—The path of the righteous is like the first gleam of dawn, shining ever brighter till the full light of day.—"You are the light of the world. A city on a hill cannot be hidden. Neither do people light a lamp and put it under a bowl. Instead they put it on its stand, and it gives light to everyone in the house. In the same way, let your light shine before men, that they may see your good deeds and praise your Father in heaven." . . . "The righteous will shine like the sun in the kingdom of their Father."—The god of this age has blinded the minds of unbelievers, so that they cannot see the light of the gospel of the glory of Christ, who is the image of God. God, who said, "Let light shine out of darkness," made his light shine in our hearts to give us the light of the knowledge of the glory of God in the face of Christ.—His face was like the sun shining in all its brilliance.—The people walking in darkness have seen a great light; on those living in the land of the shadow of death a light has dawned. . . . "Arise, shine, for your light has come, and the glory of the Lord rises upon you."

Phil. 2:15-16; Prov. 4:18; Matt. 5:14-16; 13:43; 2 Cor. 4:4, 6; Rev. 1:16; Isa. 9:2; 60:1.

aug /8

The Lord abhors dishonest scales, but accurate weights are his delight. . . . Honest scales and balances are from the Lord; all the weights in the bag are of his making.—"Do not use dishonest standards when measuring length, weight or quantity. Use honest scales and honest weights. . . . "I am the Lord your God who brought you out of Egypt."—Do not have two differing weights in your bag—one heavy, one light. Do not have two differing measures in your house—one large, one small. You must have accurate and honest weights and measures, so that you may live long in the land the Lord your God is giving you. For the Lord your God detests anyone who does these things, anyone who deals dishonestly.—All a man's ways seem right to him, but the Lord weighs the heart.—"You have been weighed on the scales and found wanting."—Therefore we do not lose heart. Though outwardly we are wasting away, yet inwardly we are being renewed day by day. For our light and momentary troubles are achieving for us an eternal glory that far outweighs them all.—"Do not keep talking so proudly, or let your mouth speak such arrogance, for the Lord is a God who knows, and by him deeds are weighed."

Prov. 11:1; 16:11; Lev. 19:35-36; Deut. 25:13-16;
Prov. 21:2; Dan. 5:27; 2 Cor. 4:16-17; 1 Sam. 2:3.

aug/9

I said, "O Lord, have mercy on me; heal me, for I have sinned against you."—Then Saul said to Samuel, "I have sinned. I violated the Lord's commands and instructions."—David said to Nathan, "I have sinned against the Lord." Nathan replied, "The Lord has taken away your sin." —Pharaoh summoned Moses and Aaron. "This time I have sinned," he said unto them.— Balaam said to the angel of the Lord, "I have sinned."—"I will . . . go back to my father and say to him: Father, I have sinned against heaven and against you.—All have sinned and fall short of the glory of God. . . . Therefore, just as sin entered the world through one man, and death through sin, and in this way death came to all men, because all sinned.—Christ Jesus came into the world to save sinners—of whom I am the worst. But for that very reason I was shown mercy so that in me, the worst of sinners, Christ Jesus might display his unlimited patience as an example for those who would believe on him and receive eternal life.—If we claim to be without sin, we deceive ourselves and the truth is not in us. If we confess our sins, he is faithful and just and will forgive us our sins and purify us from all unrighteousness.

Ps. 41:4; 1 Sam. 15:24; 2 Sam. 12:13; Exod. 9:27; Num. 22:34; Luke 15:18; Rom. 3:23; 5:12; 1 Tim. 1:15-16; 1 John 1:8-9.

aug/10

"Surely, as I have planned, so it will be, and as I have purposed, so it will stand. . . . This is the plan determined for the whole world; this is the hand stretched out over all nations. For the Lord Almighty has purposed, and who can thwart him?" . . . "My purpose will stand, and I will do that I please. . . . What I have said, that will I bring about; what I have planned, that will I do."—For there is a proper time and procedure for every matter.—Who is like me and who can challenge me?" . . . Therefore, hear what the Lord has planned . . . and what he has purposed. . . . Therefore, hear what the Lord has planned against Babylon, what he has purposed against the land of the Babylonians." . . . "The Lord's purposes against Babylon stand."—We know that in all things God works for the good of those who love him, who have been called according to his purpose.—He made known to us the mystery of his will according to his good pleasure, which he purposed in Christ. . . . The plan of him who works out everything in conformity with the purpose of his will.—Join with me in suffering for the gospel, by the power of God, who has saved us and called us to a holy life—not because of anything we have done but because of his own purpose and grace.

Isa. 14:24, 26-27; 46:10-11; Eccl. 8:6; Jer. 49:19-20; 50:45; 51:29; Rom. 8:28, Eph. 1:9, 11; 2 Tim. 1:8-9.

aug/11

Answer me when I call to you, O my righteous God. Give me relief from my distress; be merciful to me and hear my prayer.—"His mercy extends to those who fear him, from generation to generation. . . . He has helped his servant Israel, remembering to be merciful." . . . "Be merciful, just as your Father is merciful." . . . "'God, have mercy on me, a sinner'"—"I will have mercy on whom I will have mercy, and I will have compassion on whom I have compassion." It does not, therefore, depend on man's desire or effort, but on God's mercy. Therefore God has mercy on whom he wants to have mercy.—But because of his great love for us, God, who is rich in mercy, made us alive in Christ.—Let us then approach the throne of grace with confidence, so that we may receive mercy and find grace to help us in our time of need.—Praise be to the God and Father of our Lord Jesus Christ! In his great mercy he has given us new birth into a living hope through the resurrection of Jesus Christ from the dead, and into an inheritance that can never perish.—The Lord is full of compassion and mercy.—For this reason [Jesus] had to be made like his brothers in every way, in order that he might become a merciful and faithful high priest in service to God.

Ps. 4:1; Luke 1:50, 54; 6:36; 18:13; Rom. 9:15-16, 18; Eph. 2:4-5; Heb. 4:16; 1 Peter 1:3-4; James 5:11; Heb. 2:17.

aug /12

Although a wicked man commits a hundred crimes and still lives a long time, I know it will go better with God-fearing men, who are reverent before God. Yet because the wicked do not fear God, it will not go well with them, and their days will not lengthen like a shadow.—Tell the righteous it will be well with them, for they will enjoy the fruit of their deeds. Woe to the wicked! Disaster is upon them!—"Did not your father have food and drink? He did what was right and just, so all went well with him. He defended the cause of the poor and needy, and so all went well. Is that not what it means to know me?" declares the Lord. . . . "We will obey the Lord our God, . . . so that it will go well with us, for we will obey the Lord our God."—Blessed are all who fear the Lord, who walk in his ways. You will eat the fruit of your labor; blessings and prosperity will be yours.—"But when all goes well with you, remember me and show me kindness; mention me to Pharaoh and get me out of this prison." —"Honor your father and mother," which is the first commandment with a promise, "that it may go well with you and that you may enjoy long life on the earth."—People were overwhelmed with amazement. "He has done everything well," they said.

Eccl. 8:12-13; Isa. 3:10-11; Jer. 22:15-16; 42:6; Ps. 128:2; Gen. 40:14; Eph. 6:2-3; Mark 7:37.

aug/13

I delight greatly in the Lord, my soul rejoices in my God. For he has clothed me with garments of salvation and arrayed me in a robe of righteousness.—"You have a few people in Sardis who have not soiled their clothes. They will walk with me, dressed in white, for they are worthy. He who overcomes will, like them, be dressed in white." . . . Then each of them was given a white robe. . . . After this I looked and there . . . was a great multitude that no one could count, from every nation, tribe, people and language, standing before the throne and in front of the Lamb. They were wearing white robes and were holding palm branches in their hands. Then one of the elders asked, "These in white robes—who are they, and where did they come from?" I answered, . . . "These are they who have come out of the great tribulation; they have washed their robes in the blood of the Lamb."—"When the king came in to see the guests, he noticed a man there who was not wearing wedding clothes. 'Friend,' he asked, 'how did you get in here without wedding clothes?' The man was speechless.—The angel said to those who were standing before [Joshua], "Take off his filthy clothes." Then he said to Joshua, "See, I have taken away your sin, and I will put rich garments on you."

Isa. 61:10; Rev. 3:4-5; 6:11; 7:9, 13-14; Matt. 22:11-12; Zech. 3:4-5.

aug/14

"By me kings reign and rulers make laws that are just; by me princes govern, and all nobles who rule on earth."—See, a king will reign in righteousness and rulers will rule with justice. [He] will be like a shelter from the wind and a refuge from the storm. . . . Say to Zion, "Your God reigns!"—"The Lord will reign for ever and ever."—The Lord reigns, . . . and is armed with strength. . . . Say, among the nations, "The Lord reigns."—"The kingdom of the world has become the kingdom of our Lord and of his Christ, and he will reign for ever and ever." . . . "We give thanks to you, Lord God Almighty, who is and who was, because you have taken your great power and have begun to reign." . . . "Hallelujah! For our Lord God Almighty reigns. Let us rejoice and be glad and give him glory!" . . . "Just and true are your ways, King of the ages." . . . "He is the Lord of lords and King of kings." . . . On his robe and on his thigh he has this name written: KING OF KINGS AND LORD OF LORDS. . . . Blessed and holy are those who have part in the first resurrection. . . . They will be priests of God and of Christ and will reign with him for a thousand years. . . . They will see his face, . . . and they will reign for ever and ever.—If we endure, we will also reign with him.

Prov. 8:15-16; Isa. 32:1-2; 52:7; Exod. 15:18; Pss. 93:1; 96:10; Rev. 11:15, 17; 19:6-7; 15:3; 17:14; 19:16; 20:6; 22:4-5; 2 Tim. 2:12.

aug/15

The Lord is my shepherd, I shall lack nothing . . . Fear the Lord, you his saints, for those who fear him lack nothing. The lions may grow weak and hungry, but those who seek the Lord lack no good thing.—Jesus asked them, "When I sent you without purse, bag or sandals, did you lack anything?" "Nothing," they answered.—Our desire is not that others might be relieved while you are hard pressed, but that there might be equality. At the present time your plenty will supply what they need, so that in turn their plenty will supply what you need. Then there will be equality, as it is written: "He that gathered much did not have too much, and he that gathered little did not have too little." . . . This service . . . is not only supplying the needs of God's people but is also overflowing in many expressions of thanks to God.—He has watched over your journey through this vast desert. These forty years the Lord your God has been with you, and you have not lacked anything.—I have learned to be content whatever the circumstances. I know what it is to be in need, and I know what it is to have plenty. I have learned the secret of being content in any or every situation, whether well fed or hungry. . . . I can do everything through him who gives me strength.

Pss. 23:1; 34:9-10; Luke 22:35; 2 Cor. 8:13-15; 9:12; Deut. 2:7; Phil. 4:11-13.

aug/16

"**Here** I am! I stand at the door and knock. If anyone hears my voice and opens the door, I will go in and eat with him, and he with me." . . . "These are the words of him who is holy and true, who holds the key of David. What he opens, no one can shut; and what he shuts, no one can open."—Before this faith came, we were held prisoners by the law, locked up until faith should be revealed.—"Woe to you, teachers of the law and Pharisees, you hypocrites! You shut the kingdom of heaven in men's faces. You yourselves do not enter, nor will you let those enter who are trying to."—"Enemies of mine who do not want me to be king over them." . . . "O Jerusalem, Jerusalem, you who kill the prophets and stone those sent to you, how often I have longed to gather your children together, as a hen gathers her chicks under her wings, but you were not willing!"—"Listen to all that the people are saying to you; it is not you they have rejected as their king but me. As they have done from the day I brought them up out of Egypt until this day, forsaking me and serving other gods."—"'I bound the whole house of Israel and the whole house of Judah to me,' declares the Lord, 'to be my people for my renown and praise and honor. But they have not listened.'"

Rev. 3:20, 7; Gal. 3:23; Matt. 23:13; Luke 19:27; 13:34; 1 Sam. 8:7-8; Jer. 13:11.

aug/17

Enoch walked with God 300 years. . . . Enoch walked with God; then he was no more, because God took him away. . . . "Go, walk through the length and breadth of the land, for I am giving it to you." . . . "The Lord, before whom I have walked, will send his angel with you and make your journey a success."—Walk in all the way that the Lord your God has commanded you, so that you may live and prosper and prolong your days in the land that you will possess.—Whether you turn to the right or to the left, your ears will hear a voice behind you saying, "This is the way, walk in it." . . . Those who hope in the Lord, . . . they will walk and not be faint.—Since we live by the Spirit, let us keep in step with the Spirit.—If we claim to have fellowship with him yet walk in the darkness, we lie and do not live by the truth. But if we walk in the light, as he is in the light, we have fellowship with one another, and the blood of Jesus, his Son, purifies us from every sin. . . . This is how we know we are in him. Whoever claims to live in him must walk as Jesus did.—My feet stand on level ground; in the great assembly I will praise the Lord. . . . You have delivered my soul from death and my feet from stumbling, that I may walk before God in the light of life.

Gen. 5:22, 24; 13:17; 24:40; Deut. 5:33; Isa. 30:21; 40:31; Gal. 5:25; 1 John 1:6-7; 2:5-6; Pss. 26:12; 56:13.

aug/18

"The Lord our God is merciful and forgiving, even though we have rebelled against him. . . . We do not make requests of you because we are righteous, but because of your great mercy." —Have mercy on me, O God, according to your unfailing love; according to your great compassion, blot out my transgressions. . . . Answer me, O Lord, out of the goodness of your love; in your great mercy turn to me.—Therefore, I urge you, brothers, in view of God's mercy, to offer your bodies as living sacrifices, holy and pleasing to God—which is your spiritual worship.—Speak and act as those who are going to be judged by the law that gives freedom, because judgment without mercy will be shown to anyone who has not been merciful. Mercy triumphs over judgment!—By your Spirit you admonished [your people] through your prophets. Yet they paid no attention, so you handed them over to the neighboring peoples. But in your great mercy you did not put an end to them, or abandon them, for you are a gracious and merciful God.—Christ Jesus came into the world to save sinners—of whom I am the worst. But for that very reason I was shown mercy so that in me, the worst of sinners, Christ Jesus might display his unlimited patience. . . .

Dan. 9:9, 18; Pss. 51:1; 69:16; Rom. 12:1; James 2:12-13; Neh. 9:30-31; 1 Tim. 1:15-16.

aug / 19

I the Lord do not change.—Jesus Christ is the same yesterday and today and forever. . . . "In the beginning, O Lord, you laid the foundations of the earth, and the heavens are the work of your hands. They will perish, but you remain; they will all wear out like a garment. You will roll them up like a robe; like a garment they will be changed. But you remain the same, and your years will never end."—Every good and perfect gift is from above, coming down from the Father of the heavenly lights, who does not change like shifting shadows.—"I am with you and will watch over you wherever you go, and I will bring you back to this land. I will not leave you until I have done what I have promised you."—"God is not a man, that he should lie, nor a son of man, that he should change his mind. Does he speak and then not act? Does he promise and not fulfill? I have received a command to bless; he has blessed, and I cannot change it."—He whose walk is blameless and who does what is righteous, . . . honors those who fear the Lord, who keeps his oath even when it hurts.—[Melchizedeck] became a priest with an oath when God said to him: "The Lord has sworn and will not change his mind: 'You are a priest forever.'". . . Jesus lives forever, he has a permanent priesthood.

Mal. 3:6; Heb. 13:8; 1:10-12; James 1:17; Gen. 28:15; Num. 23:19-20; Ps. 15:2, 4; Heb. 7:21, 24.

aug/20

"For hardship does not spring from the soil, nor does trouble sprout from the ground. Yet man is born to trouble as surely as sparks fly upward. . . . From six calamities he will rescue you; in seven no harm will befall you."—Praise to the God and Father of our Lord Jesus Christ, the Father of compassion and the God of all comfort, who comforts us in all our troubles, so that we can comfort those in any trouble with the comfort we ourselves have received from God.—"Peace I leave with you; my peace I give you. I do not give to you as the world gives. Do not let your hearts be troubled and do not be afraid."—The Lord is a refuge for the oppressed, a stronghold in times of trouble. Those who know your name will trust in you, for you, Lord, have never forsaken those who seek you. . . . Redeem Israel, O God, from all their troubles!—An evil man is trapped by his sinful talk, but a righteous man escapes trouble. —"Some pour out gold from their bags and weigh out silver on the scales; they hire a goldsmith to make it into a god, and they bow down and worship it. . . . Though one cries out to it, it does not answer; it cannot save him from his troubles."—The past troubles will be forgotten and hidden from my eyes. . . . The former things will not be remembered."

Job 5:6-7, 19; 2 Cor. 1:3-4; John 14:27; Pss. 9:9-10; 25:22; Prov. 12:13; Isa. 46:6-7; 65:16-17.

aug/21

There is a river whose streams make glad the city of God, the holy place where the Most High dwells. God is within her, she will not fall; God will help her at break of day. . . . Where can I go from your Spirit? Where can I flee from your presence? If I go up to the heavens, you are there; if I make my bed in the depths, you are there. If I rise on the wings of the dawn, if I settle on the far side of the sea, even there your hand will guide me, your right hand will hold me fast.—"Shout and be glad, O Daughter of Zion. For I am coming, and I will live among you," declares the Lord. "Many nations will be joined with the Lord in that day and will become my people. I will live among you and you will know that the Lord Almighty has sent me to you."—For the Lord your God moves about in your camp to protect you and to deliver your enemies to you.—"Where two or three come together in my name, there am I with them."—Jesus himself stood among them and said to them, "Peace be with you."—Among the lampstands was someone "like a son of man," dressed in a robe reaching down to his feet. . . . He placed his right hand on me and said: . . . "I am the First and the Last. I am the Living One."—With the doors locked for fear of the Jews, Jesus came and stood among them.

Pss. 46:4-5; 139:7-10; Zech. 2:10-11; Deut. 23:14; Matt. 18:20; Luke 24:36; Rev. 1:13, 17; John 20:19.

aug/22

Depart, depart, go out from there! Touch no unclean thing! Come out from it and be pure, you who carry the vessels of the Lord. . . . "Bring all your brothers, from all the nations, to my holy mountain . . . as an offering to the Lord. . . . Bring them, as the Israelites bring their grain offerings, to the temple of the Lord in ceremonially clean vessels."—In a large house there are articles not only of gold and silver, but also of wood and clay; some for noble purposes and some for ignoble. If a man cleanses himself from the latter, he will be an instrument for noble purposes, made holy, useful to the Master and prepared to do any good work.—Does not the potter have the right to make out of the same lump of clay some pottery for noble purposes and some for common use?—Remove the dross from the silver, and out comes material for the silversmith.—Israel is swallowed up; now she is among the nations like a worthless thing.—The pot [the potter] was shaping from the clay was marred in his hands; so the potter formed it into another pot, shaping it as seemed best to him. . . . "I have broken Moab like a jar that no one wants. . . . How shattered she is!"—I am forgotten by them as though I were dead; I have become like broken pottery.

Isa. 52:11; 66:20; 2 Tim. 2:20-21; Rom. 9:21; Prov. 25:4; Hos. 8:8; Jer. 18:4; 48:38-39; Ps. 31:12.

aug/23

"If you are willing and obedient, you will eat the best from the land."—"'If you obey me fully and keep covenant, then out of all nations you will be my treasured possession.'" . . . Then [Moses] took the Book of the Covenant and read it to the people. They responded, "We will do everything the Lord has said; we will obey."—The people said to Joshua, "We will serve the Lord our God and obey him."—Don't you know that when you offer yourselves to someone to obey him as slaves, you are slaves to the one whom you obey—whether you are slaves to sin, which leads to death, or to obedience, which leads to righteousness? But thanks be to God that, though you used to be slaves to sin, you wholeheartedly obeyed the form of teaching to which you were entrusted.—Although [Jesus] was a son, he learned obedience from what he suffered and, once made perfect, he became the source of eternal salvation for all who obey him.—Chosen according to the foreknowledge of God the Father, by the sanctifying work of the Spirit, for obedience to Jesus Christ and sprinkling by his blood. . . . Now that you have purified yourselves by obeying the truth so that you have sincere love for your brothers, love one another deeply, from the heart.

Isa. 1:19; Exod. 19:5; 24:7; Josh. 24:24; Rom. 6:16-17; Heb. 5:8-9; 1 Peter 1:2, 22.

aug/24

Ears that hear and eyes that see—the Lord has made them both.—The eyes of those who see will no longer be closed, and the ears of those who hear will listen. . . . He wakens me morning by morning, wakens my ear to listen as one being taught. The Sovereign Lord has opened my ears, and I have not been rebellious.—O my people, hear my teaching; listen to the words of my mouth.—"He who has ears, let him hear." . . . "Though seeing, they do not see; though hearing, they do not hear or understand. . . . 'They hardly hear with their ears.' . . . But blessed are your eyes because they see, and your ears because they hear."—The time will come when men will not put up with sound doctrine. Instead, to suit their own desires, they will gather around them a great number of teachers to say what their itching ears want to hear. They will turn their ears away from the truth and turn aside to myths.—"The eyes of the Lord are on the righteous and his ears attentive to their prayer."—"He who has an ear, let him hear what the Spirit says to the churches. To him who overcomes, I will give the right to eat from the tree of life, which is in the paradise of God."—I cried out to God for help; I cried out to God to hear me.

Prov. 20:12; Isa. 32:3; 50:4-5; Ps. 78:1; Matt. 11:15; 13:13, 15-16; 2 Tim. 4:3-4; 1 Peter 3:12; Rev. 2:7; Ps. 77:1.

aug/25

Depart, depart, go out from there! Touch no unclean thing!—"Do not touch my anointed ones; do my prophets no harm."—Saul also went to his home in Gibeah, accompanied by valiant men whose hearts God had touched.—This is what the Lord Almighty says: "Whoever touches you touches the apple of his eye."—[Jesus] healed many, so that those with diseases were pushing forward to touch him.—A woman who had been subject to bleeding for twelve years . . . said to herself, "If I only touch his cloak, I will be healed." Jesus turned and saw her. "Take heart, daughter," he said, "your faith has healed you." And the woman was healed from that moment. . . . People brought all their sick to him and begged him to let the sick just touch the edge of his cloak, and all who touched were healed. . . . A man with leprosy came and knelt before him and said, "Lord, if you are willing, you can make me clean." Jesus reached out his hand and touched the man. "I am willing," he said. "Be clean!" Immediately he was cured of his leprosy.—The Lord reached out his hand and touched my mouth and said to me, "Now, I have put my words in your mouth."—The one who was born of God keeps him safe, and the evil one does not touch him.

Isa. 52:11; Ps. 105:15; 1 Sam. 10:26; Zech. 2:8; Mark 3:10; Matt. 9:21-22; 14:35-36; 8:2-3; Jer. 1:9; 1 John 5:18.

aug/26

I am honored in the eyes of the Lord and my God has been my strength. . . . Lift up your eyes and look to the heavens: Who created all these? He who brings out the starry host one by one, and calls them each by name. Because of his great power and mighty strength, not one of them is missing.—My son, give me your heart and let your eyes keep to my ways.—[Hagar] gave this name to the Lord who spoke to you: "You are the God who sees me," for she said, "I have now seen the One who sees me."—Blessed are your eyes because they see, and your ears because they hear. . . . "The eye is the lamp of the body. If your eyes are good, your whole body will be full of light. But if your eyes are bad, your whole body will be full of darkness."—A land flowing with milk and honey . . . a land the Lord your God cares for; the eyes of the Lord your God are continually on it from the beginning of the year to its end. . . . Because you obey the Lord your God, keeping all his commands that I am giving you today and doing what is right in his eyes.—The commands of the Lord are radiant, giving light to the eyes. . . . The eyes of the Lord are on the righteous.—"I counsel you to buy from me . . . salve to put on your eyes, so you can see."

Isa. 49:5; 40:26; Prov. 23:26; Gen. 16:13; Matt. 13:16; 6:22-23; Deut. 11:9, 12; 13:18; Pss. 19:8; 34:15; Rev. 3:18.

aug/27

"When men are brought low and you say, 'Lift them up!' then he will save the downcast."—To you, O Lord, I lift up my soul; in you I trust O my God. . . . Lift up your heads, O you gates; be lifted up, you ancient doors, that the King of glory may come in. . . . Hear my cry for mercy as I call to you for help, as I lift up my hands toward your Most Holy Place. . . . I cry aloud to the Lord; I lift up my voice to the Lord for mercy.—"Just as Moses lifted up the snake in the desert, so the Son of Man must be lifted up, that everyone who believes in him may have eternal life." . . . "But I, when I am lifted up from the earth, will draw all men to myself." He said this to show the kind of death he was going to die.—"When these things begin to take place, stand up and lift up your heads, because your redemption is drawing near."—I want men everywhere to lift up holy hands in prayer, without anger or disputing.—Strengthen your feeble arms and weak knees. "Make level paths for your feet," so that the lame may not be disabled, but rather healed.—The Spirit lifted me up, and I heard behind me a loud rushing sound. . . . The Spirit lifted me up between earth and heaven and in visions of God he took me to Jerusalem.

Job 22:29; Pss. 25:1; 24:7; 28:2; 142:1; John 3:14; 12:32-33; Luke 21:28; 1 Tim. 2:8; Heb. 12:12; Ezek. 3:12; 8:3.

aug/28

"How can I, your servant, talk with you, my lord? My strength is gone and I can hardly breathe." Again the one who looked like a man touched me and gave me strength. "Do not be afraid, O man highly esteemed," he said. "Peace! Be strong now; be strong. When he spoke to me, I was strengthened and said, "Speak, my lord, since you have given me strength."—"In quietness and trust is your strength." . . . Those who hope in the Lord will renew their strength. . . . Awake, awake, O Zion, clothe yourself with strength. —Wait for the Lord; be strong and take heart, and wait for the Lord.—Being strengthened with all power according to his glorious might so that you may have great endurance and patience.—I can do everything through him who gives me strength.—The Lord stood at my side and gave me strength, so that through me the message might be fully proclaimed and all the Gentiles might hear it—"Wake up! Strengthen what remains and is about to die."—God is our refuge and strength, an ever present help in trouble. . . . Blessed are those whose strength is in you. . . . They go from strength to strength till each appears before God in Zion.—If you falter in times of trouble, how small is your strength!

Dan. 10:17-19; Isa. 30:15; 40:31; 52:1; Ps. 27:14; Col. 1:11; Phil. 4:13; 2 Tim. 4:17; Rev. 3:2; Pss. 46:1; 84:5, 7; Prov. 24:10.

aug/29

"I am the Lord your God, who has set you apart from the nations. You must therefore make a distinction between clean and unclean animals and between clean and unclean birds. . . . You are holy unto me because I, the Lord, am holy, and I have set you apart from the nations to be my own."—"You singled out [Israel] from all the nations of the world to be your own inheritance, just as you declared through your servant Moses when you, O Sovereign Lord, brought our fathers out of Egypt."—Do not be yoked together with unbelievers. For what do righteousness and wickedness have in common? Or what fellowship can light have with darkness? What harmony is there between Christ and Belial? What does a believer have in common with an unbeliever? What agreement is there between the temple of God and idols? For we are the temple of the living God. As God has said, "I will live with them and walk among them, and I will be their God, and they will be my people. Therefore come out from them and be separate."—Therefore [Jesus] is able to save completely those who come to God through him, because he always lives to intercede for them. Such a high priest meets our need—one who is holy, blameless, pure, set apart from sinners, exalted above the heavens.

Lev. 20:24-26; 1 Kings 8:53; 2 Cor. 6:14-17; Heb. 7:25-26.

aug/30

"Be strong, do not fear." . . . The burning sand will become a pool, the thirsty ground bubbling springs. . . . "I will make rivers flow on barren heights, and springs within the valleys. I will turn the desert into pools of water, and the parched ground into springs." . . . This is what the Lord says: "They will neither hunger nor thirst, nor will the desert heat or the sun beat upon them. He who has compassion on them will guide them and lead them beside springs of water." . . . "The Lord will guide you always; he will satisfy your needs in a sun-scorched land and will strengthen your frame. You will be like a well-watered garden, like a spring whose waters never fail."—Jesus answered [the Samaritan woman], "Everyone who drinks this water will be thirsty again, but whoever drinks the water I give him will never thirst. Indeed, the water I give him will become in him a spring of water welling up to eternal life."—Like cold water to a weary soul is good news from a distant land. Like a muddied spring or a polluted well is a righteous man who gives way to the wicked.—The Lord will write in the register of the peoples: "This one was born in Zion." As they make music they will sing, "All my fountains are in you." . . . He will drink from a brook beside the way; therefore he will lift up his head.

Isa. 35:4, 7; 41:18; 49:8, 10; 58:11; John 4:13-14; Prov. 25:25-26; Pss. 87;6-7; 110:7.

aug/31

"Before long, the world will not see me any more, but you will see me."—We live by faith, not by sight.—"I am going to the Father, where you can see me no longer." . . . "I will remain in the world no longer." . . . "I am going [to the Father's house] to prepare a place for you. And if I go and prepare a place for you, I will come back and take you to be with me that you also may be where I am."—Though you have not seen him, you love him; and even though you do not see him now, you believe in him and are filled with an inexpressible and glorious joy.—"Blessed are those who have not seen and yet have believed." . . . "From now on, you do know him, and have seen him."—"I myself will see him with my own eyes—I, and not another. How my heart yearns within me!"—Your eyes will see the king in his beauty.—Look, he is coming with the clouds, and every eye shall see him. . . . They will see his face, and his name will be on their foreheads.—Then we shall see face to face.—"My eyes have seen the King, the Lord Almighty,"—"But as I told you, you have seen me and still you do not believe."—No one who continues in sin has either seen him or known him.

John 14:19; 2 Cor. 5:7; John 16:10; 17:11; 14:2-3; 1 Peter 1:8; John 20:29; 14:7; Job 19:27; Isa. 33:17; Rev. 1:7; 22:4; 1 Cor. 13:12; Isa. 6:5; John 6:36; 1 John 3:6.

"God is exalted in his power.
Who is a teacher like him?"

Bob Taylor

sept/1

I will sing of your strength. . . . Your saints will extol you. They will tell of the glory of your kingdom and speak of your might, so that all men may know of your mighty acts, and the glorious splendor of your kingdom. . . . Say to God, "How awesome are your deeds! So great is your power that your enemies cringe before you."—"By his power he churned up the sea. . . . Who then can understand the thunder of his power?" . . . "God is exalted in his power. Who is a teacher like him?"—Come and see what God has done, how awesome his works in man's behalf. He turned the sea into dry land, they passed through the river on foot—come, let us rejoice in him. He rules forever by his power.—Since the creation of the world God's invisible qualities—his eternal power and divine nature—have been clearly seen.—"My grace is sufficient for you, for my power is made perfect in weakness."—"You will receive power when the Holy Spirit comes upon you; and you will be my witnesses."—"Power and strength be to our God for ever and ever." . . . I heard what sounded like the roar of a great multitude in heaven shouting, "Hallelujah! Salvation and glory and power belong to our God."—I am filled with power, with the Spirit of the Lord.

Pss. 59:16; 145:10-12; 66:3; Job 26:12, 14; 36:22; Ps. 66:5-7; Rom. 1:20; 2 Cor. 12:9; Acts 1:8; Rev. 7:12; 19:1; Mic. 3:8.

sept/2

One thing I ask of the Lord, this is what I seek: that I may dwell in the house of the Lord all the days of my life, to gaze upon the beauty of the Lord and to seek him in his temple.—They devoted themselves to the apostles' teaching and to the fellowship, to the breaking of bread and to prayer. Everyone was filled with awe, and many wonders and miraculous signs were done by the apostles.—Brothers, . . . one thing I do: Forgetting what is behind and straining toward what is ahead, I press on toward the goal to win the prize for which God has called me heavenward in Christ Jesus.—"Martha, Martha," the Lord answered, "you are worried and upset about many things, but only one thing is needed. Mary has chosen what is better, and it will not be taken away from her."—Jesus looked at him and loved him. "One thing you lack," he said. "Go, sell everything you have and give to the poor, and you will have treasure in heaven. Then come, follow me." At this the man's face fell. He went away sad, because he had great wealth.—He replied, ". . . One thing I do know. I was blind but now I see!"—"Be sure to fear the Lord and serve him faithfully with all your heart; consider what great things he has done for you."—"Don't be afraid; just believe, and she will be healed."

Ps. 27:4; Acts 2:42-43; Phil. 3:13-14; Luke 10:41-42; Mark 10:21-22; John 9:25; 1 Sam. 12:24; Luke 8:50.

sept/3

David said to the whole assembly, "Praise the Lord your God." So they all praised the Lord, the God of their Fathers; they bowed low and fell prostrate before the Lord.—[Those who were of Israelite descent] stood where they were and read from the Book of the Law of the Lord their God for a fourth of the day, and spent another fourth in confession and in worshiping the Lord their God.—The four living creatures said, "Amen," and the elders fell down and worshiped.—"A time is coming and has now come when the true worshipers will worship the Father in spirit and truth, for they are the kind of worshipers the Father seeks. God is Spirit, and his worshipers must worship in spirit and in truth."—We who worship by the Spirit of God, who glory in Christ Jesus, and who put no confidence in the flesh.—Ascribe to the Lord the glory due his name; worship the Lord in the splendor of his holiness. . . . Exalt the Lord our God and worship at his footstool; he is holy.—"All this I will give you," [the devil] said, "if you will bow down and worship me." Jesus said to him, "Away from me, Satan! For it is written: 'Worship the Lord your God, and serve him only.'"

---

1 Chron. 29:20; Neh. 9:3; Rev. 5:14; John 4:23-24; Phil. 3:3; Pss. 29:2; 99:5; Matt. 4:9-10.

sept/4

"Even to your old age and gray hairs I am he, I am he who will sustain you."—For troubles without number surround me; my sins have overtaken me, and I cannot see. They are more than the hairs of my head, and my heart fails within me. . . . Those who hate me without reason outnumber the hairs of my head.—How beautiful! Your eyes behind your veil are doves. Your hair is like a flock of goats descending from Mount Gilead.—"As surely as the Lord lives," [King David] said, "not one hair of your son's head will fall to the ground."—"Foreigners sap his strength, but he does not realize it. His hair is sprinkled with gray, but he does not notice." —"Do not swear by your head, for you cannot make even one hair white or black."—"Are not five sparrows sold for two pennies? Yet not one of them is forgotten by God. Indeed, the very hairs of your head are all numbered."—A woman who had lived a sinful life . . . brought an alabaster jar of perfume, and as she stood behind [Jesus] at his feet weeping, she began to wet his feet with her tears. Then she wiped them with her hair, kissed them and poured perfume on them.—His head and hair were white like wool, as white as snow.

Isa. 46:4; Pss. 40:12; 69:4; Song of Songs 4:1; 2 Sam. 14:11; Hos. 7:9; Matt. 5:36; Luke 12:6-7; 7:37-38; Rev. 1:14.

sept/5

Sorrow is better than laughter, because a sad face is good for the heart. The heart of the wise is in the house of mourning, but the heart of fools is in the house of pleasure.—"I will turn their mourning into gladness; I will give them comfort and joy instead of sorrow."—The sorrows of those will increase who run after other gods.—Even if I caused you sorrow by my letter, I do not regret it. . . . Now I am happy, not because you were made sorry, but because your sorrow led you to repentance. For you became sorrowful as God intended. Godly sorrow brings repentance that leads to salvation and leaves no regret, but worldly sorrow brings death. . . . As servants of God we commend ourselves in every way . . . sorrowful, yet always rejoicing.—He began to be sorrowful and troubled. Then he said to them, "My soul is overwhelmed with sorrow to the point of death. Stay here and keep watch with me."—The ransomed of the Lord will . . . enter Zion with singing; everlasting joy will crown their heads. Gladness and joy will overtake them, and sorrow and sighing will flee away.—"The dwelling of God is with men, and he will live with them. . . . He will wipe every tear from their eyes. There will be no more death or mourning or crying or pain, for the old order of things has passed away."

Eccl. 7:3-4; Jer. 31:13; Ps. 16:4; 2 Cor. 7:8-10; 6:4, 10; Matt. 26:37-38; Isa. 35:10; Rev. 21:3-4.

sept/6

The Lord God had planted a garden in the east, in Eden. . . . Then the man and his wife heard the sound of the Lord God as he was walking in the garden in the cool of the day.—You are a garden fountain, a well of flowing water streaming down from Lebanon. Awake, north wind, and come, south wind! Blow on my garden, that its fragrance may spread abroad. Let my lover come into his garden and taste its choice fruits.—"The Lord will guide you always; he will satisfy your needs in a sun-scorched land. . . . You will be like a well-watered garden, like a spring whose waters never fail."—On the other side there was an olive grove, and [Jesus] and his disciples went into it. Now Judas, who betrayed him, knew the place, because Jesus had often met there with his disciples. . . . At the place where Jesus was crucified, there was a garden, and in the garden a new tomb, in which no one had ever been laid. . . . "Woman," [Jesus] said, "why are you crying? Who is it you are looking for?" Thinking he was the gardener, she said, "Sir, if you have carried him away, tell me where you have put him, and I will get him."—On each side of the river stood the tree of life, bearing twelve crops of fruit, yielding its fruit every month. And the leaves of the tree are for the healing of the nations.

Gen. 2:8; 3:8; Song of Songs 4:15-16; Isa. 58:11; John 18:1-2; 19:41; 20:15; Rev. 22:2.

sept/7

God made two great lights—the greater light to govern the day and the lesser light to govern the night. He also made the stars. . . . [The Lord God] took Abram outside and said, "Look at the heavens and count the stars—if indeed you can count them." Then he said to him, "So shall your offspring be."—He determines the number of the stars and calls them each by name.—And so from this one man, and he as good as dead, came descendants as numerous as the stars in the sky and as countless as the sand on the seashore.—Praise him, sun and moon, praise him, all you shining stars.—"Is not God in the heights of heaven? And see how lofty are the highest stars!" . . . "How can one born of a woman be pure? If even the moon is not bright and the stars are not pure in his eyes, how much less man." . . . "The morning stars sang together and all the angels shouted for joy."—"Those who are wise will shine like the brightness of the heavens, and those who lead many to righteousness, like the stars for ever and ever."—The Magi from the east came to Jerusalem and asked, "Where is the one who has been born king of the Jews? We saw his star in the east and have come to worship him." . . . When they saw the star, they were overjoyed.

Gen. 1:16; 15:5; Ps. 147:4; Heb. 11:12; Ps. 148:3; Job 22:12; 25:4-6; 38:7; Dan. 12:3; Matt. 2:1-2, 10.

sept/8

God will bring every deed into judgment, including every hidden thing, whether it is good or evil.—He made darkness his covering, his canopy around him—the dark rain clouds of the sky. . . . Forgive my hidden faults.—He reveals deep and hidden things; he knows what lies in darkness, and light dwells with him. . . . "There is a God in heaven who reveals mysteries. . . . As for me, this mystery has been revealed to me, not because I have greater wisdom than other living men, but so that you, O king, may know the interpretation and that you may understand what went through your mind." . . . "Surely your God is the God of gods and the Lord of kings and a revealer of mysteries for you were able to reveal this mystery."—You have set our iniquities before you, our secret sins in the light of your presence.—"I will open my mouth in parables, I will utter things hidden since the creation of the world." . . . "When you give to the needy, do not let your left hand know what your right hand is doing, so that your giving may be in secret. Then your Father, who sees what is done in secret, will reward you."—"There is nothing hidden that will not be disclosed, and nothing concealed that will not be known or brought out into the open."

Eccl. 12:14; Pss. 18:11; 19:12; Dan. 2:22, 28, 30, 47; Ps. 90:8; Matt. 13:25; 6:3-4; Luke 8:17.

sept/9

Be merciful to me, O Lord, for I am in distress; my eyes grow weak with sorrow, my soul and my body with grief. . . . When my heart was grieved and my spirit embittered, I was senseless and ignorant.—The Lord was grieved that he had made man on the earth, and his heart was filled with pain. So the Lord said, "I will wipe mankind, whom I have created, from the face of the earth . . . for I am grieved that I have made them." But Noah found favor in the eyes of the Lord.—In bitterness of soul Hannah wept much and prayed to the Lord," . . . Do not take your servant for a wicked woman; I have been praying here out of my great anguish and grief." . . . "I grieved that I have made Saul king, because he has turned away from me and has not carried out my instructions."—Though he brings grief, he will show compassion, so great is his unfailing love. For he does not willingly bring affliction or grief to the children of men.—If I grieve you, who is left to make me glad but you whom I have grieved? I wrote you out of great distress and anguish of heart and with many tears, not to grieve you but to let you know the depth of my love to you. If any one has caused grief, he has not so much grieved me as he has grieved all of you, to some extent—not to put it too severely.

Pss. 31:9; 73:21; Gen. 6:6-8; 1 Sam. 1:10, 16; 15:11; Lam. 3:32-33; 2 Cor. 2:2, 4-5.

sept/10

You are all one in Christ Jesus.—"My prayer is . . . that all of them may be one, Father, just as you are in me and I am in you. . . . May they be brought to complete unity to let the world know that you sent me and have loved them even as you have loved me."—In Christ we who are many form one body, and each member belongs to all the others. We have different gifts, according to the grace given us.—We ought always to thank God for you, brothers, and rightly so, because your faith is growing more and more, and the love everyone of you has for each other is increasing.—Carry each other's burdens, and in this way you will fulfill the law of Christ.—Make my joy complete by being like-minded, having the same love, being one in spirit and purpose.—That there should be no division in the body, but that its parts should have equal concern for each other. If one part suffers, every part suffers with it; if one part is honored, every part rejoices with it. Now you are the body of Christ, and each one of you is part of it.—Encourage one another daily. . . . Let us consider how we may spur one another on toward love and good deeds. Let us not give up meeting together, as some are in the habit of doing, but let us encourage one another.

Gal. 3:28; John 17:20-21, 23; Rom. 12:5; 2 Thess. 1:3; Gal. 6:2; Phil. 2:2; 1 Cor. 12:25-27; Heb. 3:13; 10:24-25.

sept/11

"I am the Lord, who has made all things" . . .
"Has not my hand made all these things?"
—Through him all things were made, without him
nothing was made that has been made. . . . The
Holy Spirit, whom the Father will send in my
name, will teach you all things.—"All things have
been committed to me by my Father."—"Lord,
you know all things; you know that I love
you."—From him and through him and to him are
all things.—The Lord works out everything for his
own ends.—We know that in all things God works
for the good of those who love him, who have
been called according to his purpose. . . . He who
did not spare his own Son but gave him up for us
all—how will he not also, along with him,
graciously give us all things?—Always giving
thanks to God the Father for everything, in the
name of our Lord Jesus Christ.—The Father, from
whom all things came and for whom we live; and
there is but one Lord, Jesus Christ, through whom
all things came and through whom we live.—God
placed all things under his feet and appointed him
to be head over everything for the Church, which
is his body, the fullness of him who fills
everything in every way.—He is before all things,
and in him all things hold together.

*Isa. 44:24; 66:2; John 1:3; 14:26; Matt. 11:27; John
21:17; Rom. 11:36; Prov. 16:4; Rom. 8:28, 32; Eph.
5:20; 1 Cor. 8:6; Eph. 1:22; Col. 1:17.*

sept/12

"To God belong wisdom and power, counsel and understanding are his." . . . "'Who is this that obscures my counsel without knowledge?'"—Blessed is the man who does not walk in the counsel of the wicked. . . . I will praise the Lord, who counsels me; even at night my heart instructs me; . . . You guide me with your counsel, and afterward you will take me into glory.—Counsel and sound judgment are mine; I have understanding and power.—For to us a child is born, to us a son is given. . . . And he will be named, Wonderful Counselor. . . . Who has understood the Spirit of the Lord, or instructed him as his counselor?—"I will ask the Father, and he will give you another Counselor, to be with you forever—the Spirit of truth. The world cannot accept him, because it neither sees him nor knows him. But you know him, for he lives with you and will be in you."—"Who has known the mind of the Lord? Or who has been his counselor?"—"I counsel you to buy from me gold refined in the fire, so you can become rich; and white clothes to wear, so you can cover your shameful nakedness, and salve to put on your eyes, so you can see."—I will restore your judges as in days of old, your counselors as at the beginning.

Job 12:13; 42:3; Pss. 1:1; 16:7; 73:24; Prov. 8:14; Isa. 9:6; 40:13; John 14:16-17; Rom. 11:34; Rev. 3:18; Isa. 1:26.

sept/13

The spirits of prophets are subject to the control of prophets. For God is not a God of disorder but of peace. . . . Everything should be done in a fitting and orderly way.—"Every morning and evening they present burnt offerings and fragrant incense to the Lord. They set out the bread on the ceremonially clean table and light the lamps on the gold lampstand every evening. We are observing the requirements of the Lord our God."—"Is not my house right with God? Has he not made with me an everlasting covenant, arranged and secured in every part?"—Many, O Lord my God, are . . . the things you planned for us no one can recount to you; were I to speak . . . of them . . . they would be too many to declare. . . . Direct my footsteps according to your word; let no sin rule over me.—"This is what the Lord says: Put your house in order, because you are going to die; you will not recover."—He pondered and searched out and set in order many proverbs.—Since I myself have carefully investigated everything from the beginning, it seems good also to me to write an orderly account for you, most excellent Theophilus.—Though I am absent from you in body, I am with you in spirit and delight to see how orderly you are and how firm your faith in Christ is.

---

1 Cor. 14:32-33, 40; 2 Chron. 13:11; 2 Sam. 23:5; Pss. 40:5; 119:133; Isa. 38:1; Eccl. 12:9; Luke 1:3; Col 2:5.

sept/14

"The Lord, the Lord, the compassionate and gracious God, slow to anger, abounding in love and faithfulness."—O Lord, . . . how priceless is your unfailing love! Both high and low among men find refuge in the shadow of your wings. They feast on the abundance of your house.—"I am come that they may have life, and have it to the full."—God's abundant provision of grace and of the gift of righteousness reign in life through the one man, Jesus Christ.—The grace that is reaching more and more people may cause thanksgiving to overflow to the glory of God.—Now to him who is able to do immeasurably more than all we ask or imagine, according to his power that is at work with us.—The grace of our Lord was poured out on me abundantly, along with the faith and love that are in Christ Jesus.—He saved us through the washing of rebirth and renewal by the Holy Spirit, whom he poured on us generously through Jesus Christ our Savior.—Through my being with you again your joy in Christ Jesus will overflow on account of me.—Out of the most severe trial, their overflowing joy and their extreme poverty welled up in rich generosity.—"Be on your guard against all kinds of greed: a man's life does not consist in the abundance of his possessions."

Exod. 34:6; Ps. 36:6-8; John 10:10; Rom. 5:17; 2 Cor. 4:15; Eph. 3:20; 1 Tim. 1:14; Titus 3:6; Phil. 1:26; 2 Cor. 8:2; Luke 12:15.

sept/15

His anger lasts only a moment, but his favor lasts a lifetime.—The angel went to [Mary] and said, "Greetings, you who are highly favored! The Lord is with you. . . . Don't be afraid, Mary, you have found favor with God."—The boy Samuel continued to grow in stature and in favor with the Lord and with men.—This is a people without understanding; so their Maker has no compassion on them, and their Creator shows them no favor. . . . "Though in anger I struck you, in favor I will show you compassion."—Let love and faithfulness never leave you; bind them around your neck, write them on the tablet of your heart. Then you will win favor and a good name in the sight of God and man. . . . Whoever finds me finds life. . . . His favor is like a rain cloud in spring. . . . A king's rage is like the roar of a lion, but his favor is like dew on the grass.—For surely, O Lord, you bless the righteous; you surround them with your favor as with a shield.—Jesus grew in wisdom and stature, and in favor with God and men.—Every day [the believers] continued to meet together in the temple courts. They broke bread in their homes and ate together with glad and sincere hearts, praising God and enjoying the favor of all the people.

Ps. 30:5; Luke 1:28, 30; 1 Sam. 2:26; Isa. 27:11; 60:10; Prov. 3:3-4; 8:35; 16:15; 19:12; Ps. 5:12; Luke 2:52; Acts 2:46-47.

sept/16

"To do your will, O my God, is my desire; your law is within my heart." . . . Teach me to do your will, for you are my God.—"Not everyone who says to me, 'Lord, Lord,' will enter the kingdom of heaven, but only he who does the will of my Father who is in heaven." . . . "Your will be done on earth as it is in heaven." . . . "My Father, if it is not possible for this cup to be taken away unless I drink, may your will be done."—" 'Here I am—it is written about me in the scroll—I have come to do your will, O God.'"—"Whoever does God's will is my brother and sister and mother."—The Spirit intercedes for the saints in accordance with God's will. . . . Test and approve what God's will is—his good, pleasing and perfect will.—The Lord Jesus Christ, who gave himself for our sins to rescue us from the present evil age, according to the will of our God and Father.—Like slaves of Christ, doing the will of God from your heart.—He is always wrestling in prayer for you, that you may stand firm in all the will of God, mature and fully assured.—Those who suffer according to God's will should commit themselves to their faithful Creator and continue to do good.—The world and its desires pass away, but the man who does the will of God lives forever.

Pss. 40:8; 143:10; Matt. 7:21; 6:10; 26:42; Heb. 10:7; Mark 3:35; Rom. 8:27; 12:2; Gal. 1:3-4; Eph. 6:6; Col. 4:12; 1 Peter 4:19; 1 John 2:17.

sept/17

Wisdom is supreme; therefore get wisdom. Though it cost you all you have, get understanding. . . . How much better to get wisdom than gold, to choose understanding rather than silver!—To the man who pleases him, God gives wisdom, knowledge and happiness.—If any of you lacks wisdom, he should ask God, who gives generously to all without finding fault, and it will be given to him. . . . The wisdom that comes from heaven is first of all pure; then peace loving, considerate, submissive, full of mercy and good fruit, impartial and sincere.—Christ the power of God and the wisdom of God. . . . Christ Jesus, who has become for us widsom from God. . . . We speak of God's secret wisdom, a wisdom that has been hidden and that God destined for our glory before time began.—The child grew and became strong; he was filled with wisdom, and the grace of God was upon him. . . . "I will give you words and wisdom that none of your adversaries will be able to resist or contradict."—[The Jews] began to argue with Stephen, but they could not stand up against his wisdom or the Spirit by which he spoke.—Through the Church, the manifold wisdom of God should be made known to the rulers and authorities.

Prov. 4:7; 16:16; Eccl. 2:26; James 1:5; 3:17; 1 Cor. 1:24, 30; 2:7; Luke 2:40; 21:15; Acts 6:9-10; Eph. 3:10.

sept/18

The path of the righteous is like the first gleam of dawn, shining ever brighter till the full light of day.—"Those who are wise will shine like the brightness of the heavens, and those who lead many to righteousness, like the stars for ever and ever."—"Arise, shine! for your light has come, and the glory of the Lord rises upon you."—"The Lord make his face shine upon you and be gracious to you."—"You will pray to him, and he will hear you; . . . and light will shine on your ways."—We have the word of the prophets made more certain, and you will do well to pay attention to it, as to a light shining in a dark place, until the day dawns and the morning star arises in your hearts.—Become blameless and pure, children of God without fault in a crooked and depraved generation, in which you shine like stars in the universe as you hold out the word of life.—From Zion, perfect in beauty, God shines forth. . . . O God, make your face shine upon us, that we may be saved.—The light shines in the darkness, but the darkness has not understood it.—"Let your light shine before men, that they may see your good deeds and praise your Father in heaven." . . . "The righteous will shine like the sun in the kingdom of their Father."

Prov. 4:18; Dan. 12:3; Isa. 60:1; Num. 6:25; Job 22:27-28; 2 Peter 1:19; Phil. 2:15-16; Pss. 50:2; 80:3; John 1:5; Matt. 5:16; 13:43.

sept/19

[David] prepared a place for the ark of God and pitched a tent for it.—You prepare a table before me in the presence of my enemies.—Penalties are prepared for mockers, and beatings for the backs of fools.—When Christ came into the world, he said: "Sacrifice and offering you did not desire, but a body you prepared for me." . . . God is not ashamed to be called their God, for he has prepared a city for them.—Jesus said, "You will indeed drink from my cup, but to sit at my right or left is not for me to grant. These places belong to those for whom they have been prepared by my Father." . . . "Then the King will say to those on his right, 'Come, you who are blessed by my Father; take your inheritance, the kingdom prepared for you since the creation of the world.'"—"No eye has seen, no ear has heard, no mind has conceived what God has prepared for those who love him."—I saw the Holy City, the new Jerusalem, coming down out of heaven from God, prepared as a bride beautifully dressed for her husband.—In a large house there are articles not only of gold and silver, but also of wood and clay; . . . if a man cleanses himself . . . , he will be an instrument for noble purposes, made holy, useful to the Master and prepared to do any work.

1 Chron 15:1; Ps. 23:5; Prov. 19:29; Heb. 10:5; 11:16; Matt. 20:23; 25:34; 1 Cor. 2:9; Rev. 21:2; 2 Tim. 2:20-21.

sept/20

No man knows when his hour will come: As fish are caught in a cruel net, or birds are taken in a snare, so are men trapped by evil times that fall unexpectedly upon them.—"As it was in the days of Noah, so also it will be in the days of the Son of Man."—"As Moses lifted up the snake in the desert, so the Son of Man must be lifted up, that everyone who believes in him may have eternal life."—"As the weeds are pulled up and burned in the fire, so it will be at the end of the age."—As you used to offer the parts of your body in slavery to impurity and to ever-increasing wickedness, so now offer them in slavery to righteousness leading to holiness. . . . As you who were at one time disobedient to God have now received mercy as a result of their disobedience, so they too have now become disobedient in order that they too may now receive mercy as a result of God's mercy to you.—So then, just as you received Christ Jesus as Lord, continue to live in him, rooted and built up in him.—As far as the east is from the west, so far has he removed our transgressions from us. As a father has compassion on his children, so the Lord has compassion on those who fear him; for he knows how we are formed, he remembers that we are dust. . . . As the deer pants for streams of water, so my soul pants for you, O God.

Eccl. 9:12; Luke 17:26; John 3:14-15; Matt. 13:40; Rom. 6:19; 11:30-31; Col. 2:6-7; Pss. 103:12-14; 42:1.

sept/21

How great is the love the Father has lavished on us, that we should be called the children of God! And this is what we are! . . . Dear friends, now we are children of God, and what we will be has not yet been made known.—When the time had fully come, God sent his Son, born of a woman, born under law, to redeem those under law, that we might receive the full rights of sons. Because you are sons, God sent the Spirit of his Son into our hearts, the Spirit who calls out, *"Abba, Father."*—[God] chose us in him before the creation of the world to be holy and blameless in his sight. In love he predestined us to be adopted as sons through Jesus Christ, in accordance with his pleasure and will—to the praise of his glorious grace, which he has freely given us in the one he loves.—The Spirit himself testifies with our spirit that we are God's children. Now if we are children, then we are heirs—heirs of God and co-heirs with Christ, if indeed we share in his sufferings in order that we may also share in his glory. . . . We ourselves, who have the first fruits of the Spirit, groan inwardly as we wait eagerly for our adoption as sons, the redemption of our bodies.—To all who received him, to those who believed in his name, he gave the right to become children of God . . . born of God.

1 John 3:1-2; Gal. 4:4-6; Eph. 1:4-6; Rom. 8:16-17, 23; John 1:12-13.

sept/22

Aaron was set apart, he and his descendants forever, to consecrate the most holy things, to offer sacrifices before the Lord, to minister before him and to pronounce blessings in his name forever.—The Lord said to Moses and Aaron, "Separate yourselves from this assembly so I can put an end to them at once."—Depart, depart, go out from there! Touch no unclean thing! Come out from it and be pure, you who carry the vessels of the Lord. . . . Your iniquities have separated you from your God; your sins have hidden his face from you, so that he will not hear.—Paul, a servant of Christ Jesus, called to be an apostle and set apart for the gospel of God.—When God, . . . set me apart from birth, and called me by his grace.—"Come out from them and be separate," says the Lord. "Touch no unclean thing, and I will receive you."—Blessed is the man who does not walk in the counsel of the wicked or stand in the way of sinners or sit in the seat of mockers. But his delight is in the law of the Lord, and on his law he meditates day and night.—Such a high priest meets our need—one who is holy, blameless, pure, set apart from sinners, exalted above the heavens . . . Who sat down at the right hand of the throne of the Majesty in heaven.

1 Chron. 23:13; Num. 16:20-21; Isa. 52:11; 59:2; Rom. 1:1; Gal. 1:15; 2 Cor. 6:17; Ps. 1:1-2; Heb. 7:26; 8:1.

sept/23

"I the Lord do not change."—"The Lord has sworn and will not change his mind."—Lord, who may dwell in your sanctuary? Who may live on your holy hill? He whose walk is blameless . . . who despises a vile man but honors those who fear the Lord, who keeps his oath even when it hurts.—"Praise be to the name of God for ever and ever; wisdom and power are his. He changes times and seasons."—God, who is enthroned forever, will hear them and afflict them—men who never change their ways and have no fear of God.—They exchanged the truth of God for a lie, and worshiped and served created things rather than the Creator.—They exchanged their Glory for an image of a bull, which eats grass. They forgot the God who saved them, who had done great things in Egypt.—"The more the priests increased, the more they sinned against me; they exchanged their glory for something disgraceful."—The trumpet will sound, the dead will be raised imperishable, and we shall be changed. For the perishable must clothe itself with the imperishable.—The Lord Jesus Christ, who, by the power that enables him to bring everything under his control, will transform our lowly bodies so that they will be like his glorious body.

Mal. 3:6; Heb. 7:21; Ps. 15:1-2, 4; Dan. 2:20-21; Ps. 55:19; Rom. 1:25; Ps. 106:20-21; Hos. 4:7; 1 Cor. 15:52-53; Phil. 3:20-21.

sept/24

"I am God Almighty; walk before me and be blameless." . . . "The Lord, before whom I have walked, will send his angel with you." . . . Enoch walked with God 300 years.—"I will walk among you and be your God, and you will be my people."—You have delivered my soul from death and my feet from stumbling, that I may walk before God in the light of life. . . . Teach me your way, O Lord, and I will walk in your truth. —Whether you turn to the right or to the left, your ears will hear a voice behind you, saying, "This is the way; walk in it."—We walk by faith, not by sight.—This is the message we have heard from him and declare to you: God is light; in him is no darkness at all. If we claim to have fellowship with him yet walk in the darkness, we lie and do not live by the truth. But if we walk in the light, as he is in the light, we have fellowship with one another, and the blood of Jesus, his Son, purifies us from every sin. . . . If anyone obeys his word, God's love is truly made complete in him. This is how we know we are in him: Whoever claims to live in him must walk as Jesus did.—Do two walk together unless they have agreed to do so?—Those who walk uprightly enter into peace; they find rest as they lie in death.

Gen. 17:1; 24:40; 5:22; Lev. 26:12; Pss. 56:13; 86:11; Isa. 30:21; 2 Cor. 5:7; 1 John 1:5-7; 2:5-6; Amos 3:3; Isa. 57:2.

sept/25

Now listen, you rich people, weep and wail because of the misery that is coming upon you. Your wealth has rotted, and moths have eaten your clothes. Your gold and silver are corroded. Their corrosion will testify against you and eat your flesh like fire.—"'This is what I'll do. I will tear down my barns and build bigger ones, and there I will store all my grain and my goods. And I'll say to myself, "You have plenty of good things laid up for many years. Take life easy; eat, drink and be merry."' "But God said to him, 'You fool! This very night your life will be demanded from you. Then who will get what you have prepared for yourself?'"—"You say, 'I am rich; I have acquired wealth and do not need a thing.' But you do not realize that you are wretched, pitiful, poor, blind and naked. I counsel you to buy from me gold refined in the fire."—"Whoever wants to save his life will lose it, but whoever loses his life for me and for the gospel, will save it. What good is it for a man to gain the whole world, yet forfeit his soul? Or what can a man give in exchange for his soul?"—I consider everything a loss compared to the surpassing greatness of knowing Christ Jesus my Lord, for whose sake I have lost all things. I consider them rubbish, that I may gain Christ.

James. 5:1-3; Luke 12:18-20; Rev. 3:17-18; Mark 8:35-36; Phil. 3:8.

sept/26

"Hear, O my people, and I will speak. I have no need of a bull from your stall or of goats from your pens, for every animal of the forest is mine, and the cattle on a thousand hills. If I were hungry I would not tell you, for the world is mine, and all that is in it."—Jesus [said], "Destroy this temple, and I will raise it again in three days." The Jews replied, "It has taken forty-six years to build this temple, and you are going to raise it in three days?" But the temple he had spoken of was his body.—"If you do not worship [the image], you will be thrown immediately into a blazing furnace. Then what god will be able to rescue you from my hand?" [They] replied to the king," . . . We do not need to defend ourselves before you in this matter. If we are thrown into the blazing furnace, the God we serve is able to save us from it, and he will rescue us from your hand, O king. But even if he does not, we want you to know, O king, that we will not serve your gods or worship the image of gold you have set up."—He replied, "Go tell that fox, 'I will drive out demons and heal people today and tomorrow, and on the third day I will reach my goal.' In any case, I must keep going today and tomorrow and the next day—for surely no prophet can die outside Jerusalem!"

Ps. 50:7, 9-10, 12; John 2:19-21; Dan. 3:15-18; Luke 13:32-33.

sept/27

"God sent me ahead of you to preserve for you a remnant on earth and to save your lives by a great deliverance."—O Lord, you will keep us safe and protect us from such people forever. . . . Love the Lord, all his saints! The Lord preserves the faithful, but the proud he pays back in full. . . . The Lord will keep you from all harm—he will watch over your life; the Lord will watch over your coming and going, both now and forevermore. . . . The Lord watches over all who love him.—He is a shield to those whose walk is blameless, for he guards the course of the just and protects the way of his faithful ones.—Whoever tries to keep his life will lose it, and whoever loses his life will preserve it.—May God himself, the God of peace, sanctify you through and through. May your whole spirit, soul and body be kept blameless at the coming of our Lord Jesus Christ. The one who calls you is faithful and he will do it.—To him who is able to keep you from falling and to present you before his glorious presence without fault and with great joy—to the only God our Savior be glory, power and authority, through Jesus Christ our Lord.—O Lord, you preserve both man and beast. How priceless is your unfailing love!

Gen. 45:7; Pss. 12:7; 31:23; 121:7-8; 145:20; Prov. 2:7-8; Luke 17:33; 1 Thess. 5:23-24; Jude 24-25; Ps. 36:6-7.

sept/28

"My ears had heard of you, but now my eyes have seen you. Therefore I despise myself and repent in dust and ashes."—"Your eyes will see the king in his beauty."—"Sir, . . . we would like to see Jesus." . . . "Anyone who has seen me has seen the Father. . . . Believe me when I say that I am in the Father and the Father is in me."—At present we do not see everything subject to him. But we see Jesus, who was made a little lower than the angels, now crowned with glory and honor because he suffered death, so that by the grace of God he might taste death for everyone.—"My eyes have seen your salvation, which you have prepared in the sight of all people."—The life appeared; we have seen it and testify to it. We proclaim to you what we have seen and heard. —By faith [Moses] left Egypt, not fearing the king's anger; he persevered because he saw him who is invisible.—In the year that King Uzziah died, I saw the Lord seated on a throne. . . . "Woe is me!" I cried. "I am ruined! For I am a man of unclean lips, and I live among a people of unclean lips, and my eyes have seen the King, the Lord Almighty."—We know that when he appears, we shall be like him, for we shall see him as he is.

Job 42:6; Isa. 33:17; John 12:21; 14:9, 11; Heb. 2:8-9; Luke 2:30; 1 John 1:2-3; Heb. 11:27; Isa. 6:15; 1 John 3:2.

sept/29

The city clerk . . . said, . . . "Therefore, since these facts are undeniable, you ought to be quiet and not do anything rash."—By the grace given me I say to every one of you: Do not think of yourself more highly than you ought, but rather think of yourself with sober judgment, in accordance with the measure of faith God has given you. . . . We who are strong ought to bear with the failings of the weak and not to please ourselves.—[Timothy], although I hope to come to you soon, I am writing you these instructions so that, if I am delayed, you will know how people ought to conduct themselves in God's household, which is the church of the living God, the pillar and foundation of the truth.—What kind of people ought you to be? You ought to live holy and godly lives as you look forward to the day of God and speed its coming.—This is how we know what love is: Jesus Christ laid down his life for us. And we ought to lay down our lives for our brothers.—If anyone has caused grief, he has not so much grieved me as he has grieved all of you, to some extent—not to put it too severely. The punishment inflicted on him by the majority is sufficient for him. Now instead, you ought to forgive and comfort him, so that he will not be overwhelmed by excessive sorrow.

Acts 19:35-36; Rom. 12:3; 15:1; 1 Tim. 3:14-15; 2 Peter 3:11-12; 1 John 3:16; 2 Cor. 2:5-7.

sept/30

"In breeding season I once had a dream in which I looked up and saw the male goats mating with the flock were streaked, speckled, or spotted. The angel of God said to me in a dream, 'Jacob.' I answered, 'Here I am.' And he said, . . . 'I am the God of Bethel, where you anointed a pillar and where you made a vow to me. Now leave this land at once and go back to your native land.'" . . . Joseph had a dream, and when he told it to his brothers they hated him all the more . . . because of his dream and what he had said. Then he had another dream, and he told it to his brothers. . . . The cupbearer and the baker, . . . who were being held in prison—had a dream the same night, and each dream had a meaning of its own. . . . Joseph came to them the next morning. . . . "We both had dreams," they answered, "but there is no one to interpret them." Then Joseph said, "Do not interpretations belong to God? Tell me your dreams."—Daniel could understand visions and dreams of all kinds. . . . "This was the dream, and now we will interpret it to the king. . . . The great God has shown the king what will take place in the future. The dream is true and the interpretation is trustworthy." . . . [Daniel had] the ability to interpret dreams, explain riddles and solve difficult problems.

Gen. 31:10-13; 37:5, 8-9; 40:5-6, 8; Dan. 1:17; 2:36, 45; 5:12.

oct / 1

"He raises the poor from the dust and lifts the needy from the ash heap; he seats them with princes and has them inherit a throne of honor."—He lifted me out of the slimy pit, out of the mud and mire; he set my feet on a rock and gave me a firm place to stand. He put a new song in my mouth, a hymn of praise to our God. Many will see and fear and put their trust in the Lord.—I went down to the potter's house, and I saw him working at his wheel. But the pot he was shaping from the clay was marred in his hands; so the potter formed it into another pot, shaping it as seemed best to him.—The Twelve were with him, and also some women who had been cured of evil spirits and diseases: Mary (called Magdalene) from whom seven demons had come out.—What a wretched Man I am! Who will rescue me from this body of death? Thanks be to God—through Jesus Christ our Lord!—You are a chosen people, a royal priesthood, a holy nation, a people belonging to God, that you may declare the praises of him who called you out of darkness into his wonderful light. Once you were not a people, but now you are the people of God.—But by the grace of God I am what I am, and his grace to me was not without effect.—[He] will transform our lowly bodies so that they will be like his glorious body.

1 Sam. 2:8; Ps. 40:2-3; Jer. 18:3-4; Luke 8:1-2; Rom. 7:24-25; 1 Peter 2:9-10; 1 Cor. 15:10; Phil. 3:21.

Resist him, standing firm in the faith.

oct /2

"You have heard that it was said, 'eye for eye, and tooth for tooth.' But I tell you, Do not resist an evil person. If someone strikes you on the right cheek, turn to him the other also."—"I will give you words and wisdom that none of your adversaries will be able to resist or contradict. . . . By standing firm you will save yourselves." —These men began to argue with Stephen, but they could not stand up against his wisdom or the Spirit by which he spoke. . . . "You stiff-necked people, with uncircumcised hearts and ears! You are just like your fathers: You always resist the Holy Spirit."—One of you will say to me, "Then why does God still blame us? For who resists his will?" But who are you, O man, to talk back to God?—Submit yourselves, then, to God. Resist the devil, and he will flee from you. Come near to God and he will come near to you.—Be self-controlled and alert. Your enemy the devil prowls around like a roaring lion looking for someone to devour. Resist him, standing firm in the faith, because you know that your brothers throughout the world are undergoing the same kind of sufferings.—Have nothing to do with them. . . . these men oppose the truth—men of depraved minds, who, as far as the faith is concerned, are rejected.

Matt. 5:38; Luke 21:15, 19; Acts 6:9-10; 7:51; Rom. 9:19-20; James 4:7-8; 1 Peter 5:8-9; 2 Tim. 3:5, 8.

oct/3

"Friend deceives friend, and no one speaks the truth. They have taught their tongues to lie; they weary themselves with sinning."—"You have burdened me with your sins and wearied me with your offenses." . . . God said, "This is the resting place, let the weary rest"; and, "This is the place of repose"—but they would not listen.—"Come to me, all you who are weary and burdened, and I will give you rest."—Of making many books there is no end, and much study wearies the body.—The Lord is the everlasting God, the Creator of the ends of the earth. He will not grow tired or weary. . . . He gives strength to the weary and increases the power of the weak. . . . Those who hope in the Lord will renew their strength. They will run and not grow weary, they will walk and not faint. . . . The Sovereign Lord has given me an instructed tongue, to know the word that sustains the weary.—"I will refresh the weary and satisfy the faint."—The king, and all the people with him arrived at their destination exhausted. And there he refreshed himself.—Let us not become weary in doing good, for at the proper time we will reap a harvest if we do not give up.—"There the wicked cease from turmoil, and there the weary are at rest."

Jer. 9:5; Isa. 43:24; 28:12; Matt. 11:28; Eccl. 12:12; Isa. 40:28-29, 31: 50:4; Jer. 31:25; 2 Sam. 16:14; Gal. 6:9; Job 3:17.

oct/4

Let the wicked forsake his way and the evil man his thoughts. Let him turn to the Lord, and he will have mercy upon him, and to our God, for he will freely pardon.—In accordance with your great love, forgive the sin of these people, just as you have pardoned them from the time they left Egypt until now. The Lord replied, "I have forgiven them as you asked."—"Why do you not pardon my offenses, and forgive my sins? For I will soon lie down in the desert; you will search me, but I will be no more."—"Why should I forgive you? Your children have forsaken me and sworn by gods that are not gods." . . . "In those days, at that time," declares the Lord, "search will be made for Israel's guilt, but there will be none and for the sins of Judah, but none will be found, for I will forgive the remnant I spare."—Who is a God like unto you, that pardons sin, and forgives the transgression of the remnant of his inheritance? You do not stay angry forever, but delight to show mercy.—Hezekiah prayed for them, saying, "May the Lord, who is good, pardon everyone who sets his heart on seeking God."—For the sake of your name, O Lord, forgive my iniquity, though it is great.—"I will cleanse them from all the sin they have committed against me and will forgive all their sins of rebellion against me."

Isa. 55:7; Num. 14:19-20; Job 7:21; Jer. 5:7; 50:20; Mic. 7:18; 2 Chron. 30:18; Ps. 25:11; Jer. 33:8.

oct /5

Zion said, "The Lord has forsaken me, the Lord has forgotten me." "Can a mother forget the baby at her breast and have no compassion on the child she has borne? Though she may forget, I will not forget you! See, I have engraved you on the palms of my hands; your walls are ever before me" . . . "I, the God of Israel, will not forsake them" . . . "I will turn the darkness into light before them and make the rough places smooth. These things will I do; I will not forsake them."—Those who know your name will trust in you, for you, Lord, have never forsaken those who seek you. . . . The Lord loves the just and will not forsake his faithful ones; they will be protected forever.—The Lord your God is a merciful God; he will not abandon or destroy you or forget the covenant with your forefathers, which he confirmed with them by oath.—About the ninth hour Jesus cried out in a loud voice, "Eloi, Eloi, lama, sabachthani?" —which means, "My God, my God, why have you forsaken me?"—The Lord himself goes before you and he will be with you, he will never leave you or forsake you. Do not be afraid; do not be discouraged.—God has said, "Never will I leave you; never will I forsake you." So we say with confidence, "The Lord is my helper; I will not be afraid. What can man do unto me?"

Isa. 49:14-16; 41:17; 42:16; Pss. 9:10; 37:28; Deut. 4:31; Matt. 27:46; Deut. 31:8; Heb. 13:5-6.

oct/6

You shall have no other gods before me.—The Lord our God, the Lord is one. Love the Lord your God with all your heart and with all your soul and with all your strength. . . . Love the Lord your God, listen to his voice, and hold fast to him.—Let those who love the Lord hate evil.—Do not love the world or anything in the world. If anyone loves the world, the love of the Father is not in him. For everything in the world—the cravings of sinful man, the lust of the eyes and the boasting of what he has and does—comes not from the Father but from the world. . . . If anyone says, "I love God," yet hates his brother, he is a liar. For anyone who does not love his brother, whom he has seen, cannot love God whom he has not seen. . . . Love one another, for love comes from God.—Love each other as I have loved you."—Perfect love drives out fear, because fear has to do with punishment. The man who fears is not made perfect in love.—"If you love me, you will obey what I command."—Love does no harm to its neighbor. Therefore love is the fulfillment of the law.—I hold this against you: you have forsaken your first love.—Keep yourselves in God's love as you wait for the mercy of our Lord Jesus Christ to bring you to eternal life.

Exod. 20:3; Deut. 6:4-5; 30:20; Ps. 97:10; 1 John 2:15-16; 4:20-21, 7; John 15:12; 1 John 4:18; John 14:15; Rom. 13:10; Rev. 2:4; Jude 21.

oct /7

"Come to me, all you who are weary and burdened, and I will give you rest. . . . Learn from me! . . . My burden is light."—My guilt has overwhelmed me like a burden too heavy to bear.—Have I become a burden to you?"—He asked the Lord, . . . "What have I done to displease you that you put the burden of all these people on me?" . . . The Lord said to Moses, . . . "I will come down and speak with you there, and I will take of the Spirit that is on you. This will help you carry the burden of the people, so that you will not have to carry it alone.—Mighty God, you have shattered the yoke that burdens them. . . . In that day their burden will be lifted from your shoulders, their yoke from your neck. . . . The Lord Almighty has sworn, . . . "His yoke will be taken from my people, and his burden removed from their shoulders."—Jesus replied, "And you experts in the law, woe to you, because you load people down with burdens they can hardly carry, and you yourselves will not lift one finger to help them.—[God] says, "I removed the burden from their shoulders; their hands were set free".—Carry each other's burdens, and in this way you will fulfill the law of Christ.—Cast your cares on the Lord, and he will sustain you.

Matt. 11:28-30; Ps. 38:4; Job 7:20; Num. 11:11, 16-17; Isa. 9:4; 10:27; 14:24-25; Luke 11:46; Ps. 81:6; Gal. 6:2; Ps. 55:22.

oct /8

For Christ's sake, I delight in weaknesses, in insults, in hardships, in persecutions, in difficulties. For when I am weak, then I am strong. . . . We are glad whenever we are weak but you are strong.—Whose weakness was turned to strength.—Dying, and yet we live on; . . . sorrowful, yet always rejoicing; poor, yet making many rich; having nothing, and yet possessing everything.—I know your afflictions and your poverty—yet you are rich!—I have been crucified with Christ and I no longer live, but Christ lives in me. The life I live in the body, I live by faith in the Son of God, who loved me and gave himself for me.—Count yourselves dead to sin but alive to God in Christ Jesus.—"Unless a kernel of wheat falls to the ground and dies, it remains only a single seed. But if it dies, it produces many seeds. The man who loves his life will lose it, while the man who hates his life in this world will keep it for eternal life."—Now faith is being sure of what we hope for and certain of what we do not see. This is what the ancients were commended for.—"If only there was someone to arbitrate between us to lay his hand upon us both."—We have one who speaks to the Father in our defense—Jesus Christ, the Righteous One.

---

2 Cor. 12:10; 13:9; Heb. 11:34; 2 Cor. 6:9-10; Rev. 2:9; Gal. 2:20; Rom. 6:11; John 12:24-25; Heb. 11:1-2; Job 9:33; 1 John 2:1.

oct/9

"Be perfect, therefore, as your heavenly Father is perfect."—"As for God, his way is perfect."—The law of the Lord is perfect, reviving the soul.—Test and approve what God's will is—his good, pleasing and perfect will.—[Job] was blameless and upright, he feared God and shunned evil.—Aim for perfection.—You will keep in perfect peace him whose mind is steadfast, because he trusts in you.—The path of the righteous is like the first gleam of dawn, shining ever brighter till the full light of day.—"May they be brought to complete unity to let the world know that you sent me and have loved them as you have loved me."—We proclaim him, admonishing and teaching everyone with all wisdom, so that we may present everyone perfect in Christ. To this end I labor, struggling with all his energy, which so powerfully works in me. . . . Epaphras, who is one of you and a servant of Christ Jesus, sends greetings. He is always wrestling in prayer for you, that you may stand firm in all the will of God, perfect and fully assured.—There is no fear in love. But perfect love drives out fear, because fear has to do with punishment. The man who fears is not made perfect in love.

Matt. 5:48; 2 Sam. 22:31; Ps. 19:7; Rom. 12:2; Job 1:1; 2 Cor. 13:11; Isa. 26:3; Prov. 4:18; John 17:23; Col. 1:28-29; 4:12; 1 John 4:18.

oct/10

Be on your guard: stand firm in the faith; be men of courage; be strong.—It is for freedom that Christ has set us free. Stand firm, then, and do not let yourselves be burdened again by a yoke of slavery.—Stand firm in one spirit, contending as one man for the faith of the gospel without being frightened in any way by those who oppose you. . . . My brothers, you whom I love and long for, my joy and crown, that is how you should stand firm in the Lord, dear friends!—In all our distress and persecution we were encouraged about you because of your faith. For now we really live, since you are standing firm in the Lord. —Stand firm and hold to the teachings we passed on to you, whether by word of mouth or by letter.—Put on the full armor of God, so that when the day of evil comes, you may be able to stand your ground, and after you have done everything, to stand. Stand firm then.—Some trust in chariots and others in horses, but we trust in the name of the Lord our God. They are brought to their knees and fall, but we rise up and stand firm.—"There is a place near me where you may stand on a rock."—All of you are standing today in the presence of the Lord your God. . . . in order to enter into a covenant with the Lord your God.

1 Cor. 16:13; Gal 5:1; Phil. 1:27-28; 4:1; 1 Thess. 3:7-8; 2 Thess. 2:15; Eph. 6:13-14; Ps. 20:7-8; Exod. 33:21; Deut. 29:10, 12.

oct/11

Sin entered the world through one man, and death through sin, and in this way death came to all men, because all sinned.—The Lord saw how great man's wickedness on the earth had become, and that every inclination of the thoughts of his heart was only evil all the time. The Lord was grieved that he had made man on the earth, and his heart was filled with pain.—Righteousness exalts a nation, but sin is a disgrace to any people.—You know my folly, O God; my guilt is not hidden from you.—A man of sorrows . . . was pierced for our transgressions, he was crushed for our iniquities. The Lord has laid on him the iniquity of us all.—Christ Jesus came into the world to save sinners.—I have not come to call the righteous, but sinners.—Christ died for our sins according to the Scriptures.—Jesus Christ, the Righteous One. He is the atoning sacrifice for our sins and not only for ours but also for the sins of the whole world. If we confess our sins, he is faithful and just and will forgive us our sins and purify us from all unrighteousness.—"I have swept away your offenses like a cloud, your sins like the morning mist."—Blessed is he whose transgressions are forgiven, whose sins are covered.

Rom. 5:12; Gen. 6:5-6; Prov. 14:34; Ps. 69:5; Isa. 53:3, 5-6; 1 Tim. 1:15; Matt. 9:13; 1 Cor. 15:3; 1 John 2:1-2; 1:9; Isa. 44:22; Ps. 32:1.

oct/12

Christ redeemed us from the curse of the law by becoming a curse for us.—You are not your own; you were bought at a price.—God will redeem my soul from the grave; he will surely take me to himself.—You have been set free from sin and have become slaves to righteousness.—O Lord, my Rock and my Redeemer.—"Know that I, the Lord, am your Savior, your Redeemer, the Mighty One of Jacob."—"Their Redeemer is strong; the Lord Almighty is his name."—The Lord redeems his servants; no one who takes refuge in him will be condemned.—"I know that my Redeemer lives, and that in the end he will stand upon the earth."—No man can redeem the life of another or give to God a ransom for him—the ransom for a life is costly, no payment is ever enough. . . . Put your hope in the Lord, for with the Lord is unfailing love, and with him is full redemption. He himself will redeem Israel from all their sins.—He entered the Most Holy Place once for all by his own blood, having obtained eternal redemption. Those who are called may receive the promised eternal inheritance—now that he had died as a ransom to set them free from the sins committed.—They sang a new song before the throne.

Gal. 3:13; 1 Cor. 6:19-20; Ps. 49:15; Rom. 6:18; Ps. 19:14; Isa. 60:16; Jer. 50:34; Ps. 34:22; Job 19:25; Pss. 49:7-8; 130:7-8; Heb. 9:12, 15; Rev. 14:3.

oct/13

"**D**oes not man have hard service on earth? Are not his days like those of a hired man?" . . . "My days are swifter than a weaver's shuttle, and they come to a hopeless end. Remember, O God, that my life is but a breath" . . . "My days are swifter than a runner; they fly away without a glimpse of joy. They skim past like boats of papyrus, like eagles swooping down on their prey." . . . "Man born of woman is of few days and full of trouble. He springs up like a flower and withers away; like a fleeting shadow, he does not endure." . . . "Man's days are determined; you have decreed the number of his months and have set limits he cannot exceed."—Who knows what is good for a man in life, during the few and meaningless days he passes through like a shadow?—"Like a weaver I have rolled up my life, and he has cut me off from his loom."—"All men are like grass, and all their glory is like the flowers of the field, the grass withers and the flowers fall, but the word of the Lord stands forever."—"Like water spilled on the ground, which cannot be recovered, so we must die."—"You have made my days a mere handbreadth; the span of my years is as nothing before you. Each man's life is but a breath." . . . Teach us to number our days aright, that we may gain a heart of wisdom.

Job 7:1, 6-7; 9:25-26; 14:1-2, 5; Eccl. 6:12; Isa. 38:12; 1 Peter 1:24-25; 2 Sam. 14:14; Pss. 39:5-6; 90:12.

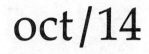

oct/14

As the mountains surround Jerusalem, so the Lord surrounds his people, both now and forevermore. . . . You hem me in, behind and before; you have laid your hand upon me. . . . The angel of the Lord encamps around those who fear him, and he delivers them. . . . The Lord's unfailing love surrounds the man who trusts in him. . . . You are my hiding place; you will protect me from trouble and surround me with songs of deliverance.—O Lord God Almighty, who is like you? You are mighty, O Lord, and your faithfulness surrounds you.—Then the angel who was speaking to me left and another angel came to meet him and said to him, "Run, tell that young man, 'Jerusalem will be a city without walls because of the great number of men and livestock in it. And I myself will be a wall of fire around it', declares the Lord, 'and I will be its glory within'."—Then King Nebuchadnezzar leaped to his feet in amazement and asked his advisers, "Wasn't it three men that we tied up and threw into the fire?" They replied, "Certainly, O king." He said, "Look! I see four men walking around in the fire, unbound and unharmed, and the fourth looks like a son of the gods."—Keep me as the apple of your eye; hide me in the shadow of your wings from the wicked who assail me.

Pss. 125:2; 139:5; 34:7; 32:10, 7; Ps. 89:8; Zech. 2:3-5; Dan. 3:24-25; Ps. 17:8-9.

oct/15

The heavens declare the glory of God; the skies proclaim the work of his hands. Day after day they pour forth speech; night after night they display knowledge.—By him all things were created: things in heaven and on earth, visible and invisible, whether thrones or powers or rulers or authorities; all things were created by him and for him.—By faith we understand that the universe was formed at God's command, so that what is seen was not made out of what was visible.—By the word of the Lord were the heavens made, their starry host by the breath of his mouth. . . . For he spoke, and it came to be; he commanded, and it stood firm.—The Sovereign Lord comes with power. . . . Who has measured the waters in the hollow of his hand, or with the breadth of his hand marked off the heavens? Who has held the dust of the earth in a basket, or weighed the mountains on the scales and the hills in a balance? . . . He who created the heavens, he is God; he who fashioned and made the earth, he founded it; he did not create it to be empty, but formed it to be inhabited.—Since the creation of the world God's invisible qualities—his eternal power and divine nature—have been clearly seen, being understood from what has been made, so that men are without excuse.

Ps. 19:1-2; Col. 1:16; Heb. 11:3; Ps. 33:6, 9; Isa. 40:10, 12; 45:18; Rom. 1:20.

oct/16

There they were, overwhelmed with dread, where there was nothing to dread. . . . When I am afraid, I will trust in you. In God, whose word I praise, in God I trust; I will not be afraid. What can mortal man do to me?—We say with confidence, "The Lord is my helper; I will not be afraid. What can man do to me?"—I sought the Lord, and he answered me; he delivered me from all my fears. Those who look to him are radiant; their faces are never covered with shame. . . . Therefore we will not fear, though the earth give away and the mountains fall into the heart of the sea, though its waters roar and foam and the mountains quake with their surging. . . . The Lord Almighty is with us.—Strengthen the feeble hands, steady the knees that give way; say to those with fearful hearts, "Be strong, do not fear; your God will come, . . . he will come to save you. . . . Do not fear, for I am with you; do not be dismayed. . . . I am the Lord, your God, who takes hold of your right hand and says to you, Do not fear; I will help you. Do not be afraid, . . . for I myself will help you."—When we came into Macedonia, this body of ours had no rest, but we were harrassed at every turn—conflicts on the outside, fears within. But God, who comforts the downcast, comforted us by the coming of Titus.

Pss. 53:5; 56:3-4; Heb. 13:6; Pss. 34:4, 5; 46:2-3, 7; Isa. 35:3-4; 41:10, 13-14; 2 Cor. 7:5-6.

oct/17

The fool says in his heart, "There is no God." They are corrupt, their deeds are vile; there is no one who does good. . . . Remember how the enemy has mocked you, O Lord, how foolish people have reviled your name. . . . Rise up, O God, and defend your cause; remember how fools mock you all day long.—The fear of the Lord is the beginning of knowledge, but fools despise wisdom and discipline. . . . Whoever spreads slander is a fool. . . . A fool finds pleasure in evil conduct, but a man of understanding delights in wisdom. . . . The way of a fool seems right to him, but a wise man listens to advice. A fool shows his arrogance at once, but a prudent man overlooks an insult. . . . Every prudent man acts out of knowledge, but a fool exposes his folly. . . . The wisdom of the prudent is to give thought to their ways, but the folly of fools is deception. Fools mock at making amends for sin, but good will is found among the upright. A wise man fears the Lord and shuns evil, but a fool is hotheaded and reckless. . . . Though you grind a fool in a mortar, grinding him like grain with a pestle, you will not remove his folly from him. . . . "Wisdom is more precious than rubies, and nothing you desire can compare with her."—Christ, . . . the wisdom of God.

Pss. 14:1; 74:18, 22; Prov. 1:7; 10:18, 23; 12:15-16; 13:16; 14:8-9, 16; 27:22; 8:11; 1 Cor. 1:24.

oct/18

"I chose you to go and bear fruit—fruit that will last."—All over the world this gospel is producing fruit and growing. . . . May [you] please him in every way: bearing fruit in every good work, growing in the knowledge of God.—The fruit of the Spirit is love, joy, peace, patience, kindness, goodness, faithfulness, gentleness and self-control. Against such things there is no law.—I delight to sit in his shade, and his fruit is sweet to my taste.—From the fruit of his lips a man is filled with good things as surely as the work of his hands rewards him. . . . From the fruit of his mouth a man's stomach is filled; with the harvest from his lips he is satisfied. The tongue has the power of life and death, and those who love it will eat its fruit. . . . The fruit of the righteous is a tree of life, and he who wins souls is wise.—"Produce fruit in keeping with repentance."—Tell the righteous it will be well with them, for they will enjoy the fruit of their deeds.—Through Jesus, therefore, let us continually offer to God a sacrifice of praise—the fruit of lips that confess his name.—He will flourish like the grain. He will blossom like a vine, and his fame will be like wine from Lebanon. . . . I am like a green pine tree; your fruitfulness comes from me.

John 15:16; Col. 1:6, 10; Gal. 5:22-23; Song of Songs 2:3; Prov. 12:14; 18:20-21; 11:30; Matt. 3:8; Isa. 3:10; Heb. 13:15; Hos. 14:7-8.

oct/19

Though now for a little while you may have had
to suffer grief in all kinds of trials, these have come
so that your faith, of greater worth than gold,
which perishes even though refined by fire—may
be proved genuine and may result in praise, glory
and honor when Jesus Christ is revealed. . . . For
you know that it was not with perishable things
such as silver and gold that you were redeemed,
. . . but with the precious blood of Christ, a lamb
without blemish or defect.—The ordinances of the
Lord are sure and altogether righteous. They are
more precious than gold, than much fine gold. . . .
O Lord, the king rejoices in your strength. . . .
You welcomed him with rich blessings and placed
a crown of pure gold on his head.—"But he knows
the way I take; when he has tested me, I will come
forth as gold." . . . "But where can wisdom be
found? It cannot be bought with the finest gold,
nor can its price be weighed in silver. . . . nor can
it be had for jewels of gold."—Blessed is the man
who finds wisdom, the man who gains
understanding, for she is more profitable than
silver and yields better returns than gold.—I
amassed silver and gold for myself. . . . Yet when
I surveyed all that my hands had done and what I
had toiled to achieve, everything was
meaningless, a chasing after the wind.

*1 Peter 1:6-7, 18; Pss. 19:9-10; 21:1, 3; Job 23:10;
28:12, 15, 17; Prov. 3:13-14; Eccl. 2:8, 11.*

oct /20

Every good and perfect gift is from above, coming down from the Father of the heavenly lights, who does not change like shifting shadows.—God's gifts and his call are irrevocable.—When you ascended on high, you led captives in your train; you received gifts from men.—"If you knew the gift of God and who it is that asks you for a drink, you would have asked him and he would have given you living water" . . . "Do not work for food that spoils, but for food that endures to eternal life, which the Son of Man will give you."—"If you then, though you are evil, know how to give good gifts to your children, how much more will your Father in heaven give the Holy Spirit to those who ask him!"—"God opposes the proud, but gives grace to the humble."—No good thing does he withhold from those whose walk is blameless.—If any of you lacks wisdom, he should ask God, who gives generously to all without finding fault, and it will be given him.—By grace you have been saved, through faith—and this not from yourselves, it is the gift of God.—"Come to me, all you who are weary and burdened, and I will give you rest."—"I have given them the glory that you gave me, that they may be one as we are one."

James 1:17; Rom. 11:29; Ps. 68:18; John 4:10; 6:27; Luke 11:13; James 4:6; Ps. 84:11; James 1:5; Eph. 2:8; Matt. 11:28; John 17:22.

oct/21

"Is it nothing to you, all you who pass by? Look around and see. Is any suffering like my suffering, that was inflicted on me?—The cords of death entangled me, the anguish of the grave came upon me; I was overcome by trouble and sorrow. Then I called on the name of the Lord, "O Lord, save me!" . . . Scorn has broken my heart and has left me helpless; I looked for sympathy, but there was none, for comforters, but I found none. . . . I pour out my complaint before him; before him I tell my trouble. . . . Look to my right and see; no one is concerned for me.—He was despised and rejected by men. . . . Surely he took up our infirmities and carried our sorrows, yet we consider him stricken by God, smitten by him, and afflicted. But he was pierced for our transgressions, he was crushed for our iniquities. Yet it was the Lord's will to crush him and cause him to suffer; . . . after the suffering of his soul, he will see the result of the light of life and be satisfied.—"Guard yourselves and all the flock of which the Holy Spirit has made you overseers. Be shepherds of the church of God, which he bought with his own blood.—In bringing many sons to glory, it was fitting that God, for whom and through whom everything exists should make the author of their salvation perfect through suffering.

Lam. 1:12; Pss. 116:3; 69:20; 142:2, 4; Isa. 53:3-5, 10-11; Acts 20:28; Heb. 2:10.

oct/22

"I was filled with delight day after day, rejoicing always in his presence, rejoicing in his whole world and delighting in mankind."—You are to rejoice before the Lord your God in everything you put your hand to.—Sing joyfully to the Lord, you righteous; it is fitting for the upright to praise him. . . . Sing to him a new song; play skillfully, and shout for joy. . . . Rejoice in the Lord, you who are righteous, and praise his holy name. —"The Ephraimites will become like mighty men, and their hearts will be glad as with wine. Their children will see it and be joyful; their hearts will rejoice in the Lord."—Rejoice in the Lord always; I will say it again; Rejoice! I rejoice greatly in the Lord that at last you have renewed your concern for me.—The apostles left the Sanhedrin, rejoicing because they had been counted worthy of suffering disgrace for the Name.—Do not be surprised at the painful trial you are suffering, as though something strange were happening to you. But rejoice that you participate in the sufferings of Christ, so that you may be overjoyed when his glory is revealed. . . . In this you greatly rejoice, though now for a little while you may have had to suffer grief in all kinds of trials. . . . You believe in him and are filled with an inexpressible and glorious joy.

Prov. 8:30-31; Deut. 12:18; Pss. 33:1, 3; 97:12; Zech. 10:7; Phil. 4:4, 10; Acts 5:41; 1 Peter 4:12-13; 1:6, 8.

oct /23

I praised the Most High; I honored and glorified him who lives forever. His dominion is an eternal dominion, his kingdom endures from generation to generation. All the peoples of the earth are regarded as nothing. He does as he pleases with the powers of heaven and the peoples of the earth. No one else can hold back his hand or say to him, "What have you done?"—You, dear children, are from God and have overcome them, because the one who is in you is greater than the one who is in the world.—"For your sake we face death all day long; we are considered as sheep to be slaughtered. No, in all these things we are more than conquerors through him who loved us.—Be strong in the Lord and in his mighty power. Put on the full armor of God so that you can take your stand against the devil's schemes. For our struggle is not against flesh and blood, but against the rulers, against the authorities, against the powers of this dark world and against the spiritual forces of evil in the heavenly realms.—They will make war against the Lamb, but the Lamb will overcome them because he is the Lord of lords and King of kings—and with him will be his called, chosen and faithful followers. . . . "They overcame him by the blood of the Lamb and by the word of their testimony."

Dan. 4:34-35; 1 John 4:4; Rom. 8:36-37; Eph. 6:10-12; Rev. 17:14; 12:11.

oct /24

Who has believed our message and to whom has the arm of the Lord been revealed? . . . His own arm worked salvation for him, and his own righteousness sustained him. . . . "My own arm worked salvation for me."—"The eternal God is your refuge, and underneath are the everlasting arms."—You are the God who performs miracles, you display your power among the peoples. With your mighty arm you redeemed your people, the descendants of Jacob and Joseph. . . . Sing to the Lord a new song, for he has done marvelous things; his right hand and his holy arm have worked salvation for him.—See, the Sovereign Lord comes with power, and his arm rules for him. . . . He tends his flock like a shepherd: he gathers the lambs in his arms and carries them close to his heart.—[Jesus] took a little child, . . . and taking him in his arms, he said to them, "Whoever welcomes one of these little children in my name welcomes me; and whoever welcomes me does not welcome me but the one who sent me." . . . He took the children in his arms, put his hands on them and blessed them.—"My righteousness draws near speedily, my salvation is on the way, and my arm will bring justice to the nations."

Isa. 53:1; 59:16; 63:5; Deut. 33:27; Pss. 77:14-15; 98:1; Isa. 40:10-11; Mark 9:36-37; 10:16; Isa. 51:5.

oct/25

"Blessed is the man whom God corrects; so do not despise the discipline of the Almighty. For he wounds, but he also binds up; he injures, but his hands also heal."—My son, do not despise the Lord's discipline and do not resent his rebuke, because the Lord disciplines those he loves, as a father the son he delights in. . . . Stern discipline awaits him who leaves the path; he who hates correction will die. . . . Do not withhold discipline from a child; if you punish him with a rod, he will not die.—Endure hardship as discipline; God is treating you as sons. For what son is not disciplined by his father? . . . We have all had human fathers who disciplined us and we respected them for it. . . . God disciplines us for our good, that we may share in his holiness.—"Therefore say to them, 'This is the nation that has not obeyed the Lord its God or responded to correction.'" . . . Correct me, O Lord, but only with justice—not in your anger, lest you reduce me to nothing. . . . "I will discipline you but only with justice; I will not let you go entirely unpunished."—All Scripture is God-breathed and is useful for teaching, rebuking, correcting and training in righteousness, so that the man of God may be thoroughly equipped for every good work.

Job 5:17-18; Prov. 3:11-12; 15:10; 23:13; Heb. 12:7, 9-10; Jer. 7:28; 10:24; 30:11; 2 Tim. 3:16-17.

oct/26

"Why do you worry about clothes? See how the lilies of the field grow. . . . If that is how God clothes the grass of the field, which is here today and tomorrow is thrown into the fire, will he not much more clothe you, O you of little faith! . . . Seek first his kingdom and his righteousness, and all these things will be given to you as well."
—Now to him who is able to do immeasurably more than we ask or imagine, according to his power that is at work in us.—You have come to Mount Zion, to the heavenly Jerusalem, the city of the living God. You have come to thousands upon thousands of angels in joyful assembly, to the church of the firstborn, whose names are written in heaven.—Since we have now been justified by his blood, how much more shall we be saved from God's wrath through him! For if, when we were God's enemies, we were reconciled to him through the death of his Son, how much more, having been reconciled, shall we be saved through his life! . . . Where sin increased, grace increased all the more.—Both high and low among men, . . . feast on the abundance of your house; you give them drink from your river of delights. . . . I will bless her with abundant provisions; her poor will I satisfy with food.

Matt. 6:28, 30, 33; Eph. 3:20; Heb. 12:22-23; Rom. 5:9-10, 20; Pss. 36:7-8; 132:15.

oct/27

"Be not afraid, Abram! I am your shield, your very great reward."—"May the Lord repay you for what you have done. May you be richly rewarded by the Lord, the God of Israel, under whose wings you have come to take refuge."—The ordinances of the Lord are sure and altogether righteous. . . . By them is your servant warned; in keeping them there is great reward. . . . Men will say, "Surely the righteous still are rewarded; surely there is a God who judges the earth."—He who sows righteousness reaps a sure reward.—"Rejoice and be glad, because great is your reward in heaven." . . . "Be careful not to do your 'acts of righteousness' before men, to be seen by them. If you do, you will have no reward from your Father in heaven." . . . "If anyone gives a cup of cold water to one of these little ones because he is my disciple, I tell you the truth, he will certainly not lose his reward."—"Love your enemies, do good to them, and lend to them without expecting to get anything back. Then your reward will be great, and you will be sons of the Most High, because he is kind to the ungrateful and wicked."—"Behold, I am coming soon! My reward is with me, and I will give to everyone according to what he has done."

Gen. 15:1; Ruth 2:12; Pss. 19:9, 11; 58:11; Prov. 11:18; Matt. 5:12; 6:1; 10:42; Luke 6:35; Rev. 22:12.

oct /28

No man has ever seen God, but God the only Son, who is at the Father's side, has made him known. The Word became flesh and lived for a while among us. We have seen his glory of the one and only Son, who came from the Father, full of grace and truth.—Beyond all question, the mystery of godliness is great: [God] appeared in a body, was vindicated by the Spirit, was seen by angels, was preached among the nations, was believed on in the world, was taken up in glory. —Philip said, "Lord, show us the Father and that will be enough for us." Jesus answered, "Don't you know me, Philip, even after I have been among you for such a long time? Anyone who has seen me has seen the Father. How can you say, 'Show us the Father'?"—The Son is the radiance of God's glory and the exact representation of his being, sustaining all things by his powerful word.—Those God foreknew he also predestined to be conformed to the likeness of his Son, that he might be the firstborn among many brothers. — When God, who set me apart from birth and called me by his grace, was pleased to reveal his Son in me so that I might preach him among the Gentiles.—"No mind has conceived what God has prepared for those who love him, but God has revealed it to us by his Spirit."

John 1:18, 14; 1 Tim. 3:16; John 14:8-9; Heb. 1:3; Rom. 8:29; Gal. 1:15-16; 1 Cor. 2:9-10.

oct/29

He will be called Wonderful Counselor, Mighty God. . . . The Lord Almighty, wonderful in counsel and magnificent in wisdom. . . . In perfect faithfulness you have done marvelous things, things planned long ago.—"Listen to this, Job; stop and consider God's wonders. . . . Do you know how the clouds hang poised, those wonders of him who is perfect in knowledge." . . . "I spoke of things I did not understand, things too wonderful for me."— "Your love for me was wonderful, more wonderful than that of women."—You are great and do marvelous deeds; you alone are God. . . . What god is so great as our God? You are the God who performs miracles. . . . The heavens praise your wonders, O Lord. . . . They saw the works of the Lord, his wonderful things in the deep. . . . Open my eyes that I may see wonderful things in your law. . . . [Give thanks] to him who alone does great wonders, His love endures forever. . . . Such knowledge is too wonderful for me, too lofty for me to attain. . . . I praise you because I am fearfully and wonderfully made; your works are wonderful, I know that full well.—"Praise the name of the Lord your God, who has worked wonders for you."

Isa. 9:6; 28:29; 25:1; Job 37:14, 16; 42:3; 2 Sam. 1:26; Pss. 86:10; 77:13; 89:5; 107:24; 119:18; 136:4; 139:6, 14; Joel 2:26.

oct /30

May the God who gives endurance and encouragement give you a spirit of unity among yourselves as you follow Christ Jesus, so that with one heart and mouth you may glorify the God and Father of our Lord Jesus Christ.—The shepherds returned, glorifying and praising God for all the things they had heard and seen.—"Father, glorify your name." Then a voice came from heaven, "I have glorified it, and will glorify it again." . . . Jesus said, "Now is the Son of Man glorified and God is glorified in him. If God is glorified in him, the God will glorify the Son in himself, and will glorify him at once." . . . [The Spirit of truth] "will bring glory to me by taking from what is mine and making it known to you." . . . Jesus looked toward heaven and prayed: "Father, the time has come. Glorify your Son, that your Son may glorify you. . . . I have brought you glory on the earth by completing the work you gave me to do." —Acclaim the Lord's majesty. . . . Give glory to the Lord. From the ends of the earth we hear singing: "Glory to the Righteous One."—"Among those who approach me I will show myself holy; in the sight of all the people I will be honored." —Whether you eat or drink or whatever you do, do it all for the glory of God.

Rom. 15:5-6; Luke 2:20; John 12:28; 13:31-32; 16:14; 17:1, 4; Isa. 24:14-16; Lev. 10:3; 1 Cor. 10:31.

oct/31

Blessed are all who take refuge in him. . . . Blessed are they who dwell in your house; they are ever praising you. . . . Blessed are they who maintain justice, who constantly do what is right. . . . Blessed are they who keep his statutes and seek him with all their heart.—"Now then, my sons, listen to me: Blessed are those who keep my ways."—Blessed are all who wait for him!—"Blessed are those who are invited to the wedding supper of the Lamb!"—"Blessed are the poor in spirit, for theirs is the kingdom of heaven. Blessed are those who mourn, for they will be comforted. Blessed are the meek, for they will inherit the earth. Blessed are those who hunger and thirst after righteousness, for they will be filled. Blessed are the merciful, for they will be shown mercy. Blessed are the pure in heart, for they will see God. Blessed are the peacemakers, for they will be called sons of God. Blessed are those who are persecuted because of righteousness, for theirs is the kingdom of heaven."—"Behold, I am coming soon! Blessed is he who keeps the words of the prophecy in this book."—"Blessed are they whose transgressions are forgiven, whose sins have been covered. Blessed is the man whose sin the Lord will never count against him."

Pss. 2:12; 84:4; 106:3; 119:2; Prov. 8:32; Isa. 30:18; Rev. 19:9; Matt. 5:3-10; Rev. 22:7; Rom. 4:7-8.

nov/1

Do not cast me away when I am old; do not forsake me when my strength is gone. . . . Even when I am old and gray, do not forsake me, O God, till I declare your power to the next generation, your might to all who are to come.—Even to your old age and gray hairs I am he, and I am he who will sustain you. I have made you and I will carry you; I will sustain you and I will rescue you.—I was young and now I am old, yet I have never seen the righteous forsaken or his children begging bread. . . . [The righteous] will still bear fruit in old age, they will stay fresh and green, proclaiming, "The Lord is upright; he is my Rock, and there is no wickedness in him." —"Blessed is the man whom God corrects; . . . you will come to the grave in full vigor, like sheaves gathered in season.—Samuel said to all Israel, . . . "As for me, I am old and gray, and my sons are here with you. I have been your leader from my youth until this day."—I then, as Paul—an old man and now also a prisoner of Christ Jesus—I appeal to you for my son Onesimus who became my son while I was in chains.—Teach the older men to be temperate, worthy of respect, self-controlled, and sound in faith, in love and in endurance. . . . Teach the older women to be reverent in the way they live.

Ps. 71:9, 18; Isa. 46:4; Pss. 37:25; 92:14-15; Job 5:17, 26; 1 Sam. 12:1-2; Philem. 9-10; Titus 2:2-3.

Worship him who made the heavens,
the earth, the sea
and the springs of water.

Bob Taylor

nov /2

The Lord will write in the register of the peoples: "This one was born in Zion." As they make music they will sing, "All my fountains are in you."—"Fear God and give him glory, because the hour of his judgment has come. Worship him who made the heavens, the earth, the sea and springs of water."—[O God,] it was you who opened up springs and streams; you dried up the ever flowing rivers. . . . He makes springs pour water into ravines; it flows between the mountains. . . . He waters the mountains from his upper chambers. . . . He turned the desert into pools of water, and the parched ground into flowing springs.—"If a man is thirsty, let him come to me and drink. Whoever believes in me, as the Scripture has said, streams of living water will flow from within him. By this he meant the Spirit." . . . "Whoever drinks the water I give him will never thirst. Indeed the water I give him will become in him a spring of water welling up to eternal life."—The teaching of the wise is a fountain of life, turning a man from the snares of death. . . . Understanding is a fountain of life to those who have it, but folly brings punishment to fools. . . . Like a muddied spring or a polluted well is a righteous man who gives way to the wicked.

Ps. 87:6-7; Rev. 14:7; Pss. 74:15; 104:10, 13; 107:35; John 7:37-39; 4:14; Prov. 13:14; 16:22; 25:26.

nov/3

"Who can forgive sins but God alone?" . . .
"You may know that the Son of Man has authority
on earth to forgive sins."—"God exalted him to
his own right hand as Prince and Savior that he
might give repentance and forgiveness of
sins."—"The Lord our God is merciful and
forgiving, even though we have rebelled against
him. . . . O Lord, forgive!"—If you, O Lord, kept
a record of sins, O Lord, who could stand? But
with you there is forgiveness; therefore you are
feared.—"Therefore, I tell you, her many sins
have been forgiven—for she loved much. But he
who has been forgiven little loves little." Then
Jesus said to her, "Your sins are forgiven." . . .
Jesus said, "Father, forgive them, for they do not
know what they are doing."—"O Lord God, hear
the supplications of your servant and of your
people Israel, when they pray. . . . Hear in
heaven, your dwelling place, and when you hear,
forgive."—If we confess our sins, he is faithful
and just and will forgive us our sins and purify us
from all unrighteousness.—In him we have
redemption through his blood, the forgiveness of
sins, in accordance with the riches of God's grace
that he lavished on us with all wisdom and
understanding.

Mark 2:7, 10; Acts 5:31; Dan. 9:9, 19; Ps. 130:3-4;
Luke 7:47-48; 23:34; 1 Kings 8:30; 1 John 1:9; Eph.
1:7-8.

nov /4

"If he remains silent, who can condemn him? If he hides his face, who can see him?"—"But whoever listens to me will live in safety and be at ease, without fear of harm." . . . Better a dry crust with peace and quiet, than a house full of feasting, with strife.—Better one handful with tranquility than two handfuls with toil and chasing after the wind.—This is what the Sovereign Lord, the Holy One of Israel, says, "In repentance and rest is your salvation, in quietness and trust is your strength." . . . The fruit of righteousness will be peace; the effect of righteousness will be quietness and confidence forever. My people will live in peaceful dwelling places, in secure homes, in undisturbed places of rest.—It is good to wait quietly for the salvation of the Lord. . . . Let him sit alone in silence.—I urge, then, first of all, that requests, prayers, and intercessions and thanksgiving be made for everyone—for kings and all those in authority, that we may live peaceful and quiet lives in all godliness and holiness. This is good and pleases God our Savior.—Your beauty should not come from outward adornment, . . . Instead, it should be that of your inner self, the unfading beauty of a gentle and quiet spirit, which is of great worth in God's sight.

Job 34:29; Prov. 1:33; 17:1; Eccl. 4:6; Isa. 30:15; 32:17-18; Lam. 3:26, 28; 1 Tim. 2:1-3; 1 Peter 3:3-4.

nov /5

His name is the Word of God.—The Word was God.—The living and enduring Word of God.—You are near, O Lord, and all your commands are true.—The one and only Son, . . . full of grace and truth.—"I am . . . the Truth"—These commands are a lamp, this teaching is a light.—In him was life, and that life was the light of the world. . . . "I am the Light of the world. Whoever follows me will never walk in darkness, but will have the light of life."—As you hold out the Word of life.—He will be called Wonderful.—When . . . the teachers of the law saw the wonderful things he did and the children shouting in the temple area, "Hosanna to the Son of David," they were indignant.—The Lord reigns forever; he has established his throne for judgment. "The word of the Lord stands forever."—He sent forth his word and healed them; he rescued them from the grave.—People brought to him all who were ill with various diseases, those suffering severe pain, the demon-possessed, the epileptics and the paralytics, and he healed them.—"From the beginning God chose you to be saved through the sanctifying work of the Spirit."

Rev. 19:13; John 1:1; 1 Peter 1:23; Ps. 119:151; John 1:14; 14:6; Prov. 6:23; John 1:4; 8:12; Phil. 2:16; Isa. 9:6; Matt. 21:15; Ps. 9:7; 1 Peter 1:25; Ps. 107:20; Matt. 4:24; 2 Thess. 2:13.

nov /6

"The God of Israel has separated you . . . and brought you near himself to do the work at the Lord's tabernacle and to stand before the community and minister to them."—What other nation is so great as to have their gods near them the way the Lord our God is near to us whenever we pray to him?—He who vindicates me is near. Who then will bring charges against me? . . . Seek the Lord while he may be found; call on him while he is near. . . . You who are far away, hear what I have done; you who are near acknowledge my power!—The Lord is close to the brokenhearted and saves those who are crushed in spirit. . . . We give thanks to you, O God, we give thanks, for your Name is near; men tell of your wonderful deeds. . . . Those who devise wicked schemes are near, but they are far from your law. Yet you are near, O Lord, and all your commands are true. . . . He has raised up for his people a horn, the praise of all his saints, of Israel, the people close to his heart.—Remember that at that time you were separate from Christ, . . . without hope and without God in the world. But now in Christ Jesus you who once were far away have been brought near through the blood of Christ.—"The kingdom of God is near you."

Num. 16:9-20; Deut. 4:6; Isa. 50:8; 55:6; 33:13; Ps. 34:18; 75:1; 119:150-151; 148:14; Eph. 2:12-13; Luke 10:9.

nov /7

"As a mother comforts her child, so will I comfort you."—His name is the Lord—and rejoice before him. A father to the fatherless, a defender of widows, is God in his holy dwelling.—"Your Maker is your husband—the Lord Almighty is his name."—A friend loves at all times, and a brother is born for adversity. —"Whoever does God's will is my brother and sister and mother."—There is a friend who sticks closer than a brother.—"You are my friends if you do what I command."—This is what the Lord Almighty says, "Whoever touches you touches the apple of his eye."—As the mountains surround Jerusalem, so the Lord surrounds his people, both now and forevermore.—"How often I have longed to gather your children together, as a hen gathers her chicks under her wings, but you were not willing."—"I will come like a thief, and you will not know at what time I will come to you." . . . "Behold, I come like a thief!"—"I am the bread of life. He who comes to me will never go hungry, and he who believes in me will never be thirsty." . . . "I am the living bread that came down from heaven." . . . "I am the good shepherd. The good shepherd lays down his life for the sheep."

Isa. 66:13; Ps. 68:4-5; Isa. 54:5; Prov. 17:17; Mark 3:35; Prov. 18:24; John 15:14; Zech. 2:8; Ps. 125:2; Matt. 23:37; Rev. 3:3; 16:15; John 6:35, 51; 10:11.

nov/8

"As long as the earth endures, seedtime and harvest . . . will never cease."—"In that day the glory of Jacob will fade; the fat of his body will waste away. It will be as when a reaper gathers the standing grain and harvests the grain with his arm—as when a man gleans heads of grain." —[Jesus] said to his disciples, "The harvest is plentiful but the workers few. Ask the Lord of the harvest, therefore, to send out workers into his harvest field."—"Let us fear the Lord our God, who gives fall and spring rains in season, who assures us of the regular weeks of harvest." . . . "The harvest is past, the summer has ended, and we are not saved."—Those who sow in tears will reap with songs of joy. He who goes out weeping, carrying his seed to sow, will return with songs of joy, carrying sheaves with him.—The people walking in darkness have seen a great light; . . . they rejoice before you as people rejoice at the harvest. . . . You have forgotten the God your Savior; . . . Therefore, though you set out the finest plants and plant imported vines, . . . the harvest will be as nothing in the day of disease and incurable pain.—Remember this: Whoever sows sparingly will also reap sparingly, and whoever sows generously will also reap generously.

Gen. 8:22; Isa. 17:4-5; Matt. 9:37-38; Jer. 5:24; 8:20; Ps. 126:5-6; Isa. 9:2-3; 17:10-11; 2 Cor. 9:6.

nov /9

All spoke well of him and were amazed at the gracious words that came from his lips.—"The words I have spoken to you are spirit and they are life." . . . "Lord, to whom shall we go? You have the words of eternal life." . . . Jesus said, "I gave them the words you gave me and they accepted them."—So the Lord spoke good and comforting words to the angel who talked with me.—The words of a man's mouth are deep waters. . . . "Lay hold of my words with all your heart; keep my commands and live." My son, pay attention to what I say; listen closely to my words. Do not let them out of your sight, keep them within your heart; for they are life to those who find them and health to a man's whole body.—The Teacher searched to find just the right words, and what he wrote was upright and true. The words of the wise are like goads, their collected sayings like firmly embedded nails—given by one Shepherd. Be warned, my son, of anything in addition to them.—"There is a judge for the one who rejects me and does not accept my words; that very word which I spoke will condemn him at the last day." . . . "If you remain in me and my words remain in you, ask whatever you wish, and it will be given you."

Luke 4:22; John 6:63, 68; 17:8; Zech. 1:13; Prov. 18:4; 4:4, 20-22; Eccl. 12:10-12; John 12:48; 15:7.

nov /10

"The Holy Spirit, whom the Father will send in my name, will teach you all things, and will remind you of everything I have said to you."
—May my tongue cling to the roof of my mouth if I do not remember you.—"Remember to extol his work, which men have praised in song."—"Remember the Lord, who is great and awesome."—You come to the help of those who gladly do right, and remember your ways.—Dear friends, remember what the apostles of our Lord Jesus Christ foretold. They said to you, "In the last times there will be scoffers who will follow their own ungodly desires."—Remember Jesus Christ, raised from the dead, descended from David. This is my gospel, for which I am suffering even to the point of being chained like a criminal.—The Lord Jesus, on the night he was betrayed, took bread, and when he had given thanks, he broke it and said, "This is my body, which is for you: do this in remembrance of me." In the same way, after supper he took the cup, saying, "This cup is the new covenant in my blood: do this, whenever you drink it, in remembrance of me."—I will always remind you of these things, even though you know them and are firmly established in the truth you now have. Remember these things.

John 14:26; Ps. 137:6; Job 36:24; Neh. 4:14; Isa. 64:5; Jude 17:18; 2 Tim. 2:8-9; 1 Cor. 11:23-25; 2 Peter 1:12, 15.

nov/11

"Have them make a sanctuary for me, and I will dwell among them. Make this tabernacle and all its furnishings exactly like the pattern I will show you." . . . So Moses finished the work. Then the cloud covered the Tent of Meeting, and the glory of the Lord filled the tabernacle.—I love the house where you live, O Lord, the place where your glory dwells. . . . If you make the Most High your dwelling—even the Lord, who is my refuge—then no harm will befall you, no disaster will come near your tent.—"Their leaves will not wither, nor will their fruit fail . . . because the water from the sanctuary flows to them."—A high priest, who sat down at the right hand of the Majesty in heaven, and who serves in the sanctuary, the true tabernacle set up by the Lord, not by man. . . . Now the first covenant had regulations for worship and also an earthly sanctuary. . . . When Christ came as high priest of the good things that are already here, he went through the greater and more perfect tabernacle that is not man-made. . . . Christ did not enter a man-made sanctuary that was only a copy of the true one.—"Him who overcomes I will make a pillar in the temple of my God." . . . I did not see a temple in the city, because the Lord God Almighty and the Lamb are its temple.

Exod. 25:8-9; 40:33-34; Pss. 26:8; 91:9-10; Ezek. 47:12; Heb. 8:1-2; 9:1, 11, 24; Rev. 3:12; 21:22.

nov/12

"I am with you and will watch over you wherever you go. . . . I will not leave you until I have done what I have promised you."—"Do not be afraid or terrified because of them, for the Lord your God goes with you; he will never leave you nor forsake you. . . . The Lord himself goes before you and he will be with you; he will never leave or forsake you. Do not be afraid; do not be discouraged."—They all ate the same spiritual food and drank the same spiritual drink; for they drank from the spiritual rock that accompanied them, and that rock was Christ.—Do not reject me or forsake me, O God my Savior. Though my father and mother forsake me, the Lord will receive me.—"Surely I will be with you always, to the very end of the age."—Then the disciples went out and preached everywhere, and the Lord worked with them and confirmed his word by the signs that accompanied it.—God has said, "Never will I leave you: never will I forsake you." So we say with confidence, "The Lord is my helper; I will not be afraid. What can man do to me?"—"You are a forgiving God, gracious and compassionate, slow to anger, and abounding in love. Therefore you did not desert them, even when they cast for themselves an image of a calf and said, "This is your god."

Gen. 28:15; Deut. 31:6, 8; 1 Cor. 10:3-4; Ps. 27:9-10; Matt. 28:20; Mark 16:20; Heb. 13:5-6; Neh. 9:17-18.

nov/13

Let the wicked forsake his way and the evil man his thoughts. . . . "For my thoughts are not your thoughts, neither are your ways my ways," declares the Lord. "As the heavens are higher than the earth, so are my ways higher than your ways and my thoughts than your thoughts."—How great are your works, O Lord, how profound your thoughts!—How precious to me are your thoughts, O God! How vast is the sum of them! Were I to count them, they would outnumber the grains of sand.—Simeon . . . said to Mary, "This child is destined to cause the falling and rising of many in Israel, and to be a sign that will be spoken against, so that the thoughts of many hearts will be revealed."—The word of God is living and active. . . . It judges the thoughts and attitudes of the heart.—Knowing their thoughts, Jesus said, "Why do you entertain evil thoughts in your hearts?"—"The Lord knows that the thoughts of the wise are futile."—If you had responded to my rebuke, I would have poured out my heart to you and made my thoughts known to you.—Search me, O God, and know my heart; test me and know my anxious thoughts. See if there is any offensive way in me, and lead me in the way everlasting.

Isa. 55:7-9; Pss. 92:5; 139:17-18; Luke 2:34-35; Heb. 4:12; Matt. 9:4; 1 Cor. 3:20; Prov. 1:23; Ps. 139:23-24.

nov/14

"Why do you discourage the Israelites from going over into the land the Lord has given them?"—Consider him who endured such opposition from sinful men, so that you will not grow weary and lose heart.—He will not falter or be discouraged till he establishes justice on earth.—I ask you, therefore, not to be discouraged because of my sufferings for you, which are your glory.—Therefore we do not lose heart. Though outwardly we are wasting away, yet inwardly we are being renewed day by day.—Jesus told his disciples a parable to show them that they should always pray and not give up.—They approach and come forward; each helps the other and says to his brother, "Be strong!" The craftsman encourages the goldsmith, and he who smooths with the hammer spurs on him who strikes the anvil.—As the time approached for him to be taken up to heaven, Jesus resolutely set out for Jerusalem.—"I know your deeds, your hard work and your perseverance. . . . You have persevered and have endured hardship for my name, and have not grown weary."—Let us fix our eyes on Jesus, . . . who for the joy set before him endured the cross, scorning its shame, and sat down at the right hand of the throne of God.

Num. 32:7; Heb. 12:3; Isa. 42:4; Eph. 3:13; 2 Cor. 4:16; Luke 18:1; Isa. 41:5-7; Luke 9:51; Rev. 2:2-3; Heb. 12:2.

nov/15

Lift up your heads, O you gates; be lifted up, you ancient doors, that the King of glory may come in. Who is this King of glory? The Lord strong and mighty; the Lord mighty in battle.—"Blessed is the man who listens to me, watching daily at my doors, waiting at my doorway."—Go, my people, enter your rooms, and shut the doors behind you.—On the evening of that first day of the week, when the disciples were together, with the doors locked for fear of the Jews, Jesus came and stood among them. . . . A week later his disciples were in the house again, and Thomas was with them. Though the doors were locked, Jesus came and stood among them.—Set a guard over my mouth, O Lord; keep watch over the door of my lips.—Suddenly there was such a violent earthquake that the foundations of the prison were shaken. At once all the prison doors flew open, and everybody's chains came loose.—I went to Troas to preach the gospel of Christ and found that the Lord had opened a door for me.—The Judge is standing at the door!—"I have placed before you an open door that no one can shut. . . . I stand at the door and knock. If anyone hears my voice and opens the door, I will go in and eat with him, and he with me."

Ps. 24:7-8; Prov. 8:34; Isa. 26:20; John 20:19, 26; Ps. 141:3; Acts 16:26; 2 Cor. 2:12; James 5:9; Rev. 3:8, 20.

nov/16

I know what it is to be in need, and I know what it is to have plenty. I have learned the secret of being content in any and every situation. . . . My God will meet all your needs according to his glorious riches in Christ Jesus.—Let us then approach the throne of grace with confidence, so that we may receive mercy and find grace to help us in our time of need. . . . You need someone to teach you the elementary truths of God's word all over again. You need milk, not solid food!—Jesus said, "It is not the healthy who need a doctor, but the sick." . . . "Your Father knows what you need before you ask him." . . . "Do not worry, saying, 'What shall we eat?' or 'What shall we drink? . . . Your Father knows that you need them. But seek his kingdom, . . . and all these things will be given to you as well."—[Jesus] welcomed the crowds and spoke to them about the kingdom of God, and healed those who needed healing.—If there is a poor man among your brothers, . . . do not be hardhearted or tight-fisted toward your poor brother. Rather be open handed and freely lend him whatever he needs.—The throne of God and of the Lamb will be in the city. There will be no more night. They will not need the light of a lamp or the light of the sun, for the Lord God will give them light.

Phil. 4:12, 19; Heb. 4:16; 5:12; Matt. 9:12; 6:8, 31-33; Luke 9:11; Deut. 15:7-8; Rev. 22:3, 5.

nov/17

[The Lord] said unto me, "You are my Son; today I have become your Father."—The angel said to Mary, ". . . You will be with child and give birth to a son, and you are to give him the name Jesus. He will be great and will be called the Son of the Most High."—"The virgin will be with child and will give birth to a son, and call him Immanuel."—"[Mary] will give birth to a son, and you are to give him the name Jesus, because he will save his people from their sins." All this took place to fulfill what the Lord had said, . . . "The virgin will be with child and will give birth to a son, and they will call him Immanuel"—which means, "God with us."—God said to [Abraham], ". . . Listen to whatever Sarah tells you, because it is through Isaac that your offspring will be reckoned."—He who had received the promises was about to sacrifice his one and only son, even though God had said to him, "It is through Isaac that your offspring will be reckoned."—He had done no violence, nor was any deceit in his mouth.—Christ suffered for you, leaving you an example, that you should follow his steps. "He committed no sin, and no deceit was found in his mouth."

Ps. 2:7; Luke 1:30-32; Isa. 7:14; Matt. 1:21-23; Gen. 21:12; Heb. 11:18; Isa. 53:9; 1 Peter 2:21.

nov/18

The word of God is living and active. Sharper than any double-edged sword, it penetrates even to dividing soul and spirit, joints and marrow; it judges the thoughts and attitudes of the heart.—The sword of the Spirit, which is the word of God.—"The seed is the word of God."—You have been born again, not of perishable seed, but of imperishable, through the living and enduring word of God.—His word is in my heart like a burning fire, shut up in my bones. I am weary of holding it in; indeed, I cannot.—These commands are a lamp, this teaching is a light.—Your word is a lamp to my feet and a light for my path.—We have the word of the prophets made more certain, and you will do well to pay attention to it, as to a light shining in a dark place, until the day dawns and the morning star rises in your hearts.—The words of the Lord are flawless, like silver refined in a furnace of clay purified seven times.—"You are already clean because of the word I have spoken unto you."—Your promises have been thoroughly tested, and your servant loves them. . . . How sweet are your promises to my taste, sweeter than honey to my mouth.—You are strong, and the word of God lives in you, and you have overcome the evil one.

Heb. 4:12; Eph. 6:17; Luke 8:11; 1 Peter 1:23; Jer. 20:9; Prov. 6:23; Ps. 119:105; 2 Peter 1:19; Ps. 12:6; John 15:3; Pss. 119:140, 103; 1 John 2:14.

nov/19

Carrying his own cross, he went out to the Place of the Skull. . . . Here they crucified him, and with him two others—one on each side and Jesus in the middle. Pilate had a notice prepared and fastened to the cross. It read, JESUS OF NAZARETH, THE KING OF THE JEWS.—Being found in appearance as a man, he humbled himself and became obedient to death—even death on a cross!—He forgave us all our sins, having canceled the written code, with its regulations, that was against us and that stood opposed to us; he took it away, nailing it to the cross.—Who for the joy set before him endured the cross, scorning its shame.—Those who want to make a good impression outwardly are trying to compel you to be circumcised. The only reason they do this is to avoid being persecuted for the cross of Christ. . . . May I never boast except in the cross of our Lord Jesus Christ, through which the world has been crucified to me, and I to the world.—Christ did not send me to baptize, but to preach the gospel—not with words of human wisdom, lest the cross of Christ be emptied of its power. For the message of the cross is foolishness to those who are perishing, but to us who are being saved it is the power of God.—"Anyone who does not take his cross and follow me is not worthy of me."

John 19:17-19; Phil. 2:8; Col. 2:13-14; Heb. 12:2; Gal. 6:12, 14; 1 Cor. 1:17-18; Matt. 10:38.

nov/20

[Jesus asked Peter,] "Who do you say I am?"
Simon Peter answered, "You are the Christ, the
Son of the living God." Jesus replied, . . . "On
this rock I will build my church, and the gates of
Hades will not overcome it."—"Be shepherds of
the church of God, which he bought with his own
blood."—Christ loved the church and gave
himself up for her to make her holy, cleansing her
by washing with water through the word, and to
present her to himself as a radiant church, without
stain or wrinkle or any other blemish, but holy
and blameless. . . . Christ is the head of the
church, his body, of which he is the Savior.—He
is the head of the body, the church; he is the
beginning and the firstborn from among the dead,
so that in everything he might have the
supremacy. . . . I rejoice in what was suffered for
you, and I fill up in my flesh what is still lacking in
regard to Christ's afflictions, for the sake of his
body, which is the church.—After all, no one ever
hated his own body, but he feeds and cares for it,
just as Christ does the church—for we are
members of his body. "For this reason a man will
leave his father and mother and will be united to
his wife, and the two will become one flesh." This
is a profound mystery—but I am talking about
Christ and the church.

Matt. 16:15-16, 18; Acts 20:28; Eph. 5:25-27, 23;
Col. 1:18, 24; Eph. 5:29-32.

nov/21

The eternal God.—Christ Jesus, . . . the King eternal.—The eternal Spirit.—"I am God Almighty."—The Son . . . sustaining all things by his powerful word.—"You will receive power when the Holy Spirit comes on you."—"You are the God who sees me."—[Jesus] knew all men. . . . he knew what was in a man.—The Spirit searches all things, even the deep things of God.—The gift of God is eternal life.—[Jesus said,] "I give them eternal life, and they shall never perish."—The one who sows to please the Spirit, from the Spirit will reap eternal life.—By his power God raised the Lord from the dead.—"Destroy this temple, and I will raise it again in three days." . . . The temple he had spoken of was his body.—The Spirit of him who raised Jesus from the dead is living in you, he who raised Christ from the dead will also give life to your mortal bodies through his Spirit, who lives in you.—May the grace of the Lord Jesus Christ, and the love of God, and the fellowship of the Holy Spirit be with you all.—"Am I only a God nearby," . . . "and not a God far away? Can anyone hide in secret places, so that I cannot see him?"

Rom. 16:26; 1 Tim. 1:16-17; Heb. 9:14; Gen. 17:1; Heb. 1:3; Acts 1:8; Gen. 16:13; John 2:24-25; 1 Cor. 2:10; Rom. 6:23; John 10:28; Gal. 6:8; 1 Cor. 6:14; John 2:19, 21; Rom. 8:11; 2 Cor. 13:14; Jer. 23:23-24.

nov/22

The Lord was with Joseph and he prospered, and he lived in the house of his Egyptian master. When his master saw the Lord was with him and that the Lord gave him success in everything he did, Joseph found favor in his eyes and became his attendant.—Carefully follow the terms of this covenant, so that you may prosper in everything you do.—Blessed is the man . . . [whose] delight is in the law of the Lord. . . . He is like a tree planted by streams of water, . . . and whose leaf does not wither. Whatever he does prospers.—Yet it was the Lord's will to crush him and cause him to suffer, and though the Lord makes his life a guilt offering, he will see his offspring and prolong his days, and the will of the Lord will prosper in his hand.—"Your beginnings will seem humble, so prosperous will your future be."—He who conceals his sins does not prosper, but whoever confesses and renounces them finds mercy.—The shepherds are senseless and do not inquire of the Lord; so they do not prosper and all their flock is scattered.—"Observe what the Lord your God requires: Walk in his ways, and keep his decrees and commands, his laws and requirements, as written in the Law of Moses, so that you may prosper in all you do and wherever you go.

Gen. 39:2-4; Deut. 29:9; Ps. 1:1-3; Isa. 53:10; Job 8:7; Prov. 28:13; Jer. 10:21; 1 Kings 2:3.

nov /23

"The younger son got together all he had, set off for a distant country and there squandered his wealth in wild living." . . . "When he came to his senses he said, . . . 'I will set out and go back to my father.' . . . So he got up and went to his father. But while he was still a long way off, his father saw him and was filled with compassion for him; He ran to his son, threw his arms around him and kissed him. . . . ['He] was dead and is alive again; he was lost and is found.'"—That is what some of you were. But you were washed, you were sanctified, you were justified in the name of the Lord Jesus Christ and by the Spirit of our God. You were dead in your transgressions and sins, in which you used to live when you followed the ways of this world and of the ruler of the kingdom of the air, the spirit who is now at work in those who are disobedient. All of us also lived among them at one time, gratifying the cravings of our sinful nature and following its desires and thoughts. Like the rest, we were by nature objects of wrath. But because of his great love for us, God, who is rich in mercy, made us alive with Christ when we were dead in transgressions—it is by grace you have been saved.—This is love: not that we loved God, but that he loved us and sent his son as an atoning sacrifice for our sins.

Luke 15:13, 17-20, 32; 1 Cor. 6:11; Eph. 2:1-5; 1 John 4:10.

nov/24

"No one ever spoke the way this man does."—All spoke well of him and were amazed at the gracious words that came from his lips.—The people were amazed at his teaching, because he taught them as one who had authority, not as teachers of the law.—"I tell you the truth, we speak of what we know, and we testify to what we have seen, but still you people do not accept our testimony. I have spoken to you of earthly things and you do not believe; how then will you believe if I speak of heavenly things?" . . . "The words I have spoken to you are spirit and they are life. Yet there are some of you who do not believe." . . . "I do nothing on my own but speak just what the Father has taught me."—You are the most excellent of men and your lips have been anointed with grace, since God has blessed you forever.— In your teaching show integrity, seriousness, and soundness of speech that cannot be condemned, so that those who oppose you may be ashamed because they have nothing bad to say about us.—"Men will have to give account on the day of judgment for every careless word they have spoken. For by your words you will be acquitted, and by your words you will be condemned."

John 7:46; Luke 4:22; Mark 1:22; John 3:11-12; 6:63-64; 8:28; Ps. 45:2; Titus 2:7-8; Matt. 12:36-37.

nov /25

"Remain in me, and I will remain in you. No branch can bear fruit by itself; it must remain in the vine. Neither can you bear fruit unless you remain in me. . . . If a man remains in me and I in him, he will bear much fruit; apart from me, you can do nothing."—We are the temple of the living God. As God has said: "I will live with them and walk among them, and I will be their God, and they will be my people." "Therefore come out from them and be separate."—"Now the dwelling of God is with men, and he will live with them. They will be his people, and God himself will be with them and be their God. He will wipe every tear from their eyes."—I have been crucified with Christ and I no longer live, but Christ lives in me.—You, however, are not controlled by the sinful nature but by the Spirit, if the Spirit of God lives in you. . . . If Christ is in you, your body is dead because of sin, yet your spirit is alive because of righteousness.—"I saw the Spirit come down from heaven as a dove and remain on him."—See that what you have heard from the beginning remains in you. If it does, you also will remain in the Son and in the Father. As for you, the anointing you received from him remains in you. . . . Remain in him. . . . Continue in him.

John 15:4-5; 2 Cor. 6:16-17; Rev. 21:3-4; Gal. 2:20; Rom. 8:9-10; John 1:32; 1 John 2:24, 27-28.

nov /26

"The god who answers by fire—he is God."—For the Lord your God is a consuming fire, a jealous God. . . . The Lord your God is the one who goes across ahead of you like a devouring fire.—Worship God acceptably with reverence and awe, for our God is a consuming fire.—"He will baptize you with the Holy Spirit and with fire."—When the day of Pentecost came, they were all together in one place. . . . They saw what seemed to be tongues of fire that separated and came to rest on each of them. All of them were filled with the Holy Spirit and began to speak in other tongues as the Spirit enabled them.—His word is in my heart like a burning fire, shut up in my bones.—[His work] will be revealed with fire, and the fire will test the quality of each man's work. If what he has built survives, he will receive a reward. If it is burned up, he will suffer loss; he himself will be saved, but only as one escaping through the flames.—I counsel you to buy from me gold refined in the fire.—"When you walk through the fire, you will not be burned, the flames will not set you ablaze. For I am the Lord, your God."—"Were not our hearts burning within us while he talked with us on the road and opened the Scriptures to us?"

1 Kings 18:24; Deut. 4:24; 9:3; Heb. 12:28-29; Matt. 3:11; Acts 2:1, 3-4; Jer. 20:9; 1 Cor. 3:13-15; Rev. 3:18; Isa. 43:2-3; Luke 24:32.

nov /27

The Lord is near to all who call on him, to all who call on him in truth.—Seek the Lord while he may be found; call on him while he is near.—Be joyful always; pray continually; give thanks in the circumstances, for this is God's will for you in Christ Jesus.—The eyes of the Lord are on the righteous and his ears are attentive to their cry. . . . The righteous cry out, and the Lord hears them; he delivers them from all their troubles.—"Be always on the watch, and pray that you may be able to escape all that is about to happen, and that you may be able to stand before the Son of Man."—Let us then approach the throne of grace with confidence, so that we may receive mercy and find grace to help us in time of need.—Come near to God and he will come near to you. . . . The prayer of a righteous man is powerful and effective. Elijah was a man just like us. He prayed earnestly that it would not rain, and it did not rain on the land for three and a half years. Again he prayed, and the heavens gave rain, and the earth produced its crops.—Dear friends, if our hearts do not condemn us, we have confidence before God and receive from him anything we ask, because we obey his commands and do what pleases him.

Ps. 145:18; Isa. 55:6; 1 Thess. 5:16-18; Ps. 34:15, 17; Luke 21:36; Heb. 4:16; James 4:8; 5:16-18; 1 John 3:21-22.

nov/28

"Everything comes from you, and we have given you only what comes from your hand." —Samuel took a stone . . . and named it Ebenezer, saying, "Thus far has the Lord helped us." . . . "Be sure to fear the Lord and serve him faithfully with all your heart; consider what great things he has done for you."—The Lord is my shepherd, I shall lack nothing. . . . The lions may grow weak and hungry, but those who seek the Lord lack no good thing. . . . The land will yield its harvest, and God, our God, will bless us. . . . The Lord God is a sun and shield; the Lord bestows favor and honor; no good thing does he withhold from those whose walk is blameless. —So Abraham called that place, "The Lord will provide." And to this day it is said, "On the mountain of the Lord it will be provided."—"May the Lord bless his land with the precious dew from heaven above and with the deep waters that lie below; with the best the sun brings forth and the finest the moon can yield."—My God will meet all your needs according to his glorious riches in Christ Jesus.—He who did not spare his own Son, but gave him up for us all—how will he not also, along with him, graciously give us all things?

1 Chron. 29:14; 1 Sam. 7:12; 12:24; Pss. 23:1; 34:10; 67:6; 84:11; Gen. 22:14; Deut. 33:13-14; Phil. 4:19; Rom. 8:32.

nov /29

Do not consider it a hardship to set your servant free, because his service to you these six years has been worth twice as much as that of a hired hand. And the Lord your God will bless you in everything you do. . . . All these blessings will come upon you and accompany you if you obey the Lord your God: You will be blessed in the city and in the country. The fruit of your womb will be blessed, and the crops of your land and the young of your livestock—the calves of your herds and the lambs of your flocks. Your basket and your kneading trough will be blessed. You will be blessed when you come in and blessed when you go out.—"As for you, be strong and do not give up, for your work will be rewarded."—Do you see a man skilled in his work? He will serve before kings; he will not serve before obscure men.—We are God's workmanship, created in Christ Jesus to do good works, which God prepared in advance for us to do.—Because Jesus was doing these things on the Sabbath, the Jews persecuted him. Jesus said to them, "My Father is always at his work to this very day, and I, too, am working."—All Scripture is God-breathed and is useful for teaching, rebuking, correcting and training in righteousness, so that the man of God may be thoroughly equipped for every good work.

Deut. 15:18; 28:2-5; 2 Chron. 15:7; Prov. 22:29; Eph. 2:10; John 5:16-17; 2 Tim. 3:16-17.

nov /30

When I am afraid, I will trust in you. In God, whose word I praise, in God I trust; I will not be afraid.—"The Lord your God has given you the land. Go up and take possession of it. . . . Do not be afraid; do not be discouraged."—"I am the Lord, your God, who takes hold of your right hand and says to you, Do not fear; I will help you. Do not be afraid, O worm Jacob, O little Israel, for I myself will help you," declares the Lord.—Have no fear of sudden disaster or of the ruin that overtakes the wicked, for the Lord will be your confidence and will keep your foot from being snared.—A furious squall came up, and the waves broke over the boat, so that it was nearly swamped. Jesus was in the stern, sleeping on a cushion. The disciples woke him and said to him, "Teacher, don't you care if we drown?" He got up, rebuked the wind and said to the waves, "Quiet! Be still!" The wind died down, and it was completely calm. He said to his disciples, "Why are you so afraid? Do you still have no faith?"—"Do not be afraid, little flock, for your Father has been pleased to give you the kingdom."—"Do not be afraid of those who kill the body but cannot kill the soul. . . . Don't be afraid; you are worth more than many sparrows."

Ps. 56:3-4; Deut. 1:21; Isa. 41:13-14; Prov. 3:25-26; Mark 4:37-40; Luke 12:32; Matt. 10:28, 31.

I live by faith in the son of God.

dec/1

Jesus said, "Did I not tell you that if you believed, you would see the glory of God?"—It is by grace you have been saved, through faith—and this not from yourselves, it is the gift of God. —The life I live in the body, I live by faith in the Son of God, who loved me and gave himself for me.—Without faith it is impossible to please God, because anyone who comes to him must believe that he exists and that he rewards those who earnestly seek him. . . . Faith is being sure of what we hope for and certain of what we do not see.—"Whoever believes in him is not condemned, but whoever does not believe stands condemned already because he has not believed in the name of God's one and only Son."— "Everything is possible for him who believes." . . . "I do believe: help me overcome my unbelief!"—Show me your faith without deeds, and I will show you my faith by what I do. . . . You see that [Abraham's] faith and his actions were working together, and his faith was made complete by what he did. . . . "Abraham believed God, and it was credited to him as righteousness," and he was called God's friend.—[Abraham] did not waver through unbelief regarding the promise of God, but was strengthened in his faith and gave glory to God.

John 11:40; Eph. 2:8; Gal. 2:20; Heb. 11:6; 11:1; John 3:18; Mark 9:23-24; James 2:18, 22-23; Rom. 4:20.

dec/2

In my Father's house are many rooms; if it were not so, I would have told you. I am going there to prepare a place for you. And if I go and prepare a place for you, I will come back and take you to be with me that you also may be where I am."—Dear friends, now we are children of God, and what we will be has not yet been made known. But we know that when he appears, we shall be like him, for we shall see him as he is. Everyone who has this hope in him purifies himself, just as he is pure.—The Lord himself will come down from heaven, with a loud command, with the voice of the archangel and with the trumpet call of God, and the dead in Christ will rise first. After that, we who are still alive and are left will be caught up with them in the clouds to meet the Lord in the air. And so we will be with the Lord forever.—"Men of Galilee, . . . why do you stand here looking into the sky? This same Jesus, who has been taken from you into heaven, will come back in the same way as you have seen him go into heaven."—Our citizenship is in heaven. And we eagerly await a Savior from there, the Lord Jesus Christ, who, by the power that enables him to bring everything under his control, will transform our lowly bodies so that they will be like his glorious body.

John 14:2-4; 1 John 3:2-3; 1 Thess. 4:16-17; Acts 1:11; Phil 3:20-21.

dec /3

Only the high priest entered the inner room, and that only once a year, and never without blood, which he offered for himself and for the sins the people had committed in ignorance. The Holy Spirit was showing by this that the way into the Most Holy Place had not yet been disclosed as long as the first tabernacle was still standing. . . . [Jesus] did not enter by means of the blood of goats and calves; but he entered the Most Holy Place once for all by his own blood, having obtained eternal redemption.—When Jesus had cried out again in a loud voice, he gave up his spirit. At that moment the curtain of the temple was torn in two from top to bottom. The earth shook and the rock split. The tombs broke open and the bodies of many holy people who had died were raised to life.—Since we have confidence to enter the Most Holy Place by the blood of Jesus, by a new and living way opened for us through the curtain, that is, his body, and since we have a great high priest over the house of God, let us draw near to God with a sincere heart in full assurance of faith.—He was pierced for our transgressions, he was crushed for our iniquities; the punishment that brought us peace was upon him, and by his wounds we are healed.

Heb. 9:7-8, 12; Matt. 27:50-52; Heb. 10:19-22; Isa. 53:5.

dec /4

"With your blood you purchased men for God from every tribe and language and people and nation. You have made them to be a kingdom and priests to serve our God, and they will reign on the earth." . . . Blessed and holy are those who have part in the first resurrection. The second death has no power over them, but they will be priests of God and of Christ and will reign with him for a thousand years.—You are a chosen people, a royal priesthood, a people belonging to God, that you may declare the praises of him who called you out of darkness into his wonderful light. . . . You also, like living stones are being built into a spiritual house to be a holy priesthood, offering spiritual sacrifices acceptable to God through Jesus Christ.—Through Jesus, therefore, let us continually offer to God a sacrifice of praise—the fruit of lips that confess his name. And do not forget to do good and to share with others, for with such sacrifices God is pleased.—"Now if you obey me fully and keep my covenant, then out of all nations you will be my treasured possession. Although the whole earth is mine, you will be for me a kingdom of priests and a holy nation."—"May your priests be clothed with righteousness; may your saints sing for joy."

Rev. 5:9-10; 20:6; 1 Peter 2:9, 5; Heb. 13:15-16; Exod. 19:56; Ps. 132:9.

dec /5

Just as he who called you is holy, so be holy in all you do; for it is written: "Be holy, because I am holy."—If I had cherished sin in my heart, the Lord would not have listened; but God has surely listened and heard my voice in prayer.—To fear the Lord is to hate evil.—Test everything. Hold on to the good. Avoid every kind of evil. May God himself, the God of peace, sanctify you through and through. May your whole spirit, soul and body be kept blameless at the coming of our Lord Jesus Christ. The one who calls you is faithful and he will do it.—Nevertheless, God's solid foundation stands firm, sealed with this inscription, "The Lord knows those who are his," and, "Everyone who confesses the name of the Lord must turn away from wickedness." . . . If a man cleanses himself, . . . he will be an instrument for noble purposes, made holy, useful to the Master and prepared to do any good work. Flee the evil desires of youth, and pursue righteousness, faith, love and peace, along with those who call on the Lord out of a pure heart.— Because Jesus lives forever, . . . he is able to save completely those who come to God through him, because he always lives to intercede for them. Such a high priest meets our need—one who is holy, blameless, pure, set apart from sinners.

1 Peter 1:15; Ps. 66:18-19; Prov. 8:13; 1 Thess. 5:21-24; 2 Tim. 2:19, 21-22; Heb. 7:24-26.

dec/6

O Lord, our God, other lords besides you have ruled over us, but your name alone do we honor. . . . This is how you guided your people, to make for yourself a glorious name. . . . Our enemies have trampled down your sanctuary. We are yours from of old; you have not ruled over them, they have not been called by your name.—The name of the Lord is a strong tower; the righteous run to it and are safe.—"O Lord, listen! O Lord, forgive! O Lord, hear and act! For your sake, O my God, do not delay, because your city and your people bear your Name."—"The Lord turn his face toward you and give you peace. So will they put my name on the Israelites, and I will bless them."—"For the sake of his great name the Lord will not reject his people, because the Lord was pleased to make you his own."—Then all the peoples on earth will see that you are called by the name of the Lord, and they will fear you.—"[When] they ask me, 'What is his name?' Then what shall I tell them?" God said to Moses, "I am who I am. . . . I AM has sent me to you.'"—"I raised you up for this very purpose, that I might display my power in you and that my name might be proclaimed in all the earth."

Isa. 26:13; 63:14, 18-19; Prov. 18:10; Dan. 9:19; Num. 6:26-27; 1 Sam. 12:22; Deut. 28:10; Exod. 3:13-14; Rom. 9:17.

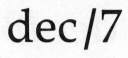

dec/7

Then will you call, and the Lord will answer; you will cry for help, and he will say: Here am I! . . . Seek the Lord while he may be found; call on him while he is near. . . . "Before they call I will answer; while they are yet speaking I will hear."—There is no difference between Jew or Gentile—the same Lord is Lord of all and richly blesses all who call on him, for, "Everyone who calls on the name of the Lord will be saved." —"'Call to me and I will answer you and tell you great and unsearchable things you do not know.'"—Answer me when I call to you, O my righteous God. Give me release from distress; be merciful to me and hear my prayer. . . . "Call upon me in the day of trouble; I will deliver you, and you will honor me." . . . I call to God, and the Lord saves me. Evening, morning and noon I cry out in distress, and he hears my voice. . . . You are kind and forgiving, O Lord, abounding in love to all who call to you. . . . In the day of my trouble I will call to you, for you will answer me. . . . "He will call upon me, and I will answer him; I will be with him in trouble, I will deliver him and honor him. With long life will I satisfy him and show him my salvation."—"You will call and I will answer you; you will long for the creature your hands have made."

Isa. 58:9; 55:6; 65:24; Rom. 10:12; Jer. 33:3; Pss. 4:1; 50:15; 155:16-17; 86:5, 7; 91:15-16; Job 14:15.

dec/8

The fruit of the Spirit is . . . joy.—We also rejoice in God through our Lord Jesus Christ, through whom we have now received reconciliation. . . . For the kingdom of God is not a matter of eating and drinking, but of righteousness, peace and joy in the Holy Spirit.—"This day is sacred to our Lord. Do not grieve, for the joy of the Lord is your strength." —"I have told you this that my joy may be in you and that your joy may be complete."—We work with you for your joy, because it is by faith you stand firm.—Though you have not seen him, you love him; and even though you do not see him now, you believe in him and are filled with an inexpressible and glorious joy.—You have made known to me the path of life; you fill me with joy in your presence, with eternal pleasure at your right hand.—Sorrowful, yet always rejoicing . . . I am greatly encouraged; in all our troubles my joy knows no bounds. [Titus] told us about your longing for me, your deep sorrow, your ardent concern for me, so that my joy was greater than ever.—Strengthened with all power according to his glorious might so that you may have great endurance and patience, and joyfully giving thanks to the Father.

Gal. 5:22; Rom. 5:11; 14:17; Neh. 8:10; John 15:11; 2 Cor. 1:24; 1 Peter 1:8; Ps. 16:11; 2 Cor. 6:10; 7:4, 7; Col. 1:11.

dec /9

"The Scriptures . . . testify about me, yet you refuse to come to me to have life." . . . He came to that which was his own, but his own did not receive him. Yet to all who received him, to those who believed in his name, he gave the right to become children of God.—"All day long I have held out my hands to an obstinate people, who walk in ways not good . . . who say, 'Keep away; don't come near me!"—"There is a judge for the one who rejects me and does not accept my words; that very word which I spoke will condemn him at the last day."—Since you rejected me when I called and no one gave heed when I stretched out my hand, since you ignored all my advice, and would not accept my rebuke, I in turn will laugh at your disaster; I will mock when calamity overtakes you.—"O Jerusalem, Jerusalem, you who kill the prophets and stone those sent to you, how often I have longed to gather your children together, as a hen gathers her chicks under her wings, but you were not willing. Look, your house is left to you desolate."—"While you were doing all these things, declares the Lord, I spoke to you again and again, but you did not listen; I called you, but you did not answer."—See to it that you do not refuse him who speaks . . . from heaven.

John 5:39-40; 1:11-12; Isa. 65:2, 5; John 12:48; Prov. 1:24-27; Matt. 23:37-39; Jer. 7:13; Heb. 12:25.

dec/10

That evening after sunset the people brought to Jesus all the sick, . . . and [he] healed many who had various diseases.—This was to fulfill what was spoken through the prophet Isaiah: "He took up our infirmities and carried our diseases." —Lazarus now lay sick, . . . So the sisters sent word to Jesus, "Lord, the one you love is sick." When he heard this, Jesus said, "This sickness will not end in death. No, it is for God's glory so that God's Son may be glorified through it."—Is any one of you sick? He should call the elders of the church to pray over him and anoint him with oil in the name of the Lord. And the prayer offered in faith will make the sick person well; the Lord will raise him up.—"I am the Lord who heals you."—The Lord will sustain him on his sickbed and restore him from his bed of illness.—On each side of the river stood the tree of life, bearing twelve crops of fruit, yielding its fruit every month. And the leaves of the tree are for the healing of the nations. . . . "There will be no more death or mourning or crying or pain, for the old order of things has passed away."—Do not be wise in your own eyes; fear the Lord and shun evil. This will bring health to your body and nourishment to your bones.

Mark 1:32, 34; Matt. 8:17; John 11:2-4; James 5:14-15; Exod. 15:26; Ps. 41:3; Rev. 22:2; 21:4; Prov. 3:7-8.

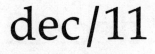

dec/11

Do not . . . encroach on the fields of the fatherless, for their Defender is strong; he will take up their case against you.—Defend the cause of the fatherless, plead the cause of the widow. . . . Woe to those who make unjust laws, . . . making widows their prey and robbing the fatherless. What will you do on the day of reckoning?—His name is the Lord—and rejoice before him. A father to the fatherless, a defender of widows, is God in his holy dwelling. . . . Defend the cause of the weak and fatherless; maintain the rights of the poor and oppressed.—"Though you were a powerful man, owning land—an honored man, living on it. And you sent widows away empty-handed and broke the strength of the fatherless." . . . "If I have kept bread to myself, not sharing it with the fatherless. . . . If I have raised my hand against the fatherless, . . . then let my arm fall from the shoulder."—Religion that God our Father accepts as pure and faultless is this: to look after orphans and widows in their distress and to keep oneself from being polluted by the world.—"Your Father knows what you need before you ask him. This is how you should pray: 'Our Father in heaven, hallowed be your name.'"

Prov. 23:10-11; Isa. 1:17; 10:1-3; Pss. 68:4-5; 82:3; Job. 22:8-9; 31:18, 21-22; James 1:27; Matt. 6:8-9.

dec/12

"Do not worry saying, 'What shall we eat?' or 'what shall we drink?' or 'What shall we wear?' . . . Your heavenly Father knows that you need them. But seek first his kingdom and his righteousness, and all these things will be given to you as well."—[Jesus] asked them, "What were you arguing about on the road?" But they kept quiet because on the way they had argued about who was the greatest. Sitting down, Jesus called the Twelve and said, "If anyone wants to be first, he must be the very last, and the servant of all."—"When you enter a house, first say, 'Peace to this house.' If a man of peace is there, your peace will rest on him; if not, it will return to you."—The first thing Andrew did was to find his brother Simon and tell him, "We have found the Messiah" (that is, the Christ).—"If you are offering your gift at the altar and there remember that your brother has something against you, leave your gift there in front of the altar. First go and be reconciled to your brother, then come and offer your gift."—"Bring the best of the firstfruits of your soil to the house of the Lord."—"Honor your father and mother"—which is the first commandment with a promise, "that it may go well with you and that you may enjoy long life on the earth."

Matt. 6:31-34; Mark 9:33-35; Luke 10:5-6; John 1:41; Matt. 5:23-24; Exod. 23:19; Eph. 6:2-3.

dec/13

He who vindicates me is near. Whom then will bring charges against me? Let us face each other! Who is my accuser?—"The accuser of our brothers, who accuses them before our God day and night. . . . They overcame him by the blood of the Lamb and by the word of their testimony."—Be self-controlled and alert. Your enemy the devil prowls around like a roaring lion looking for someone to devour. Resist him, standing firm in the faith.—Stand firm in one spirit, contending as one man for the faith of the gospel without being frightened in any way by those who oppose you. This is a sign to them that they will be destroyed, but that you will be saved—and that by God.—Thanks be to God, who always leads us in triumphal procession in Christ. . . . The weapons we fight with are not the weapons of the world. On the contrary, they have divine power to tear down strongholds.—It is written, "For your sake we face death all the day long; we are considered as sheep to be slaughtered." . . . In all these things we are more than conquerors through him who loved us.— Jesus said, "I saw Satan fall like lightning from heaven. I have given you authority to trample on snakes and scorpions, and to overcome all the power of the enemy; nothing will harm you."

Isa. 50:8; Rev. 12:10-11; 1 Peter 5:8-9; Phil. 1:27-28; 2 Cor. 2:14; 10:4; Rom. 8:36-37; Luke 10:18-19.

dec/14

Should you then seek great things for yourself?
Seek them not.—For those who are self-seeking
and who reject the truth and follow evil, there will
be wrath and anger.—He who seeks good finds
good will, but evil comes to him who searches for
it. . . . The discerning heart seeks knowledge, but
the mouth of a fool feeds on folly.—[Love] is not
self-seeking.—"Life is more than food and the
body more than clothes. . . . Seek his kingdom,
and these things will be given to you as well." . . .
"The Son of Man came to seek and to save what
was lost."—"I am not seeking glory for myself;
but there is one who seeks it, and he is the
judge."—"Day after day they seek me out; they
seem eager to know my ways."—Such is the
generation of those who seek him, who seek your
face, O God of Jacob. . . . My heart says of you,
"Seek his face!" Your face, Lord, I will seek.—"He
who seeks finds."—O God, you are my God,
earnestly I seek you. . . . Blessed are they who
keep his statutes and seek him with all their
heart.—I love those who love me, and those who
seek me find me.—"There is, however, some good
in you, for you rid the land of the Asherah poles
and set your heart on seeking God."

---

*Jer. 45:5; Rom. 2:8; Prov. 11:27; 15:14; 1 Cor. 13:5;
Luke 12:23, 31; 19:10; John 8:50; Isa. 58:2, Pss. 24:6;
27:8; Matt. 7:8; Pss. 63:1; 119:2; Prov. 8:17; 2
Chron. 19:3.*

dec/15

Jacob also went on his way, and the angels of God met him. When Jacob saw them, he said, "This is the camp of God!"—"'If God places no trust in his servants, if he charges his angels with error, how much more those who live in houses of clay, whose foundations are in the dust.'"—The angel of the Lord encamps around those who fear him, and he delivers them. . . . If you make the Most High your dwelling, . . . he will command his angels concerning you to guard you in all your ways; they will lift you up in their hands, so that you will not strike your foot against a stone.— "There is rejoicing in the presence of the angels of God over one sinner who repents." . . . "Those who are considered worthy of taking part in that age and in the resurrection from the dead will neither marry nor be given in marriage, and they can no longer die; for they are like angels."—"When the Son of Man comes in his glory, and all the angels with him, he will sit on his throne in heavenly glory." . . . "Do you think I cannot call on my Father, and he will at once put at my disposal more than twelve legions of angels?"—"He who overcomes will . . . be dressed in white. I will never erase his name from the book of life, but will acknowledge his name before my Father and his angels."

Gen. 32:1-2; Job 4:18; Pss; 34:7; 91:9, 11-12; Luke 15:10; 20:35-36; Matt. 25:31; 26:53; Rev. 3:5.

dec/16

God said, "Let us make man in our image, in our likeness. . . . So God created man in his own image, in the image of God he created him; male and female he created them.—Just as we have borne the likeness of the earthly man, so we shall bear the likeness of the man from heaven.—If you have any encouragement from being united with Christ, . . . then make my joy complete by being like-minded, having the same love. . . . [Christ Jesus] made himself nothing, taking the very nature of a servant, being made in human likeness.—What the law was powerless to do in that it was weakened by the sinful nature, God did by sending his own Son in the likeness of sinful man to be a sin offering.—Love is made complete among us so that we will have confidence on the day of judgment, because in this world we are like him. . . . We know that when he appears, we shall be like him, for we shall see him as he is.—We, who with unveiled faces all reflect the Lord's glory, are being transformed into his likeness with ever-increasing glory, which comes from the Lord, who is the Spirit.—The throne of God and of the Lamb will be in the city, and his servants will serve him. They will see his face, and his name will be on their foreheads.

Gen. 1:26-27; 1 Cor. 15:49; Phil. 2:1-2, 7; Rom. 8:3; 1 John 4:17; 3:2; 2 Cor. 3:18; Rev. 22:3-4.

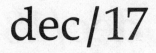

dec/17

"A bruised reed he will not break, and a smoldering wick he will not snuff out." . . . "For a brief moment I abandoned you, but with deep compassion I will bring you back. In a surge of anger I hid my face from you for a moment, but with everlasting kindness I will have compassion on you," says the Lord your Redeemer.—If you, O Lord, kept a record of sins, O Lord, who could stand? But with you there is forgiveness; therefore you are feared. . . . Their hearts were not loyal to him, they were not faithful to his covenant. Yet he was merciful; he atoned for their iniquities and did not destroy them.—"Though I completely destroy all nations among which I scatter you, I will not completely destroy you. I will discipline you but only with justice; I will not let you go entirely unpunished.'"—God is faithful: he will not let you be tempted beyond what you can bear. But when you are tempted, he will also provide a way out so that you can stand up under it.—"I am in deep distress. Let us fall into the hands of the Lord, for his mercy is great; but do not let me fall into the hands of men."—He does not treat us as our sins deserve or repay us according to our iniquities. For as high as the heavens are above the earth, so great is his love for those who fear him.

Isa. 42:3; 54:7; Pss. 130:3, 4; 78:37-38; Jer. 30:11; 1 Cor. 10:13; 2 Sam. 24:14; Ps. 103:10-11.

dec/18

"I will ransom them from the power of the grave; I will redeem them from death. Where, O death, are your plagues? Where, O grave is your destruction?"—[Jesus] suffered death, so that by the grace of God he might taste death for everyone. . . . Since the children have flesh and blood, he too shared in their humanity so that by his death he might destroy him who holds the power of death—that is, the devil—and free those who all their lives were held in slavery by their fear of death.—It has now been revealed through the appearing of our Savior, Christ Jesus, who has destroyed death and has brought life and immortality to light through the gospel.—If we died with Christ, we believe that we will also live with him. . . . Count yourselves dead to sin but alive to God in Christ Jesus.—"I am the Living One; I was dead, and behold I am alive for ever and ever! And I hold the keys of death and Hades." . . . Blessed and holy are those who have part in the first resurrection. The second death has no power over them. . . . Death and Hades were thrown into the lake of fire. . . . "There will be no more death or mourning or crying or pain, for the old order of things has passed away."—He will swallow up death forever. The Sovereign Lord will wipe away the tears from all faces.

Hos. 13:14; Heb. 2:9, 14-15; 2 Tim. 1:10; Rom. 6:8, 11; Rev. 1:18; 20:6, 14; 21:4; Isa. 25:8.

dec/19

The Lord is my shepherd, I shall lack nothing. He makes me lie down in green pastures, he leads me beside quiet waters, he restores my soul.—Then Naomi said, "Wait, my daughter, until you find out what happens."—"See, I lay a stone in Zion, a tested stone, a precious cornerstone for a sure foundation; the one who trusts will never be dismayed." . . . This is what the Sovereign Lord, the Holy One of Israel says: "In repentance and rest is your salvation, in quietness and trust is your strength." . . . Blessed are all who wait for him!—When you are on your beds, search your hearts and be silent. . . . "Be still, and know that I am God; I will be exalted among the nations, I will be exalted in the earth." . . . He will have no fear of bad news; his heart is steadfast, trusting in the Lord. His heart is secure, he will have no fear. . . . Commit your way to the Lord; trust in him and he will do this. . . . Be still before the Lord and wait patiently for him; do not fret when men succeed in their ways, when they carry out their wicked schemes. . . . Do not fret—it leads only to evil.—"Come to me, . . . I will give you rest. Take my yoke upon you and learn from me, for I am gentle and humble in heart, and you will find rest for your souls."

Ps. 23:1-2; Ruth 3:18; Isa. 28:16; 30:15, 18; Pss. 4:4; 46:10; 112:7-8; 37:5, 7-8; Matt. 11:28-29.

dec/20

Noah . . . sent out a raven, [which did not return]. Then he sent out a dove, . . . [which] returned to him in the evening, there in its beak was a freshly plucked olive leaf! . . . The earth was completely dry.—"The priest shall order that two live clean birds and some cedar wood, scarlet yarn and hyssop be brought for the one to be cleansed."—The word of the Lord came to Elijah: ". . . You will drink from the brook, and I have ordered the ravens to feed you there."—"Who provides food for the raven when its young cry out to God and wander about for lack of food?"—He satisfies my desires with good things, so that my youth is renewed like the eagle's.—"'You yourselves have seen what I did to Egypt, and how I carried you on eagles' wings and brought you to myself.'"—Those who hope in the Lord . . . will soar on wings like eagles. . . . "I cried like a swift or thrush, I moaned like a mourning dove." —Even the sparrow has found a home, and the swallow a nest for herself, where she may have her young, a place near your altar, O Lord Almighty.—"Are not two sparrows sold for a penny? Yet not one of them will fall to the ground apart from the will of your Father. So don't be afraid; you are worth more than many sparrows."

Gen. 8:6-8, 11, 14; Lev. 14:4; 1 Kings 17:2, 4; Job 38:41; Ps. 103:5; Exod. 19:4; Isa. 40:31; 38:14; Ps. 84:3; Matt. 10:29, 31.

dec/21

"Sing about a fruitful vineyard: I, the Lord, watch over it; I water it continually. I guard it day and night so that no one may harm it." . . . "I, the Lord, have called you in righteousness; I will take hold of your hand. I will keep you."—"O Lord, the great and awesome God, who keeps his covenant of love with all who love him and obey his commands."—He will not let your foot slip—he who watches over you will not slumber; indeed, he who watches over Israel will neither slumber nor sleep. . . . He will command his angels concerning you to guard you in all your ways. . . . In the shelter of your presence you hide them from the intrigues of men; in your dwelling you keep them safe from the strife of tongues. —"He will guard the feet of his saints, but the wicked will be silenced in darkness." — Through faith you are shielded by God's power until the coming of the salvation that is ready to be revealed in the last time.—The peace of God, which transcends all understanding, will guard your hearts and your minds in Christ Jesus.—"I am with you and will watch over you wherever you go, and I will bring you back to this land. I will not leave you until I have done what I have promised you."—"The Lord bless and keep you."

Isa. 27:3; 42:6; Dan. 9:4; Pss. 121:3-4; 91:11; 31:20; 1 Sam. 2:9; 1 Peter 1:5; Phil. 4:7; Gen. 28:15; Num. 6:24.

dec/22

For the Lord is good and his love endures forever; his faithfulness continues through all generations. . . . The heavens are the work of your hands. They will perish, but you remain; they will all wear out like a garment. Like clothing you will change them and they will be discarded. But you remain the same, and your years will never end. . . . Your kingdom is an everlasting kingdom, and your dominion endures through all generations.—"Because of the increase of wickedness, the love of most will grow cold, but he who stands firm to the end will be saved." —Endure hardship with us like a good soldier of Christ Jesus. . . . Therefore I endure everything for the sake of the elect, that they too may obtain the salvation that is in Christ Jesus, with eternal glory. . . . Keep your head in all situations, endure hardship.—Among God's churches we boast about your perseverance and faith in all the persecutions and trials you are enduring. —Consider him who endured such opposition from sinful men, so that you will not grow weary and lose heart. . . . Endure hardship as discipline; God is treating you as sons. For what son is not disciplined by his father. . . . Jesus, . . . who for the joy set before him, endured the cross.

Pss. 100:5; 102:25-27; 145:13; Matt. 24:12-13; 2 Tim. 2:3, 10; 4:5; 2 Thess. 1:4; Heb. 12:3, 7, 2.

dec/23

"Blessed are the pure in heart, for they will see God."—Who may ascend the hill of the Lord? Who may stand in his holy place? He who has clean hands and a pure heart. . . . To the faithful you show yourself faithful, and to the blameless you show yourself blameless, to the pure you show yourself pure.—He who loves a pure heart and whose speech is gracious will have the king for his friend. . . . Who can say, "I have kept my heart pure; I am clean and without sin?"—We know that when he appears, we shall be like him, for we shall see him as he is. Everyone who has this hope in him purifies himself, just as he is pure.—Now that you have purified yourselves by obeying the truth so that you have sincere love for your brothers, love one another deeply, from the heart.—The wisdom that comes from heaven is first of all pure.—Blessed is the man who does not condemn himself by what he approves.— Whatever is true, whatever is noble, whatever is right, whatever is pure, whatever is lovely, whatever is admirable—if anything is excellent or praiseworthy—think about such things.—[Jesus], who gave himself for us to redeem us from all wickedness and to purify for himself a people that are his very own, eager to do what is good.

Matt. 5:8; Pss. 24:3-4; 18:25-26; Prov. 22:11; 20:9; 1 John 3:2-3; 1 Peter 1:22; James 3:17; Rom. 14:22; Phil. 4:8; Titus 2:14.

dec/24

"My servant Job will pray for you, and I will accept his prayer and not deal with you according to your folly. You have not spoken of me what is right, as my servant Job has."—I will tell you of the kindnesses of the Lord, the deeds for which he is to be praised—according to all the Lord has done for us . . . according to his compassion and many kindnesses.—The Lord said to me, "Go, show your love to your wife again, though she is loved by another and is an adulteress. Love her as the Lord loves the Israelites, though they turn to other gods and love the sacred raisin-cakes."—A woman . . . came up behind him and touched the edge of his cloak. She said to herself, "If I only touch his cloak, I will be healed." Jesus turned and saw her. "Take heart, daughter," he said, "your faith has healed you." And the woman was healed from that moment.—From time to time those who owned lands or houses sold them, brought the money from the sales and put it at the apostles' feet, and it was distributed to anyone as he had need.—Have mercy on me, O God, according to your unfailing love; according to your great compassion blot out my transgressions. . . . May the groans of the prisoners come before you; by the strength of your arm preserve those condemned to die.

Job 42:8-9; Isa. 63:7; Hos. 3:1; Matt. 9:20-22; Acts 4:34-35; Pss. 51:1; 79:11.

dec/25

For to us a child is born, to us a son is given, and the government will be on his shoulders. And he will be called Wonderful Counselor, Mighty God, Everlasting Father, Prince of Peace. Of the increase of his government and peace there will be no end. He will reign on David's throne and over his kingdom, establishing and upholding it with justice and righteousness from that time on and forever.—This is how the birth of Jesus Christ came about. His mother Mary was pledged to be married to Joseph, but before they came together, she was found to be with child through the Holy Spirit. . . . An angel of the Lord appeared to him in a dream and said, "Joseph son of David, do not be afraid to take Mary home as your wife, because what is conceived in her is from the Holy Spirit. She will give birth to a son, and you are to give him the name Jesus, because he will save his people from their sins."—An angel of the Lord appeared to [the shepherds], and the glory of the Lord shone around them, and they were terrified. But the angel said to them, "Do not be afraid. I bring you good news of great joy that will be for all the people. Today in the town of David, a Savior has been born to you; he is Christ the Lord." . . . "Glory to God in the highest, and on earth peace to men on whom his favor rests."

Isa. 9:6-7; Matt. 1:18, 20-21; Luke 2:9-11, 14.

dec/26

"Why were you searching for me?" [Jesus] asked. "Didn't you know I had to be in my Father's house?"—In everything that he undertook in the service of God's temple and in obedience to the law and the commands, he sought his God and worked wholeheartedly. And so he prospered.—"'Be strong, all you people of the land," declares the Lord, "and work. For I am with you," declares the Lord Almighty.—Make every effort to add to your faith goodness; and to goodness, knowledge; and to knowledge, self-control. . . . We are looking forward to a new heaven and a new earth, the home of righteousness . . . make every effort to be found spotless, blameless and at peace with him. —Whatever your hand finds to do, do it with all your might.—Never be lacking in zeal, but keep your spiritual fervor, serving the Lord.—Lazy hands make a man poor, but diligent hands bring wealth. . . . Diligent hands will rule, but laziness ends in slave labor. . . . The lazy man does not roast his game, but the diligent man prizes his possessions.—"'Well done, good and faithful servant! You have been faithful with a few things; I will put you in charge of many things. Come and share your master's happiness.'"

Luke 2:49; 2 Chron. 31:21; Hag. 2:4; 2 Peter 1:5-6; 3:13-14; Eccl. 9:10; Rom. 12:11; Prov. 10:4; 12:24, 27; Matt. 25:23.

dec/27

The zeal of the Lord Almighty will accomplish this.—"Hallelujah! For our Lord God Almighty reigns."—Jesus came to them and said, "All authority in heaven and on earth has been given to me."—Job replied to the Lord, "I know that you can do all things; no plan of yours can be thwarted."—"It is easier for a camel to go through the eye of a needle than for a rich man to enter the kingdom of God." Those who heard this asked, "Who can then be saved?" Jesus replied, "What is impossible with men is possible with God." —Then I praised the Most High; I honored and glorified him who lives forever. His dominion is an eternal dominion; his kingdom endures from generation to generation. All the peoples of the earth are regarded as nothing. He does as he pleases with the powers of heaven and the peoples of the earth. No one can hold back his hand or say to him: "What have you done?"—"Yes, and from ancient days I am he. No one can deliver out of my hand. When I act, who can reverse it?"—"To whom will you compare me? Or who is my equal?" says the Holy One. He who brings out the starry host one by one, and calls them each by name. Because of his great power and mighty strength, not one of them is missing.

Isa. 9:7; Rev. 19:6; Matt. 28:18; Job 42:1-2; Luke 18:25-27; Dan. 4:34-35; Isa. 43:13; 40:26.

dec/28

When Jacob awoke from his sleep, he thought,
"Surely the Lord is in this place, and I was not
aware of it." He was afraid and said, "How
awesome is this place! This is none other than the
house of God; and this is the gate of heaven."
—Balaam said to the angel of the Lord, "I have
sinned. I did not realize you were standing in the
road to oppose me. Now if you are displeased, I
will go back."—"If a person sins and does what is
forbidden in any of the Lord's commands, even
though he does not know it, he is guilty and will
be held responsible."—When Moses came down
from Mount Sinai with the two tablets of the
Testimony in his hands, he was not aware that his
face was radiant because he had spoken with the
Lord.—About midnight Paul and Silas were
praying and singing hymns to God, and the other
prisoners were listening to them.—[The Jews]
asked [the invalid], "Who is this fellow who told
you to pick [your mat] up and walk?" The man
who was healed had no idea who it was, for Jesus
had slipped away into the crowd. . . . Early in the
morning, Jesus stood on the shore, but the
disciples did not realize that it was Jesus. . . .
When [John] saw Jesus passing by, he said,
"Look, the Lamb of God!" When the two disciples
heard him say this, they followed Jesus.

*Gen. 28:16-17; Num. 22:34; Lev. 5:17; Exod. 34:29;
Acts 16:25; John 5:12-13; 21:4; 1:35-36.*

dec/29

Surely I have been a sinner from birth, sinful from the time my mother conceived me.—Your fame spread among the nations on account of your beauty, because the splendor I had given you made your beauty perfect, declares the Sovereign Lord.—Dark am I, yet lovely, O daughters of Jerusalem. . . . "Therefore I despise myself and repent in dust and ashes."—[Simon Peter] fell at Jesus' knees and said, "Go away from me, Lord; I am a sinful man!"—All beautiful you are . . . there is no flaw in you.—The forgiveness of sins, in accordance with the riches of God's grace that he lavished on us with all wisdom and understanding.—I find this law at work: When I want to do good, evil is right there with me. —Thanks be to God! He gives us the victory through our Lord Jesus Christ.—No one can redeem the life of a man or give to God a ransom for him—the ransom for a life is costly, no payment is ever enough—that a man should live on forever and not see decay.—You were bought at a price, do not become the slaves of men.— Surely I have been a sinner from birth, sinful from the time my mother conceived me.—"Flesh gives birth to flesh, but the Spirit gives birth to spirit. . . . You must be born again."

Ps. 51:5; Ezek. 16:14; Song of Songs 1:5; 4:7; Luke 5:8; Job 42:6; Eph. 1:7; Rom. 7:21; 1 Cor. 15:57; Ps. 49:7-9; 1 Cor. 7:23; Ps. 51:5; John 3:6-7.

dec/30

Lord, you have been our dwelling place throughout all generations. Before the mountains were born or you brought forth the earth and the world, from everlasting to everlasting, you are God.—The eternal God is your refuge, and underneath are the everlasting arms.—Trust in the Lord forever, for the Lord, the Lord, is the Rock eternal.—The Lord is the true God; he is the living God, the eternal King. . . . "I have loved you with an everlasting love; I have drawn you with lovingkindness."—This God is your God for ever and ever; he will be our guide even to the end.—Only the redeemed of the Lord will walk there, and the ransomed of the Lord will return. They will enter Zion with singing; everlasting joy will crown their heads.—He became the source of eternal salvation for all who obey him. . . . He entered the Most Holy Place once for all by his own blood, having obtained eternal redemption. —Our light and momentary troubles are achieving for us an eternal glory that far outweighs them all. So we fix our eyes not on what is seen, but on what is unseen. For what is seen is temporary, but what is unseen is eternal.—Now to the King eternal, immortal, invisible, the only God, be honor and glory for ever and ever. Amen.

Ps. 90:1-2; Deut. 33:27; Isa. 26:4; Jer. 10:10; 31:3; Ps. 48:14; Isa. 35:9-10; Heb. 5:9; 9:12; 2 Cor. 4:17; 1 Tim. 1:17.

dec/31

Not one of all the Lord's good promises to the house of Israel failed; every one was fulfilled. . . . "You know with all your heart and soul that not one of all the good promises the Lord your God gave you has failed. Every promise has been fulfilled; not one has failed."—Let us hold unswervingly to the hope we profess, for he who promised is faithful.—Then Samuel took a stone and set it up between Mizpah and Shem. He named it Ebenezer, saying, "Thus far has the Lord helped us."—Glorify the Lord with me; let us exalt his name together. I sought the Lord, and he answered me; he delivered me from all my fears. . . . When I was in distress, I sought the Lord; at night I stretched out untiring hands, and my soul refused to be comforted. . . . I remembered my songs in the night. My heart mused and my spirit inquired: . . . Has his unfailing love vanished forever? Has his promise failed for all time? I will meditate on all your works and consider all your mighty deeds. Your ways, O God are holy. . . . Surely goodness and love will follow me all the days of my life, and I will dwell in the house of the Lord forever. . . . Teach us to number our days aright, that we may gain a heart of wisdom.—Jesus Christ is the same yesterday and today and forever.

Josh. 21:45; 23:14; Heb. 10:23; 1 Sam. 7:12; Pss. 34:3-4; 77:2, 6, 8, 12-13; 23:6; 90:12; Heb. 13:8.